The Well-Fed Writer – A Well-Praised Book!

"When it comes to commercial copywriting, I implore you to listen to every word that comes from Peter Bowerman. There is NOBODY I'd recommend more than Peter, and you'll see why the moment you dig into this excellent book. Peter walks the walk, applying his ideas to his everyday business. He cares enormously about helping you live the dream: his books have literally transformed the lives of tens of thousands of writers."

Michael A. Stelzner, Author
Writing White Papers: How to Capture Readers and Keep Them Engaged
www.WritingWhitePapers.com

"When the first edition of *The Well-Fed Writer* first came out, I said it provided the best advice on how to make more money writing for corporate clients I had ever read. This new edition—expanded, up-to-date, and with even more sound strategies for freelance success—allows me to reaffirm my original opinion."

Bob Bly, Copywriter
Author of 75 books, including
Secrets of a Freelance Writer

"Peter has more experience helping writers make a good living than just about anyone I know. So I wasn't surprised to find this updated edition of TWFW packed solid with valuable tips and strategies. His chapter on cold calling, particularly, is a must-read. As a 15-year copywriting veteran, I can tell you, there's more practical advice here than in any other book of its kind I've ever read."

Steve Slaunwhite, Copywriter, Author
Start and Run a Copywriting Business (and other writing titles)
Publisher, **www.ForCopywritersOnly.com**

"Over the years, I've recommended TWFW to countless aspiring copywriters who were eager for practical steps to take to find clients. With this new updated edition, it's still far and away the best single source of information and inspiration for getting started as an independent writer for business clients."

Marcia Yudkin, Author and Copywriting Coach
www.yudkin.com

"If you want to live the six-figure freelance writing dream, and are looking for the real nuts and bolts of HOW to do it, without the hype and hysteria, this latest book by Peter Bowerman is exactly what you need. Solid substance from cover to cover."

Nick Usborne, Copywriter
Author, *Net Words*
Editor, **www.FreelanceWritingSuccess.com**

"If you only invest in a one resource on commercial freelancing, make it this one. It will deliver 1000 times over in new business. Just when I thought Peter Bowerman had left no detail untouched, he's outdone himself. This updated edition includes tons of examples from successful writers. It's a welcome replacement for my dog-eared copy!"

Casey Hibbard, Author
Stories That Sell: Turn Satisfied Customers into Your Most Powerful Sales and Marketing Asset
www.StoriesThatSellGuide.com

"This book is an incredibly comprehensive resource for starting your own freelance writing business. And in classic Bowerman style, it's encouraging to the core. On virtually every page, you can just about hear Peter whispering, 'Come on, you can do this!!' in your ear. A terrific update to Peter's original WFW titles."

Pete Savage, Co-Author
The Wealthy Freelancer
www.TheWealthyFreelancer.com

"Writers, get this book! It can't instantly solve your financial problems, but it *can* put you back in control of your commercial writing life—*and* future. This updated edition of TWFW shows you, step by step, how to enter this sturdy, flexible, rewarding field. Aside from showcasing the many kinds of commercial writing and the best ways to market your services, what's most valuable is the book's confident, helpful tone and the many examples and strategies from other freelancers. Congratulations, Peter. Well done!

Lucy V. Parker, Author
How to Start a Home-Based Writing Business (5th edition)

"If you're seeking a comprehensive blueprint for starting your own high-profit writing practice (not an oxymoron!), you need this book. And as 'The Queen of Cold Calling,' I can say that Bowerman truly grasps the process and 'gets' the power of this oft-misunderstood marketing strategy."

Wendy Weiss
The Queen of Cold Calling
www.wendyweiss.com

"Peter's book more than fulfills the promise it makes. Do what he suggests and you too *will* become self-supporting through your writing. Bowerman writes with lightness and humor, and gives away every single success secret he knows in clear, easy-to-follow prose. Truly a must-read for any writer or anyone who wants to be."

Anne Wayman, Writer, Ghostwriter, Writing coach
Editor, www.AboutFreelanceWriting.com

"Everybody who is wrangling words for a living ought to have this book on their shelves. It offers a great primer for the business and terrific tools to keep the enterprise rolling along. Subscribers to FreelanceSuccess.com refer to Peter frequently as the guru of freelancing for corporate entities."

Jennie Phipps, Editor & Publisher
Freelance Success
www.FreelanceSuccess.com

"Peter thinks of every excuse you have not to be successful—and blasts them! He tells you how to hit it big in a small town, how to start out part-time when you have a full-time job, and how to overcome resistance to your healthy rates. You'll get the scoop on social media, countless places to sell your services, how to succeed with email marketing, and more. If you want to earn top dollar freelance writing, you need this guide."

Linda Formichelli, Writing coach, Author
The Renegade Writer: A Totally Unconventional Guide to Freelance Writing Success
www.TheRenegadeWriter.com

"*The Well-Fed Writer* has always been a wonderful tool, and this new edition is just what writers need to give them the competitive edge they need in today's economy!"

Moira Allen, Editor, www.Writing-World.com
Author, *Starting Your Career as a Freelance Writer*

"Grab a packet of Post-it notes and a highlighter before you pick up this book. It's chock full of hundreds of examples of how commercial freelancers are earning a living in a marketplace glutted with mediocre writers. An added bonus: Bowerman's writing style. His liberal use of sub-heads, lists and sidebars makes the book an easy read—techniques you can use when writing for your clients."

Joan Stewart, Editor
The Publicity Hound
www.PublicityHound.com

"How I wish that back in 1982, someone could have shoved a copy of TWFW under my nose and said, 'You want to be a working writer? Go write marketing and informational copy for businesses and stop chasing the magazine/newspaper dream. Here's how, step by step.' Eventually, I figured that out, but Peter would have taken years off the process."

Shel Horowitz, Copywriter
Author of seven books, including
Grassroots Marketing for Authors and Publishers
www.FrugalMarketing.com

"Back in 2004, *The Well-Fed Writer* woke me up to the tremendous opportunity in commercial writing, showing me not only that I could make a great living doing this, but *how* to get there. This new heavily updated edition is jam-packed with practical ideas, tips and strategies for launching, running and *improving* your freelancing business. Whether just starting out or seasoned pro, I can't recommend it highly enough!"

Ed Gandia, B2B Copywriter
Co-Author, *The Wealthy Freelancer*
www.TheWealthyFreelancer.com

"Without any doubt *The Well-Fed Writer* is one of the best books on commercial writing I have read! Drawing on years of experience, Peter Bowerman shares up-to-date strategies and ideas for building a successful commercial writing business. With solid material and plenty of examples, it's no wonder so many people have become full-time writers after reading Peter's book."

Gary McLaren, Founder
www.WorldwideFreelance.com

The Well-Fed Writer:

Financial Self-Sufficiency
As a *Commercial* Freelancer
In Six Months or Less

Peter Bowerman

www.wellfedwriter.com

Fanove Publishing—Atlanta, Georgia

This book includes information from many sources and gathered from many personal experiences. It is published for general reference and is not intended to be a substitute for independent verification by readers when necessary and appropriate. The book is sold with the understanding that neither the author nor publisher is engaged in rendering any legal, psychological or accounting advice. The publisher and author disclaim any personal liability, directly or indirectly, for advice or information presented within. Although the author and publisher have prepared this manuscript with utmost care and diligence and have made every effort to ensure the accuracy and completeness of the information contained within, we assume no responsibility for errors, inaccuracies, omissions or inconsistencies.

Publisher's Cataloging In Publication

Bowerman, Peter

The Well-Fed Writer: Financial self-sufficiency as a commercial freelancer in six months or less /Peter Bowerman

– 2nd ed.

p. cm.

Includes appendices and index; revised edition, 2009.

LCCN: 2008912241

ISBN-13: 978-0-9670598-7-7 (trade paper)

1. Authorship—Marketing. 2. Authorship. I. Title

PN161.B69 2009 808.02

QBI00-500042

ATTN: QUANTITY DISCOUNTS ARE AVAILABLE TO YOUR COMPANY, EDUCATIONAL INSTITUTION OR WRITING ORGANIZATION

for reselling, educational purposes, subscription incentives, gifts or fundraising campaigns.

For more information, please contact the publisher at Fanove Publishing, 3713 Stonewall Circle, Atlanta, Georgia 30339 770/438-7200—peter@wellfedwriter.com

Dedication

To all the well-fed writers around the globe
—past, present and future.

Table of Contents

Ability to Market Yourself; And BTW: It's Nowhere NEAR as Scary as You Imagine

Discipline—I'm Lazy, Believe It or Not (Just Like You…)

Technical Expertise—If I, THE Original Techno-Moron, Can Do It…

Being a Tenacious, Flexible, Reliable, Curious, Assertive Non-Conformist…

Being Easy to Get Along With Is Your Secret Weapon

Ability to Ask Lots of Dumb Questions = Less Work & Happier Clients

Getting Ready For Self-Employment—It's All in Your Head!

Get Mental, Make Money; And Remember: You Give the Raises Around Here

Getting Your Finances in Order

Business Names, Business Plans, and Business Cards—Three Ways to Procrastinate

Creating a Portfolio from Thin Air (AND Buying an Actual Portfolio…)

The Writer's Bookshelf: The Books You Need to Sound Brilliant

Chapter Three
LEARNING TO LOVE S & M (SALES & MARKETING…)

Success is Far More About a Process than a Personality

Marketing: What It Is and What It Isn't

You're in Control of More than Enough to Succeed

The Game Is Already in Progress; Just Learn Your Lines

That "Icky Sales Thingy": Bad Experiences, Bad Associations

B2B and B2C: The Definitions and the Differences

Marketing Lessons from a Former "Love Merchant"

Eight Sales Tips for Non-Salespeople (from Sales Training Firm CEO)

Real Sales: A Single-Bullet Assassination Story

All-Star "Sales" Stories: Not What You'd Expect "Sales" to Look Like

Into the Mind of the Marketer (C'mon in, the Water's Fine…)

Why Write Anything? (Hint: Think Like a 10-Year-Old)

Tune into WIFM ("What's In It For Me?") and You Win

Sales & Marketing Cornerstones: Learn and Earn

Who's the Audience? (Still the First Question)

Features Vs. Benefits (Stop Talking About Yourself…)

It's Not Just Business, It's Human Nature

Thoughts of Resumes, Releases, Books, Drill Bits and…Love

The USP (Every Company Has One…)

Are You "Branded"?—The Basics of Standing Out

Chapter Four
WWW.YOURWEBSITE.COM

Tale of Two Writers—One with Web Site, One without. Guess Who Wins?

Writer Reluctantly Builds Site, Business Soars, Leaves Crummy Job

Acknowledgements

My sincere thanks to:

The Copy Hos, Paul, Kathy, Steve, Georgia, and Barbara, my fellow writing "peeps" and Copyopolis clan (www.copyopolis.com). Thanks for being the eternal example of integrity, competence and professionalism. You give copywriting a good name.

Chris DiNatale, fabulous graphic designer, for yet another kick-butt cover and for being such a big part of my success since 1994. (www.dinataledesign.com)

Debbie Rohde, my other design cohort in crime. Thanks for all your help and support, and most of all, your friendship. (www.rohdemd.com)

Shelley, Beth and the whole BookMasters gang for making me look so good in print, and for lifting the logistics burden from my shoulders—since 1999 (offset/galley printing, fulfillment, distribution and more; www.bookmasters.com).

Doug Rohde (Debbie's son), for his web development prowess, dogged determination when faced with a challenge, and all-round terrific attitude. (www.rohdemd.com)

Mom and Sis for happily listening to me go on and on about all this for years.

Bob Bly. If not for you, chances are excellent, none of this would ever have happened.

Hilda, fellow writer, dear friend, adopted sister and favorite truth-speaker. I'm glad you're in my life.

Richard, Buddy, Rob and Todd, my long-time homies. Thanks for your friendship, and for keeping me reasonably humble and reliably entertained.

Everyone who generously contributed to this book. The steps, stories, strategies and tips you've shared will absolutely make a difference for many, and are the empirical evidence that this gig is indeed doable.

Finally, all my readers, around the world. Thanks for supporting my work, and trusting me to be your guide. May all your writing be well-fed.

Introduction

There's no scarcity of opportunity to make a living at what you love. There is only a scarcity of resolve to make it happen.

Wayne Dyer

PICTURE THIS On a Friday morning client phone call, you pick up a job writing a marketing brochure. Several hours later, the client emails background material. In a follow-up call, the client answers some questions. After a few hours reviewing the material, you get to work—on your deck, under that great shady tree, phone by your side, tall glass of lemonade nearby.

By Wednesday morning, between the client call, background reading and crafting a first draft, you have 16 hours in the project (16 x $75 = $1,200). You email them your draft Wednesday morning, and you won't get it back until Friday.

THE PHONE KEEPS RINGING... In the meantime, you put in seven hours on a few sales sheets for a telecommunications firm (7 x $75 = $525). Then, an ad for a company in Canada (you've never met them) that takes four hours (another $300). You send it on, and bill them immediately.

Later that afternoon, a new but now-regular client calls and snags you for a brochure project the next week: 12–15 hours worth of work. That same day, one of your regulars calls, needing a few quick headlines for a store display. You've done 30+ similar projects like this. You charge your two-hour minimum, $150, grab your mini-recorder, head to the gym, knocking out half of it on the way over. That night, sitting outside at your favorite neighborhood eatery with a clipboard, you get the rest done. You get home, type them up, and send them on, having spent just over an hour total.

That's over $2,000 by Thursday, for under 30 hours of work, no running around and completely by phone and email. Plus, $1,000 worth of work lined up for next week. And that's at $75 an hour. What'll it be like at $100 or $125?

REALITY CHECK Okay, it's not always this easy or rosy. You'll have your share of $500 weeks, and you may have to meet clients in person. This is no get-rich-quick thing. In the beginning, you'll be working a lot harder for a lot less, and there's a lot of prospecting, marketing, and paperwork to do. But, stick to it, develop the right work habits, and weeks like the above will come soon and often.

Good money, flexible hours, stimulating work. You control your day, your time off, your life. Do you have outside interests? *Would you* if you had more time of your own?

Want a raise? Simple. Work harder, make more phone calls, put in more hours.

This is freelance *commercial* writing: writing for businesses, large and small, and for hourly rates of $50 to $125 or more—depending on your experience and the market you're in. In the first chapter, we'll explore why this field makes so much sense—both for writers and the clients who hire them.

Have you dreamed of becoming a writer but never took it too seriously because after all, the words "starving" and "writer" are pretty much joined at the hip? Or are you already a writer but either working for someone else or struggling financially? This might just be your ticket.

MY STORY I'd love to tell you about how I knew I wanted to be a freelance commercial writer from the time I was crawling. Alas, not so. One journalism course in both high school and college. Oh, and at 15, I wrote a column covering little league baseball for three local papers on the North Shore of Massachusetts. That's it. Impressive, huh?

I'd never been a writer before I started this business. I'd never written anything for money. No writing training. I had no industry background and no advertising agency experience. I had no contacts in the industry, no client list. Nada. Zippo. Zilch. Heck, I was a Russian Studies major in college. Given all that, while my success certainly says something about me, it says just as much about the accessibility of the opportunity.

I found that in any job I'd held over the years, I gravitated to the few writing tasks that did crop up—an occasional letter or little brochure—and typically got good feedback from those around me. Do we have anything in common there?

I always wanted to be a writer, but wasn't willing to starve at it. In the early 90's, I stumbled across Bob Bly's great book, *Secrets of a Freelance Writer*, about the commercial writing field. Who knew that many companies, for some darn good reasons (stay tuned), actually hired freelancers to handle their writing tasks? Lightbulb on. This is how I'd do it. Finally, in January of 1994, after talking myself in and out of the idea about 100 times, and alternately experiencing anxiety attacks and delusions of grandeur, I took the plunge. Cold turkey. No moonlighting.

Within three and a half months, following the strategies outlined in this book, I literally had more business than I could handle, and had indeed achieved "financial self-sufficiency" (i.e., paying all my bills). That first year's tally? 19 brochures, four video scripts, two radio spots, two 40-page technical manuals, a half dozen ad campaigns and sales promotion projects, a 44-part educational CD-ROM, and a ghost-written book for a local businessman. Oh, and 45 columns published in five local papers (just fun, "grocery-money" writing).

Your Story? Is this you? Get up early, put on the suit, drive 30–45 minutes (on a good day) through glacial rush hour traffic, work in some climate-controlled windowless cubicle in a high-rise all day, deal with office politics, eat unhealthy food on the run, sit in endless boring meetings using phrases like "market space," "value-added," and "mission-critical," get stressed out, be nice to people you think are morons, leave the office late, maybe get in a rushed workout, get home by 8:30–9:00, wolf down some dinner, fall asleep in front of the TV, collapse on Friday night, run errands and do wash on Saturday, take your one to two weeks of vacation every year, and 40 more years of that.

My life is very different, and at some point early in my fourth year, I started realizing how good I actually had it: healthy income *and* a lifestyle others will drool over. And I'm living proof you don't have to be Type A to have all this (*and*, you'll undoubtedly be delighted to discover along the way here that I'm not a super-disciplined, aggressive, or technically-savvy guy and yet, I've done quite well).

Remember the $2,000 week described earlier? Even lighter weeks of $1,200 x 50 = $60K. Not all the money in the world, but if it gave you the time to truly enjoy your life and your own terms—*however* you define that—would it be enough?

100K? Absolutely possible, and likely working a lot less than in other businesses. Bust your rear for someone else for three or four years, and where will you be? More money and less time to enjoy it? Most importantly, are you doing something you like? I know, new-agey, touchy-feely BS, right? Hardly. Try it and watch your outlook on life do a 180.

"FINDING YOUR PASSION"? NOT what I'm talking about here. That's an overrated trap that keeps people stuck in jobs they hate, waiting for **THE Thing** that'll make them blissful and rapturous. For 95% of people out there, finding something they *pretty* much like to do *most* of the time would be a 100% improvement. Shoot for that, and from there, fine-tune toward the ideal. Am I passionate about writing marketing brochures? Please. Do I enjoy it? Yes. What I *am* passionate about is living my life my way.

Living my life my way means owning a house, driving a decent, late-model car, saving for retirement, taking a couple or three vacations a year, and staying out of debt. As such, this book is *not* about eking out a living as a writer. You can find that anywhere.

Don't write me asking, "I just heard the going rate for a 500-word online article was $10. How can we make a living when so many are willing to work for slave wages?" In my world, that would be akin to a high-priced lawyer setting up shop in the poor side of town and then complaining that no one wants to pay his rates.

NEW HANGOUT, NEW FRIENDS If you want to make the high wages in any craft, don't hang out with the low-priced practitioners, or you'll start believing that's as good as it gets. By and large, you can forget the online venues—where you're competing with zillions of other writers for a project type (articles) that's relatively easy to write and where "acceptable" quality is all they're looking for. Where writing has become "commoditized": many competing writers can deliver the same basic product, so Econ 101 reliably dictates that rates will drop to nothing—which they have.

Go where you're *not* competing nearly as much, where you can bring special skills (i.e., marketing savvy, exceptionally creative writing style, industry-specific knowledge, project expertise, etc.) to the table—skills that can't be easily duplicated by thousands of others. Go where the barriers to entry are a bit stiffer (I mean, how hard is it to bid on a project online?), as that will discourage the writing "hobbyists." When you think about it, it's pretty logical: *Easy Access = Low Rates.*

Most importantly, go where you're not writing articles, but rather, marketing brochures, direct mail campaigns, web site content, case studies, newsletters, white papers and a bunch of other *business*-related projects. Not articles (except perhaps, high-paying trade articles). And in the pages ahead, we'll talk about all this.

"WELL-FED WORLD" Here, you won't find lists of new markets paying five cents a word. Or the latest online job site where you can bid with dozens of other writers fighting over *The Amazing Shrinking Fee* (Watch It Get Smaller Before Your Very Eyes!). Or strategies for convincing that client to pay you $15 an hour instead of $10 ("cuz you're worth it!").

In our world, the discussion will be about when to bump hourly rates from $65 to $75, $90 to $100 or $125 to $150. Oh, and here, you get paid in 30 days, 95% of the time—with rarely the need for repeated reminder emails. What a concept.

My approach has always been to give you the tools and ideas you need to make a handsome full-time living as a commercial writer (or FLCW, *Freelance Commercial Writer*, as I refer to us throughout my books). With the emphasis on *commercial*. This is a business, and you'd be wise to consider yourself a businessperson first, writer second.

A "REAL-PEOPLE" APPROACH I'd like to think I've written a *realistic* guide to building this business, given the lazy, slug-like streak in all of us. No question, this field takes plenty of work, but as businesses go, this one is a *lot* easier than most to get off the ground. And compared with other areas of freelance writing, it's not only much easier to get into, it's much more lucrative once you do.

With an emphasis on *simple, repeatable systems*, I've created a "best-of-both-worlds" business strategy: potential for healthy financial success without killing yourself to get there. Rest assured, whether you want to work the business like a *Type A* would, or prefer (like me) to have a life *and* make a solid living, this book will show you how.

WHAT WILL WE COVER? I've made just two assumptions in writing *TWFW*: 1) that you already know you're at least a decent writer; and 2) that you want to parlay that skill into a lucrative profession. As such, I'll spend just one chapter near the end on how to actually write certain kinds of projects; the main focus of the book will be on how to build a freelance commercial writing business.

I'll be sharing with you the things that have worked for me—not the *right* answers or *only* answers. But know that what's outlined on the pages that follow is a solid blueprint for building a business of your own. Do I do everything I suggest in this book religiously? No. If I did, would I make a lot more money than I currently do? Absolutely. If you followed these guidelines to the letter, would you earn an even healthier living than I do? I'd bet on it.

By definition, my experience is limited: big city, sales background, full-time startup *and* by cold calling, a generalist, etc. Over the years, however, I've heard from thousands of people with vastly different stories, circumstances, strategies, niches, backgrounds and geographic settings. I've incorporated their stories here.

DIFFERENT SITUATIONS, DIFFERENT ANSWERS In the pages that follow, in addition to general "how-to" detail for anyone anywhere, we'll cover:

- Building the business in a small town or rural area
- Doing it part-time while working at a full-time job
- Leveraging different backgrounds into profitable writing businesses
- Building a business as an AHM (At-Home Mom)
- Building it with cold calling, email marketing, networking, and/or direct mail
- Carving out niches in nonprofit work, case studies, white papers, direct response copywriting, associations, and many others
- Building a web site to promote your business
- What to charge and how to get paid
- Powerful networking strategies that go beyond the "meet 'n greet"
- Starting and maximizing the potential of a writers' group
- What it takes to earn $125 an hour—and beyond…

All the folks represented by the stories you'll read here have one thing in common: they're quietly exploding the stereotype of the "starving writer" and making handsome livings with their words in the vast and profitable zone between poverty and seven-figure novel advances. Their accounts are filled with great ideas for *anyone, anywhere*, in any situation.

Translation? Just because you're a fearless cold caller doesn't mean there's nothing worth reading in the cold-calling section. Just because you built or can build your business full-time doesn't mean you should skip the chapter on part-time start-up. Just because you're building the business in a major metro doesn't mean the chapter on small town/remote area startup won't hold any value for you. Trust me, the part-timers and smaller market/rural area folks are tough, smart and resourceful.

YOU'LL LOVE THIS… Because I know that most writers are creative types with a predictably primal aversion to "sales" and "marketing," I've devoted an entire chapter to painlessly and enjoyably developing that crucial sales and marketing mindset (with a chapter heading of "Learning to Love S & M," you know we're going to have some fun…). Grasping these cornerstone concepts will enable you to confidently build your own business while making eloquent contributions to the writing needs of your clients. And do it all with far less effort and angst than you might imagine.

This book is, at best, a few chapters in the big juicy story of "well-fed writing." As you read it, I want you to keep asking, "What other writing opportunities might be right under my nose?" *TWFW* doesn't have all the answers, but I think it's got a lot of good ideas. We writers like good ideas—especially ones that can make us a lot of money.

TWFW is just the beginning of the conversation in many ways, not the end. Check out a few pretty killer resources available at **www.wellfedwriter.com** that won't cost you a dime. In May 2002, I launched *The Well-Fed E-PUB*, my monthly ezine, chockfull of strategies, success stories and tips from FLCW's around the globe. The "E-Newsletter" link will lead you to archived issues, and laughably-priced past-ezine compilations to get you up to speed in a hurry.

In March 2008 (in typical techno-phobic, "late-adopter" fashion), I started *The Well-Fed Writer Blog*, which has spawned wonderful dialogues that serve as mini-knowledgebases on a variety of subjects. Subscribe to them both on the site, and while you're poking around—and speaking of knowledgebases —check out the *WF KnowledgeBase*. Between these three always-evolving resources, I make sure that I'm right beside you as you move ahead with your business.

And There's More...

The book you're holding in your hands is just the largest chunk of the total resources you have at your disposal as you set out on this profitable path...

SIDE DISHES

When you're combining two roughly 300-page books into ONE 350-page book, just doing an editing job of biblical proportions only gets you so far. You still have to offload some content—which I've done, to a special link on the web site called *Side Dishes*. Throughout the book, you'll see references to **www.wellfedwriter.com/sidedishes.shtml**; it's a "side-door" link— to be used by those who've bought the book, but it's not advertised on the site. At that link, you'll find a veritable cornucopia of goodies that complement the content of this book—and at no extra charge. But, alas, my charitable spirit only goes so far...

THE DELUXE WELL-FED TOOL BOX

Whenever you see this icon 📖 throughout the book, it means the item just discussed appears in my separate ebook, *The Deluxe Well-Fed Tool Box*, an exhaustive cut 'n pastable compilation of tools, articles, and reports to dramatically streamline and simplify your path to financial self-sufficiency.

In some cases, you'll see the icon when the item in question actually appears in the book (e.g., a simple contract, expanded cold-calling script, etc.). This is done so you can cut and paste/print out your own copy of it. See Appendix C for the full contents (as well as a description of yet another waaaay cool tool, *The Well-Fed Writer Time Line*). Yes, they are separate purchases, but at prices so reasonable as to be truly laughable.

Finally, throughout the book, you'll see several abbreviated references:

TWFW: The Well-Fed Writer

FLCW: Freelance Commercial Writer (how I refer to those in our field)

E-PUB: The WELL-FED E-PUB (my monthly ezine)

Subscribe for free at **www.wellfedwriter.com**, then *E-Newsletter.*

●   ●   ●

So, why even be a FLCW? Why is this a good career direction for decent writers? My, my, my, there are *so* many good reasons. Let's go take a look...

Chapter 1

There are tons of reasons to be a FLCW or "copywriter" (I prefer FLCW—sounds more like the profession it is. Nonetheless, you'll still be referred to as a "copywriter" by many in the business, especially in the ad copy realm.)…

1) YOU LIKE TO WRITE AND ARE GOOD AT IT

Just making sure…

2) HIGH DEMAND FOR TALENT

If you're a good writer, a quick study, can think strategically about a business (more on this later), and are willing to let the world know you're out there, you'll find a receptive marketplace. But, don't believe me. Check out the sidebar called, "Wanted: Good Writers!".

3) UNLIMITED WORK

Marketing brochures, corporate image pieces, advertisements, newsletters, direct mail campaigns, industrial video/ CD-ROM scripts, trade articles, press releases, radio spots, TV commercials, event scripting, business letters, sales sheets, sales promotions, marketing manuals, technical manuals, corporate/executive profiles, case studies, annual reports, product documentation, product spec sheets, proposals— shall I go on?

And remember, most of what we see as consumers (i.e., ads, direct (okay, junk) mail, the occasional brochure) is B2C (business-to-consumer). That's dwarfed by B2B (business-to-business) marketing materials, all the materials created by businesses to market to other businesses. Finally, and huge as well, is *internal communications*—the mountain of projects created by companies "for their eyes only." More on all these later.

Every one of these—and tons more—have to be written by someone. The sheer volume of work in a good-sized metro is staggering (later, we'll discuss how even Smalltown, USA-dwellers can thrive). As a good writer, if I'm not eating well, it's my fault.

4) THE TIME IS RIGHT FOR FREELANCERS

Why don't companies do the work themselves? Well, many do have in-house creative departments. But the last few decades have been all about *downsizing* and *outsourcing*. Fewer people, less resources, smaller budgets. And it's the creative, marketing and communications departments that are often the first to get whacked.

The result? Many organizations rely on freelancers heavily—and not just because they have to. While earlier lean economic times forced companies to hire outside contractors, they quickly realized the solid economic and creative advantages of the freelance model:

No salaries, vacation time, sick days, health insurance or benefits to pay.

They buy only what they need, only when they need it.

Fresh "outsider" perspectives combat insular mindsets.

Companies get access to a wide range of talent.

A manager in a large telecommunications firm in Atlanta noted, "Most people would assume that a company of our size would do the bulk of our writing in-house and they'd be wrong. It's amazing how much writing we outsource." Even companies with in-house "creative" have crunch times. Enter a competent freelancer, and both sides win.

As we'll discover later, big corporations are just one place to find work. When I released the original *TWFW* in 2000, I was doing a lot more work with the big boys. These days, I work with a lot of smaller firms (more respect and the same money), which, by definition, are far less likely to have in-house creative resources. Sure, many handle their writing themselves, kinda sorta, and it shows. But you know why most do so?

Wanted: Good Writers! Will Pay Handsomely.

I solicited input from a number of commercial writing buyers in Atlanta and elsewhere, asking them to share their thoughts on finding good writing talent in this field. As you'll see from their comments, there's plenty of room for you if you're a good writer. See a longer list at www.wellfedwriter.com, then *Testimonials*, then click the first link.

"Without question, it is hard to find a good freelance writer. We're not lacking for choices, but really good ones are rare. It's taken us several years to build up a stable of writers spread out over the country who are talented and reliable. There are probably currently 7 or 8 freelancers on our 'A list' and we keep them very busy."

—Ken Sternad, Vice-President, Public Relations
UPS

"Finding good copywriters is probably one of the toughest challenges we have. We're a small agency, but I bet we try 3–4 new writers a year. Most experiences are very disappointing—for many different reasons. So we usually end up rewriting most copy in-house."

—Doug Warner, CEO, Fountainhead Advertising
Atlanta, Georgia

"Once you find a copywriter who is talented, strategic, creative and reliable—hold on to them for dear life! The demand for these individuals is extremely high in the fast-paced world of corporate marketing and advertising. A writer who takes the time and initiative to really get to know your business becomes a valuable asset that you just can't afford to live without."

Kristi Sumner, Marketing Director - Creative Development
Mercedes-Benz Credit Corporation

Enough Bad Writers One final note. You'd be amazed at how many really bad writers there are out there working in this field. I hear about them all the time. That's bad news and good news. Any incompetent, unreliable writer makes the next one guilty until proven innocent as well. But given the chance to prove you're indeed one of the good guys, you'll do well.

Because they're simply unaware that folks like us exist. So, we have our work cut out for us.

By the way, by small, we're talking 20–50 employees and up (forget the five-or-fewer shops; they're good for portfolio-building when starting out, but, as a rule, they can't afford our market rates). Just remember: for every multi-billion dollar behemoth, there are scores of $25-, $50-, and $100-million companies.

A few years back, I landed a $5,000 gig from a company with less than 20 employees and annual sales of barely $1 million. But, when it came to doing their first catalog—their MAIN marketing tool—in six years, they knew they needed to get it right. I've since been hired repeatedly to edit this or that web page or sales letter for $125 an hour.

THE OTHER SIDE OF "DOWNSIZING" Freelancing since 1994 has given me a different perspective on corporate downsizing. Historically, the media has highlighted this trend with one-sided screeds about Big Bad Greedy corporations, more concerned about their own selfish profiteering than their own employees.

Certainly, profits are paramount, but what gets lost in these emotional discussions are the inevitable opportunities created for the entrepreneurially-minded out there. A whole freelance segment of the population out there, sizable and growing, is richly benefiting from all this "Bad News." Bottom line: the economy taketh away, the economy giveth.

COMPETENCE = SECURITY Perhaps you're one of those displaced souls looking to carve out your own niche. Well, the time is right. If you're good, and you work hard for a few years, get your name out there, and build something solid, you'll experience true "job security"—and that security will be in *your* hands, not someone else's.

5) BE YOUR OWN BOSS

I don't do well with someone else telling me where to be every day, and *when*. If you're a morning person by edict, trapped in a night owl's body, your time has come. Sure, there are times when I feel I really should get up early and blend in with the rest of the world, but I get over it. If that sounds like you, check out the sidebar below.

NIGHT OWLS UNITE!

10:06 a.m. The phone rings. It's one of my clients getting back to me on some ad copy I faxed them late the night before. My spoon is poised over my just-poured-the-milk-in bowl of cereal as she asks if I can go over a few revisions. Getting up from the dining room table and heading north to my upstairs office, I hedge briefly, even letting a tiny whine escape my white-mustachioed lips.

Should I come out of the closet finally? Living this lie has become unbearable. After all, they like my work and aren't too likely to replace me just because I'm living an "alternative" lifestyle. Taking a deep breath, I begin. "Um, I'm sort of a night person; I stay up late and get up late and (I'm picking up steam now) I'm actually right in the middle of breakfast."

There. It's out. Gotta train 'em sometime. "Oh," she replies, caught off guard. Pause. I can see her checking her watch. "Wanna call me back?"

Fifteen minutes later, we're chatting again, and happily, she understands completely, especially when I tell her that cold cereal was on the menu. Corn flakes. "And with cereal," she commiserates, "every second counts."

You got that right. In fact, in the time it took me to walk halfway upstairs, turn around, and dig back in, I experienced an estimated 25–30% breakdown factor in my cereal bowl. Welcome to Sog City. I hate that.

Just my luck. The present work day was obviously conceived by a morning person. No one in his right mind would have everyone getting up and hitting the highways all at the same time. Hello? No wonder so many people are grumpy in the mornings and have pathological caffeine addictions. HELLO?

I recall a conversation with a former colleague—and fellow night owl— who was recounting the unpleasant and short-lived experience of a 7 a.m. college French class. After several weeks of somnambulistic agony, he finally went to the professor and dropped the course, explaining that at 7 a.m., English was as much a foreign language to him as French would ever be.

Remember: To rise with the sun is human, but to dance with the moon is divine.

Bottom line, an 8:30 a.m. meeting is rarely necessary. People may suggest it, but I'll cheerfully lie through my teeth, invoking "prior appointments" (with my pillow and blankets). Of course, if that's the only time the client can meet, then do what you've got to do. In the early start-up days, meet clients when and where they want. Once they realize that they can't live without your awesome talents, *then* start making a few of your own scheduling preferences known.

6) MINIMAL INVESTMENT/LOW OVERHEAD

Here's all you need to get started and be successful: A small office. A phone with voice mail capability. Computer. Email. Fax. Printer. Business card. Seriously, that's about it. Once you get a few bucks rolling in, spring for some nice letterhead and envelopes. Put it all together, and its one of the lowest business start-up investments going.

As Atlanta FLCW Ed Gandia reminds, "When it comes to a traditional business, no one has a problem borrowing a lot of money or investing their savings to get it off the ground. But, when it comes to a FLCW business, for some reason, nobody wants to spend any money. People need to start looking at this as a traditional business. The thought of being able to start a very profitable business with only $1,000 or $2,000 is pretty remarkable." By the way, Ed built a $3–4K/month PT writing biz *while* working a FT job, and earned over $163K in his first full year in the biz; see more on Ed in Chapter Eleven.

7) SHEER VARIETY OF WORK

In this business, every day is different and interesting, full of opportunities to learn something. Love that. Over the years, I've written brochures, ads, newsletters, direct mail, web site content, case studies and more, about telecommunications, overnight shipping, soft drinks, artificial turf, supermarkets, baggage handling, charitable activities, building materials, special needs athletic facilities, data capture technology, mortgages, bio-energy processes, security systems, a major metro's biggest arts center, mountain property, apartment buildings, beer packaging, an inner-city dance troupe, the "green" initiatives of a carpet manufacturer, specialty medical apparel, executive search, fiber optics, financial planning, family therapy, chocolate chip cookies, credit cards, accounting software, high-end interior design, and about a thousand other things.

In talks I give, people often whine, "I don't want to write about soft drinks, mortgages, or security systems." My reply: "What if someone were paying you $75, $85, $100 an hour to learn and write about their business?" Pause. Um, yeah, okay, sure. I thought so. Another serious plus to the variety? You never have to deal with any particular set of office politics for very long. You get in, get it done and get out.

8) HEALTHY INCOME

I say a reasonably intelligent person with moderate writing ability and drive can sleepwalk their way to $30K annually. If you're good, and reasonably aggressive about getting the word out, you should easily hit $50–60K. And once you get a good reputation, and the referrals start coming in, who knows? There are a pretty healthy number of writers in this business grossing $100K or more.

Maybe you're a purist, and writing for Corporate America just feels so mercenary. Well, it's about trade-offs. Living the "starving artist" lifestyle *does* have its advantages: you get to live this romantic, angst-ridden existence, and feel vastly superior to all the "sellouts."

Of course, there is the "starving" part. Call me crazy, but I like decent clothes, nice digs, a good meal out, and a couple of nice vacations a year. I'm funny that way.

Some interesting (and lucrative!) gigs over the years: week-long on-site gigs crafting snappy headlines/tags for supermarket signage (~$5,000). Non-technical web content for a specialty medical site ($125 an hour; 100+ hours). Broad marketing campaign for an international charity (~$12,000 for 100 hours). 1500-word music CD-liner overview piece ($2,400). Twelve-page, image-heavy brochure for artificial-turf manufacturer ($3,700). Monthly six-page newsletter for telecomm giant ($4,500 monthly).

Some years back, I landed a pile of work with a global staffing company through an interesting "middleman" client: an internal marketing communications firm, hired by the staffing giant to execute a bunch of projects, and in turn, choosing to outsource the writing to a freelancer.

Over six weeks, I did three web articles (~$2,700); two simple one-sided sales sheets ($850); two 30- to 40-page benefits guides (~$6,500); two newsletter articles ($1,800); and various flyers, letters, and posters (~$2,100).

Roughly $14K. Oh, and another $1,700 from another client I'd "high-balled" to discourage him, since I didn't need the work. Please proceed, he said. Sheesh.

Once established, streaks like this just aren't that rare. For a longer piece on the juicy run with the global staffing client, visit **www.wellfedwriter.com/ sidedishes.shtml**, and look for "A Savory 'Well-Fed Writing' Scenario."

FINANCE YOUR DREAMS Go the "purist" route (i.e., writing only articles and books), and you could easily end up moonlighting to make ends meet. If writing's the goal, doesn't it make more sense to write for a *good* living, even if it's not your choice of subjects, than stay in some job you hate? I'm just sayin'... Then, with the bills paid, you've got the time and space to pursue your "bliss writing": that future Oscar, Pulitzer, Emmy, or Tony-award-winning screenplay, novel, TV series, or Broadway play.

9) TOTALLY DIFFERENT FINANCIAL PARADIGM

Compared with most "freelance writing," commercial writing enjoys a very different financial paradigm: *you're paid for all your time.* Compare that to, say, magazine writing. In that world, writers query an editor with a story idea, and if accepted, are told what they'll be paid—a flat fee. Time—as in, how many hours it'll take them to complete an assignment—is never discussed. The understanding is, whether the job takes them 15 or 50 hours, they'll make the same (and often low) fee.

If you have magazine experience, imagine this scenario: the editor of a publication for which you've written several pieces responds positively to a recent query. Once on the phone, the conversation turns to money. He says, "Let's try something a little different this time. Figure out how many hours you think it'll take to do the piece. Factor in time for research, background reading, travel, meetings, brainstorming, interviewing, writing, and editing. Then multiply the hours by $75 and give me a figure."

After you picked your jaw up off the floor, and stopped pinching yourself, imagine you did just that, returned with a number, and he said, "Fine." Welcome to Fantasy Island, right? Yet, in commercial writing, that description is pretty much right on the money.

10) THE OPPORTUNITY TO LEVERAGE WHAT YOU KNOW

Few working commercial freelancers started in this field without leveraging some past career or professional experience. I put my sales background to work. Over the years, I've talked to attorneys, engineers, scientists, healthcare administrators, medical researchers, nonprofit executives, university professors, software specialists, teachers, accountants, and many others who got tired of working in their field but didn't mind working *with* their field. If that's you, and you don't mind writing about that field, that's a huge plus.

And that experience can often be an adequate substitute for a big writing portfolio. Think about it from the client side. If you need some writing projects done, and you've got this person knocking on your door who knows your industry, its corporate culture and its vernacular, and can write about it well, you just basically eliminated the learning curve.

Many folks solicit work from their own former companies for these very reasons.

You may eventually transition into writing for other fields, but at the outset, why not establish a solid business base writing about what you already know, using years of established contacts?

11) IMPRESS PEOPLE AT COCKTAIL PARTIES

A writer is very interesting to people. I've joked about this with a friend of mine whose profession seems to have the opposite effect on people. When she tells people she sells ear plugs for a living, well … where do you go from there? "How interesting. I need to get a refill."

WHAT'S YOUR STORY?

STAFF WRITER? Maybe you're writing for a company but looking to go solo. Given your grasp of the commercial writing milieu, while you definitely have an advantage over those who've never written in this field, you're still looking for a roadmap to self-sufficiency. This can get you there.

JOURNALIST? Love the business of writing but long to make more money *and* enjoy better working conditions? A former journalist turned business owner shared this:

> *Thanks to low pay and often lousy working conditions,*
> *most journalists seek a career change within a few years.*

With their experience at expressing ideas in a clear, concise, logical manner and working on deadline, they're positioned to do well in the commercial writing market, where there's a huge demand for good, solid, coherent writing skills.

RESTLESS MOM? Maybe you're an at-home mom seeking a flexible, lucrative side business that meshes with motherhood. Capitalizing on your past career experience and perhaps seeking writing projects in your former field—a common success strategy—can make this a perfect fit. (Check out the at-home mom profiles in Appendix B.)

NEW COLLEGE GRAD? Just graduated, but not at all sure that working for The Man works for you? Having little professional experience will make it tougher, but low "right-out-of-college" overhead will dramatically hasten the ramp-up to profitability.

55+? Taken voluntary (or involuntary!) early retirement? Looking for your next career adventure, and always enjoyed writing? Healthy income potential and "on-my-own-terms" lifestyle flexibility makes this field an appealing draw for those either nearing or smack dab in the midst of "retirement." Check out the "Attn: 55+" link at **www.wellfedwriter.com.**

THE DOWNSIDES:

THE CLIENT IS THE BOSS Clients may want to change what you think is good into something awful. While they have final say, don't be afraid to challenge them if you feel they're making a mistake. Smart clients expect and appreciate your input. Got some good creative suggestions—even non-writing related ones? Speak up. Recommend a direction different from their original vision that they end up using effectively, and you'll go from copywriter to valued consultant. Which, in turn, can lead to repeat gigs and higher fees.

Suzanne Ryan (**www.thegourmetcopywriter.com**) sent this some time back:

I'd handed in a draft to a client two weeks earlier. No word, even after a follow-up email. I felt I "got" the company and their message. I called, prepared to hear I'd missed the mark, but found out my copy was spot on. Turns out my Q&A session, coupled with other questions I posed in the draft made them rethink their positioning and services.

*I'd proved to be a catalyst and more of an asset than I
intended. Given this "added value," they thought I was
undercharging!*

Also, here's the trade-off in our field: You write what others want, not
what you want. If I get a column published, I'll be lucky to earn $100.
Yet, a simple tri-fold brochure could easily make me $600–1,000+. I
don't romanticize the field and won't promise you total creative fulfillment
from it. But, fact is, as mentioned, I've had plenty of fun, interesting, and
yes, creative projects over the years. That also happened to pay very well.

Many newcomers (*especially* those hailing from the media or academia)
will grandly sniff, "Well, I couldn't write about anything I didn't believe in."
Sigh. Could you believe in apartments? Artificial turf? Fiber optics? Tea bags?

THE LIMITS OF COMPENSATION As a freelancer, you're paid for your
time. Come up with a tagline that becomes a company's new signature
slogan on all their materials and in their advertising and, as a rule, all
you'd receive is payment for your time.

That said, if it was discussed in advance, a high-profile piece of work
like that could warrant what's known as "value billing": a higher fee
than just the hours expended because of the promotional value of that
slogan. This is a very familiar concept in creative circles, so don't be shy
about pressing the point if it's appropriate.

GET OUT! This business, if done from home, can significantly reduce
human contact. So, how to counteract the inevitable loneliness, isola-
tion, and slow creep of social atrophy? In these amazingly high-tech
times, once you've secured new clients, you'll be able to do most of the
work by phone and email. Fewer meetings, minimal running around.

While that probably sounds pretty fabulous to commuter slaves, solitary
days followed by solitary nights aren't healthy. So get out: take a class,
take up kick-boxing, volunteer, have dinner with friends, etc. And keep
an eye out for other freelancers. Make friends, swap cards, grab lunch.
I'd wager they'd welcome the opportunity to expand their social circle.

•   •   •

So, what are the qualities that will boost your odds of success? And what are
the early steps to getting your business off the ground? Right this way….

Chapter 2

So, what qualities are good predictors of future success as a FLCW?

WRITING ABILITY: While you *do* need to be a good writer for this business (no one pays lousy writers $60–100 an hour—not more than once, anyway), you don't have to be brilliant. If you are brilliant, it can open doors to fun arenas like ads or direct mail, which require tight, snappy, and creative copy. But, plenty of fields—healthcare, financial services, manufacturing, high tech, and others—simply need clear, concise copywriting.

A popular part of my live seminars is the hands-on "sample review," where attendees paw through samples. Few see ones they wouldn't feel comfortable writing. For decent writers, it all seems pretty doable, because, well, it is.

GOT THE CHOPS? Before you take the FLCW leap, solicit input from those with zero attachment to protecting your feelings. Don't ask your mother or best friends; you already know what they're going to say. That's why you asked them. Ideally, get an opinion from someone who could hire you, or a more established FLCW (besides me, please). Call an ad agency or graphic design firm to locate seasoned FLCW's. But, what happens if you don't get back glowing reports? Should you punt? Not necessarily. Read on...

Can I Become a Better Writer?

Came across this great snippet from the 8/22/07 edition of Marcia Yudkin's excellent *Marketing Minute* (to subscribe: **http://www.yudkin.com/markmin.htm**):

Over the years, many people have asked me to look at their writing. "I need to know, do I have talent or not," they say.

Their request is seriously flawed, I'd reply. Anyone can become a better writer. When I taught English 101 at various colleges, I saw proof of this. Students with hackneyed, half-dead writing turned in lively, interesting essays by the end of the semester.

Stanford psychology professor Carol Dweck, [author of] **Mind-set: The New Psychology of Success***, reports research showing that in education, the arts and business, people who believe talent is fixed and inborn do not fully develop their potential and do not recover easily from setbacks. Those who believe talent can be developed, regardless of apparent starting point, not only achieve more but also prompt greater achievement in their children and staff.*

Her best news: You can change your mind-set about talent or intelligence. In only two months, kids who were taught that the brain, like a muscle, improves with exercise saw their math scores rocket from F's to B's.

SHOULD I TAKE A WRITING COURSE? If your hunt for second opinions reveals you could benefit from one, ask those same folks for recommendations. I can recommend two courses offered through AWAI (American Writers and Artists Institute): *Secrets of Writing for the Business-to-Business Market* and *Michael Masterson's The Six-Figure Copywriting Course.*

The first is ideally suited to a huge segment of the commercial writing project universe: business-to-business communications (B2B). The second, while focused on "direct response copywriting" (i.e., the long-letter style of direct mail typically used by purveyors of health products, real estate investing programs, and the like, as well as nonprofit fundraisers), will help you in any kind of persuasive writing. I've gotten plenty of feedback on both, and all has been positive.

One caveat: AWAI's marketing campaigns can get pretty hype-y, which is a shame, given that their materials are solid. Don't enroll because you believe you'll "Retire This Year." Buy it because it'll offer good training that will move your career forward (read "Full Disclosure" copy at **http://www.wellfedwriter.com/awai.shtml#1**). For more details:

Secrets of Writing for the Business-to-Business Market
http://www.thewriterslife.com/business/findoutmore/

Michael Masterson's The Six-Figure Copywriting Course
www.thewriterslife.com/wellfedwriter

DEGREES OF TALENT Listen. Perhaps you're *not* good enough (at least not yet) to get in the door of the Fortune 500's, but understand that *other* "Theory of Relativity." There are tons of small- to medium-sized companies with either no marketing materials or stuff so gruesome it'd make your hair stand on end. Being able to take them to the next level of clarity and coherence—if not on the par with a brochure for BellSouth, an ad for Verizon or web content for DuPont—can often make a dramatic difference for them. And a healthy—though perhaps not six-figure—income for you.

Just being able to write nice sentences or to clean up poorly written ones won't earn you $75 to $100+ an hour. For those rates, you need to be able to think strategically about a client's business—part and parcel of developing the marketing mindset we'll explore in the next chapter. And as for how to command the industry's top rates, stay tuned for Chapter Thirteen, "How Do I Make $125 an Hour? (or More!)."

DESIGN EXPERTISE (NOT!): During the "sample reviews" described above, THE most common question I get (as they swallow hard) is, "Are we designing these as well?" The relief is palpable when I reply, "Absolutely not. We just write." Clients never expect design from writers.

When folks I mentor say they're planning on learning design to offer the whole package, my usual response is, "Why?" Unless you're only working with smaller clients, for whom simple design is perfectly adequate, it'll take a long time to match the skills of a 10- to 20-year veteran (not to mention all the ins and outs of the printing side). Far better to make those folks your allies than your competitors. One man's opinion.

Do I Need Ad Agency Experience To Succeed In This Business?

I saw this fable rear its ugly head some years back in an Amazon review (excerpted) of the original *TWFW*, written by a woman who worked for an ad agency:

> *While reading books is good, most people cannot be good commercial writers unless they first work in an agency with seasoned professionals. It's all about apprenticeship & mentoring.*

I heard that years back when starting out. *Whatever.* Presupposing that someone is a decent writer, it just ain't so. I and countless other successful FLCW's—all similarly and allegedly *hobbled*—are living proof of that.

Part of the problem could be the term "copywriting," which in advertising, means writing ad copy. If that's what she meant, sure, mentoring and connections definitely count. Yet, you can make piles of money in this field and never write an ad. Moreover, ad agency cred on your résumé is no guarantee of writing talent. Read on…

Stumbling Giants A few years back, I got a call from a graphic designer who'd been contacted that morning by a huge, national high-tech company rolling out a new service in two weeks. Their big-bucks ad agency with offices worldwide had taken five weeks to come up with *one* lame concept. One. (Always deliver two or three, at least…)

The company took one look and sent their high-priced *artistes* back to the drawing board. A week later, they returned with one more, only a minor variation from the first and just as lame. I remember thinking, *Amazing. I wish my readers could hear this.*

The firm, staring at a swiftly-approaching media deadline, called my guy on Thursday morning and asked, *Um, can you come up with concepts for, oh, six different campaigns by, say, next Wednesday? And the first three by Monday?* We jumped on it, met all our deadlines, gave them several ideas for each, and they loved all our work. Touchdown.

For the record, some of the coolest and most effective marketing stuff ever created comes out of agencies every day. Respect them, sure; just don't be intimidated. And check out veteran adman Luke Sullivan's killer book, *Hey Whipple, Squeeze This*. It will absolutely make you a better and more creative writer and help you avoid common creative mistakes—in ad copy *and* commercial writing. Sullivan echoes one of my mantras: A lot of lousy stuff gets produced out there with big companies' names on it.

ABILITY TO MARKET ONESELF: This business is, first and foremost, a sales and marketing venture. While, in the beginning, it'll be 100/0% marketing/writing, over time, it'll balance out, then go the other way. Never sold anything in your life? Fret not. In the next chapter, we'll cover all this in fear-banishing detail. Remember: in this business, you are the product, and when you're selling *you* and what you know you do well, it's a whole other ball game.

DISCIPLINE: People afraid to leave the corporate nest (as if job security was a fact) often say, *I'm not very disciplined. I need to stick where things are more secure.* Hey, right now, you're on the other side and all you see in the plus column is this vague yet desirable goal of working for yourself. On the minus side are all the ways you could fail, go broke, lose your salary, benefits, house, car, wife, dog, etc.

People say, "Oh, you must be so disciplined." Please. Get a taste of the freelance life, and discipline ceases to be an issue. Why? Because you'll do *anything* to keep the gig going. Realize you can make a living at this— and in your PJs—and those nightmares of losing everything are quickly replaced by an even more horrifying notion: *The Return of the 9-to-5* (shudder). That'll get your butt outta bed in the morning, I promise you.

TECHNICAL EXPERTISE: Minimal. Know how to use *Microsoft® Word*? Send email? With an attachment (raising the bar)? That's about it. Seriously. I'm a "Minimum Daily Requirement" technical guy: I learn the least I can possibly get away with, and I've done just fine. Get comfy with *MS PowerPoint* and you'll be more marketable, but know that my *PP* skills are primitive at best and I've done just fine.

TENACITY: A thick skin and a healthy dose of "stick-tuit-iveness" are essential. Start-up can be lonely, unprofitable and full of naysayers. About four years after I started my business, I passed a cubicle in the office of my biggest client—with a familiar nameplate. "Did you used to have an ad agency?" I asked. "I did," was the reply, "but thanks to the huge recession in the creative industry back then (*a fact I was blissfully unaware of at the time*), I had to shut my doors."

Ah…now I remembered her. She was one of several people who told me that, with no ad agency experience or writing background, I'd have a heck of a time making it. Thanks for sharing. I was self-sufficient in four months. If I'd believed them, it would've been true. Now, this is no overnight venture. If you're going full-time out of the gate, have at least eight to twelve months of expenses set aside. Married at-home mom with a financial support system? This business can make a lot of sense.

FLEXIBILITY: Do you crave structure? If so, this business can be frustrating. Hit the inevitable slow periods, and it can pummel your attitude and self-concept. Women—being more multi-dimensional—generally adapt better. As a man, I'm more likely to define myself by what I do for a living. If I have no work, who am I? Learn to work hard during the feasts and kick back a bit during the famines, and you'll be fine.

RELIABILITY: A few years back, I was tied up on a huge project, forcing my long-time graphic design ally to hire another writer. She was complaining mightily that his first draft was overdue and typo-laden, saying, "I'm getting another round from him today, and I'm crossing my fingers that it'll be better." That's what many creative pros have come to expect from writers. Not this writer.

I've been saying this forever: Do what you say you're going to do, show up when you say you're going to show up (not 10 minutes late), deliver when you say you're going to deliver (and make it error-free) and you'll absolutely set yourself apart from 90% of the competition. No kidding. And because *you need no experience whatsoever to be reliable and dependable*, for those starting out, this is your secret weapon.

San Antonio, TX FLCW Michelle Zavala echoes this:

> *Some of the simplest things make a client sit up and take notice. One prospect was shocked when I said 'I'll call you next Tuesday at 10,' and I did. He was wowed with my ability to honor my word and follow through. And that contributed to him moving from 'potential' to 'regular' client.*

CURIOSITY: Love learning about new and different people, places, and things? Like trying exotic ethnic restaurants, traveling to unusual places, reading National Geographic, or dating three different people at a time? If so (not counting the last part…okay, maybe counting the last part), you'll like this field.

FLCW's know a lot about a lot, and that makes life interesting. A brochure for a medical apparel firm is followed by an ad for a mountain property developer, a case study for a building materials company, and then a direct mail piece for an accounting software program. All at a handsome wage.

ORGANIZATIONAL SKILLS: An anal-retentive nature can be a very good friend in this business. There's a healthy amount of minutiae to keep track of, but never too much.

EASY TO GET ALONG WITH: The surest way to keep clients coming back is to make it an easy, enjoyable and ultimately beneficial experience for them. Lose the attitude. Many average writers make good livings because they're easy-going and accommodating, while talented scribes often struggle for work because they're such arrogant pains in the butt.

Atlanta FLCW Boyd Baker has this to say about attitude:

> *My favorite design firm calls me when they're against the wall and need something yesterday. I don't stress or complain but find time for them. Because I work fast and am flexible, they're glad they called and that's what I want. I'm building a relationship. Would I rather have a longer lead time? Sure, but that's not what they're offering today. Today the special is Hurry Up and Write and I'm bellying up to the bar. They repay me by keeping me on the top of their "go-to" list when new projects come along.*

EXCITED ABOUT WHAT YOU'RE DOING: No, I don't bound out of bed with an ear-to-ear grin every morning, but I look forward to getting to work. If what you're doing doesn't turn you on, find something that does. Otherwise, you'll be a drag to be around.

ASSERTIVENESS: Be willing to fight for what's best for a project in the face of a client's revisions. Remember, (most) clients hire you because you possess skills they don't. During my first year, clients would ask, "What do you think? You're the professional." And inside, I'm screaming, "Me?!? The professional? I was selling dating club memberships a year ago (the sad truth)!! What do I know?!?" Of course, I'd just wisely rub my chin, and begin, "Well, given the target audience and the objective of the piece, my recommendation is…" Fake it till you make it.

"DOCILE" COPYWRITERS NEED NOT APPLY If I feel a client's off base on something, I speak up. Good clients will appreciate that conviction and the commitment to a quality outcome. The morons won't, but that's their problem, not yours. If you just obediently go along with every lame-brained copy change your clients suggest, they may just start wondering how good you really are. Then again, when the *Client From Hell* is insisting on one idiotic change after another, it's completely acceptable to have expediency trump any nobler commitment to creative integrity and want to get done, paid and gone.

ABILITY TO ASK LOTS OF DUMB QUESTIONS: I ask tons of questions at the beginning, many of which may make me seem like a dim bulb. I also happen to nail my first drafts about 95% of the time. Clients notice and appreciate it. One said, "That's why we like working with you. You take the time to find out exactly what we want and end up hitting the mark most every time." There you have it.

Asking questions is the great equalizer when facing any unfamiliar subject. Get them talking. They'll usually end up telling you what to write, how to write it, and even serve up a golden concept. By definition, you come into every project "in the middle." Questions help you be a quick study. Much more on this later.

DON'T FREAK OUT! Any project kickoff meeting will be with people who, by definition, have been stewing in the subject forever (especially high-tech). As such, they'll often assume knowledge you don't have and throw unfamiliar jargon at you at breakneck speed. Overwhelm sets in. All your "I'm-not-good-enough" stuff starts bubbling up. Don't panic. Ask a bunch of questions, take notes (ideally, record the meeting) and get some printed source material. Get home, review it all, ask a few more questions and I promise that in about 95% of cases, you'll feel 95% better.

While not always, clients can be extraordinarily disorganized; often, multiple contributors to one piece come in with their own objectives, goals, and agendas. Just to cover themselves, they'll often overload you with beaucoup extraneous information (hint: ask which is less-important "background," the "steep you in their world," and which is crucial "source" —which you'll use to write your copy). The first time it happens, you'll be looking for the life preserver. Hang in there. It's like breaking a code. It'll come.

HUMILITY/GOOD LISTENING SKILLS: There's a wonderful saying in spiritual self-growth circles: "Before enlightenment, chopping wood, carrying water. After enlightenment, chopping wood, carrying water." Be humble, no matter your level of accomplishment and success. Some copywriters, however, just can't muster it up.

They walk into a new situation and, in no time flat, are just sure they *know* what the client wants. Then, their first draft misses. Well. Obviously, the client 1) doesn't know what he wants, and/or 2) can't appreciate good writing, when in fact, the writer just didn't listen. Approach this business with humility. You'll be viewed as easy to work with (priceless) + have less anxiety + get more jobs done faster = make more money.

SMALL CAN LEAD TO BIG I have a colleague who declares, "I don't pick up a pen for less than $500." Good for her, but I doubt she was always like that. If you can pick up $200 for a few hours work, why not? Small jobs done well can lead to big jobs later—and not necessarily from that same client. On several occasions, I've been referred by clients for whom I'd done small jobs (or no jobs!) to colleagues with much bigger projects on tap.

DISCRETION: In the course of this work, you'll be exposed to mighty sensitive stuff (e.g., details of a company's product launch, consumer demographics, multi-million-dollar proposals, etc.)—information competitors would practically kill for. Zip it. Don't even discuss it innocently, minus the names. Not worth it. If the client or your market gets even a whiff that you've got loose lips, you might as well find a new line of work.

PRIDE IN A JOB WELL DONE: I'm successful, in large part, because I'm unwilling to turn in substandard work. Which, empirically, is not a sentiment shared by every writer. Make sure it's not only your best effort, but error/typo-free as well. Clients care.

During a recent copywriting workshop I did for the marketing folks of a software firm, one attendee shared this: an event production company vying for their business was making a pitch via *PowerPoint*. There on one slide was a single typo. The decision maker got up and left, saying over her shoulder, "Thanks for coming. Seeya." It matters.

So, those are the ideal qualities of a successful FLCW. Next? What are the steps you can take—mentally, physically, financially—to get yourself prepared for taking the plunge?

Ready for Self-Employment?

IT'S ALL IN YOUR HEAD Okay, mostly. Making the transition from long-time paycheck-drawing, cubicle-dwelling, spirit-drained soul to happy, smiling, skipping, humming freelancer is a big step. Having come directly from other chapters of self-employment prior to writing, I have to remember that many folks have major psychological hurdles to overcome.

Yes, a steady paycheck is real, not in your head, but a steady paycheck from freelancing is just as real to thousands out there—even if not to you quite yet.

Ask virtually any successful self-employee (i.e., two to three+ successful years) where true job security lies, and most will unhesitatingly say self-employment. *In competence there is security.* If you're good at something people are willing to pay well for, and you're willing to let those kinds of people know about it on a fairly consistent basis, you'll always eat well.

Most importantly, when you work for yourself, you control your outcome (*and* your income), not some bean-counter, for whom your job is just another line item, to be snipped out, if need be. Sure, if you're married with family and serious obligations, then you need to take care of business. But my book and ezine are full of stories of folks who cut the apron strings, and are making as much or more writing, while seriously loving their lives like they never came close to doing before.

A LIFESTYLE BOOK I half-jokingly tell people my books aren't really about writing; they're about creating a lifestyle. True. It's really as much about creating a life on your terms as it is about writing for a living. Fact: there are precious few careers that will inspire enough passion to justify lousy hours, major stress, idiot coworkers/bosses, or even just *commuting*, if all the rest of it is okay. You're far better off going for the lifestyle. One week of no alarm clocks, leisurely breakfasts, and working to your own rhythms, and you'll be weeping tears of joy.

TAKE FULL RESPONSIBILITY Successfully launching your own business is a game for adults. When you work for someone else, you can cut corners and likely get away with it. Do that here and you're only cheating yourself.

But if you're not used to being completely self-motivated, starting your own venture can be daunting. The nitty-gritty of building a business is hard, repetitive, grueling, and generally unprofitable work at the beginning. The good news? It can happen fast if you hit it hard, and even faster in this business because of its lower startup costs. Establish and maintain good habits at the outset and freelancing doesn't have to be difficult.

"The 4-Hour Workweek"

I looked like one of those nodding-head dogs as I was reading this great book by Timothy Ferris. Not all his advice is feasible for everyone, and there are a few "yeah, right" moments, but I love how he challenges traditional assumptions of work—its nature, setting, rules, and goals.

I realized that on some levels I was already following his advice: working smarter (i.e., creating passive income streams) and more efficiently (i.e., outsourcing anything you can to others who charge a lot less than you per hour); inserting mini-retirements throughout your life (while you've got the energy and health to enjoy them), rather than rolling the dice on the big "retirement payoff" after your body, health, and energy level are well into their decline; and just generally not accepting how "work" is supposed to look.

No matter where you are work-wise—even if you're a long-time cubicle-dweller looking to break out—you'll enjoy it. Even if you don't follow in his footsteps completely, at the very least, look at it as a roto-tiller and fertilizer for your mental soil—getting it prepped and enriched for self employment.

GET MENTAL, MAKE MONEY Making good money takes mental preparation. Reminds me of the classic joke: Salaried guy asks, "How can you stand *not* knowing what you're going to make every month?" Self-employed guy: "How can you stand *knowing* what you're going to make?" Amen to that. But, the self-employment mindset isn't automatic.

Many people come to the FLCW arena as starving writers. Take someone used to 500-word articles for $5 from online job sites, and drop him into our world, where *low-end* rates are $50 an hour. The predictable initial elation is quickly followed by hard swallowing and difficulty making that mental leap. But start believing you're worth it and begin exuding that, and people will buy it and *you*. Look at this email from Maryland FLCW Holly Minor:

> *Thanks to your book, I charge as much as $80 an hour now (I'd been meekly asking for $35 to $50 before) and am working most of the time. Every job seems to lead to another.*

Asking more seems to make people value my work more, too. Because of my rates, they just assume I'm great.

While I proudly carry my portfolio to all meetings, I haven't shown it in more than a year. People just seem comforted knowing it's there (it could be empty for all they know.) Hah! I'm having a ball.

Perhaps your fear is this: "Writing for a Fortune 500 company feels way out of my league. How do I know I'm good enough?" One reader touched on this in an email:

I've written for years—columns, articles, book reviews—so knew I could write. But, there wasn't a lot of money involved in that writing.

Ah. So when there's little money, you don't worry as much about having it be so incredibly good. But when the pay is a lot higher, so is the bar on expectations. And that cranks up the insecurity. Sure, clients *do* want a quality product, and they're paying for the right to expect that. But that's beside the point…

Give these people credit. If a client hires you, it's because she has talked to you and/or seen your work and decided you're capable of doing the job. With a few colorful exceptions, these people are not stupid and self-destructive. They don't willfully make their lives and jobs more difficult, nor in the case of employees do they care to risk the wrath of their superiors by choosing a clueless copywriter.

YOU'RE IN CONTROL   An interesting thing happened in my fourth year in the business. When I first started my business, my goals were modest: *make a full-time living (i.e., no moonlighting)*. Done. Second-year goal? A vague, "enough to pay the bills and then some." Got it. Year three was a little different. I started out great guns, set an ambitious monthly goal and was crankin' for six months. All I did differently was set a number. But then, my ADD kicked in, and my income dropped. I got back on track and finished the year strongly, but there's a bunch of good news here.

First: You control your income. Want a raise? Work a little harder. Make more calls. Meet more people. Network more. Your income *will* rise. Of course, the flip side is just as true. Slip into typical lazy, instant-gratification-seeking human being mode, and the well starts going dry. But even the downside is a wonderful reminder that we run the show.

Sure. I made less money for several months, but I also took time to have a life. I sang in a choir in the summer. I started Tai Chi. I took a couple of nice trips. All because my time was my own. And I paid all my bills *and* put money in the bank.

LITTLE CHANGE, BIG DIFFERENCE The following year, one slight adjustment made a big difference in my income. It's all about goal setting. Now, before you amble off with fingers in ears, know that my version of goal setting isn't difficult, nor does it require huge commitments of time and energy. Five minutes to start and about two minutes a day after that. To dramatically increase your income. Ah, you're back.

I decided I wanted to make $100,000 that next year. Now, just saying "I'm going to make 100K a year" is like trying to fit a whole pizza in your mouth at once. You need to break it down into bite-sized pieces. So, I created this chart:

> **$100,000 a year**
> **$8,000 a month**
> **$2,000 a week**
> **$400 a day**
> **Where's the $400 coming from today?**

One copy on my bathroom mirror, a second tacked up next to my computer. I read it aloud in the mirror for one minute in the morning and one at night before bed. Just having it to focus on made a huge difference. My mind started working to make it a reality. When you've got to make $400 a day, you get busy. The goal naturally propels you forward and suddenly presents you with opportunities. It's eerie, but it works.

With a 100K goal, $2,000 a week became the baseline. Before, $1,000–1,200 sounded good. Now? Low. It naturally drives up your own expectations of yourself (and yes, I did reach my goal). How much is a lot of money to you? If the most you've ever made in one year is, say, 30K, then 100K is likely unrealistic. Pick a figure that excites and stretches you, but doesn't seem unreal and out of reach.

GET YOUR FINANCES IN ORDER What's your present situation? Heavy debt? Healthy cash reserves? Expensive car? High mortgage? Extravagant lifestyle? How hard is it going to be to scale back? Unless you're an amazing marketer, with tons of contacts and/or a built-in client base from your last job, count on *not* making much right out of the gate.

Go for a low-maintenance overhead. The lower your bills, the sooner you'll be financially self-sufficient. Sure, there's something to be said for being "hungry" as a source of inspiration, but if you're too stressed over the light bill, it's going to make you crazy and have you wondering why in heaven's name did I go in this direction, and wait'll I get my hands on that Peter Booberman guy.

Try to pay off or pay down credit cards. $200–300 less a month = less anxiety. Do you need that fancy car with the fancy payment? In 1993, I went from a Jeep Cherokee (i.e., chick magnet) at about $400 a month to a Ford Escort at about half that. As a single guy, I felt like I'd left some of my manhood on the table. What sort of havoc would such a vehicle wreak on my social life, I wondered. Sad, I know.

But, guess what? I probably had more dates that year because all of a sudden I was doing something that really turned me on and it showed in my confidence and attitude. That's a zillion times more important than your wheels to the people really worth your time.

BUSINESS NAMES, BUSINESS PLANS AND BUSINESS CARDS

I get plenty of email asking about *just* the right name for a business. Or how business cards should look. Or if a business plan is necessary. But, too often these discussions are just paper shuffling to avoid the necessary actions, in which case I say, S*top stalling and start calling.* But let's deal with them, *briefly …*

BUSINESS NAMES Two schools of thought:

1) A catchy name, not just *Joe Smith Writes.* Conveys being bigger than one person and shows you're creative. Of course, if Joe Smith markets himself better than the writer with the business named after the Swahili words for "river of writing," then Joe's going to do a lot better than Mr. Brilliantly Creative. While I like my company name (WriteInc.; **www.writeinc.biz**), if I were starting out today, I'd likely opt for #2.

2) YOU, the writer, are the brand (especially important with web sites). Your name as URL might be more easily remembered. Many follow this formula (**www.steveslaunwhite.com, www.jonmcculloch.com, www.bly.com**). Unless you're John Smith or Mary Brown, reserving yourname.com will probably be easier than something with "write" in it (i.e., they're probably all taken).

FLCW Who Made $163K in Year One Serves Up His "Action Plan"

Atlanta FLCW Ed Gandia (**www.edgandia.com**) has a great story. He built a part-time FLCW biz while working FT in software sales, and in his first full year as a writer, grossed over $163K. We'll hear his whole story in Chapter Eleven. As a result of his experiences, Ed knows more than just a little about preparing—mentally and financially—to launch a commercial freelancing career. And he's written a great ebook on the subject called "Stop Wishing and Start Earning" that reflects his in-the-trenches experiences. I say it's this kind of info that's most valuable to aspiring FLCW's. No theoretical fluff, just the real deal from people who've been there and done it.

Ed describes Stop Wishing and Start Earning as, "all about how to create and execute an action plan to make the leap as safely as possible. It involves all critical areas, including goal setting, finances, self-promotion, balancing a job and a part-time freelance career, etc."

"When I was trying to launch my FLCW business, many people were raving about the opportunity, but few were addressing my biggest dilemma: How do I transition from a full-time job to a full-time FLCW career? And how do I do it without risking my family's financial future? That's what I cover in this e-book."

Check it out at **www.StopWishingandStartEarning.com**.

Creativity-sparking sites for naming: **www.businessownersideacafe.com** (then Start a Business, Business Name Ideas); **www.namestormers.com** (a naming firm); and from copywriting guru Marcia Yudkin, **www.yudkin.com/generate.htm**.

BUSINESS PLANS To clarify, if by "business plan," we're talking about a list of marketing activities such as identifying prospects, cold calling, direct mail campaigns, etc., great. Go for it. But some exhaustive proposal with income/expense spreadsheets, profit/loss statements, and the like? Not necessary (though if it makes you happy to do it, knock yourself out).

At a writers conference some years back, a fellow panelist and FLCW went on and on about the importance of a comprehensive business plan.

I was puzzled. My business plan was simple: *Make tons of phone calls and follow up until I have plenty of business. When slow, repeat.* Good plan. After all, it worked in less than four months. A financial advisor hired by one of my readers urged him to do a business plan before launching the business. After weeks of agonizing, eureka! My book was his business plan. ☺

BUSINESS CARDS Make sure your card tells people what you do. Pretend you've never seen it. If someone found it later but had forgotten the conversation, would it still be clear what you do? "Writing" or "writer" should be on the card somewhere. Seems basic, but you'd be amazed at how clever people try to be—to their own detriment.

When creating a business card, brochure or web site for your business, get clear about what you are and are *not* offering. Keep that offering uncluttered. If I see one of the above that says, *I write, I do photography, graphic design, proofreading, marketing strategy, and voice-over,* my first thought is, *jack-of-all-trades, master of none.* A prospect reading such an unfocused message would likely think the same.

Key question: Where would you like to make the lion's share of your income? Writing? Then present yourself as a writer. Wait until you're in front of the client to plant other seeds, if it's appropriate: *By the way, I also do a little photography and voice-over work.* If you've got the skills, and the client has that need (and who doesn't like a single-source solution?), then go for it. Just be clear on your "main line" offering.

The only exception is if you're also truly proficient at, say, graphic design —good enough to compete with dedicated practitioners. The ability to provide true one-stop turnkey solutions will make you very marketable (and I've only crossed paths with two such folks in 15+ years). But, even in this case, consider having separate cards and sites in addition to combined ones to be able to tailor your pitch to prospects' needs.

WHERE'S YOUR PORTFOLIO? (a.k.a. Your "Book")

What's in yours? A few articles from the church newsletter, several poems, and your own brochure? Sorry, but most corporate clients won't hire you. No need for the proverbial "overstuffed-with-Fortune-100-gems" book, but get your presentation up to snuff. All the following can be done while employed elsewhere. Smaller companies will be more open to less-impressive samples and can provide juicy opportunities for upgrading your "book." And you may already have some writing samples.

Building Your "Book" While On the J-O-B

Columbus, Ohio FLCW Laura Rees (www.romacreative.net), the primary breadwinner for her family of four, left her full-time job in June 2008 after employing a clever strategy she strongly recommends to all those working full-time:

"Take advantage of any opportunities at your full-time job to get clips. I pitched a column on behalf of our company president to our local business paper and it was accepted. I ghostwrote the article for him and it ran in 08/06. My first clip! After that I kept volunteering for more writing projects at work and by the time I left, I was in charge of not only HR, but also all marketing communications efforts for the company. It gave me a great portfolio to start out my full-time freelancing efforts, and I used those clips, while I was still working, to freelance part-time."

Ben Hardesty, a technical writer at a Fortune 500 corporation, echoes Laura's sentiment: "If you use a little imagination and your knowledge of the inner workings of the company where you already work, you can find a wealth of writing opportunities. You probably won't get paid, but you won't find a quicker – or easier – way to get writing experience and build your portfolio.

"I spoke to Marketing Communications about doing some work for them, and quickly had more offers than I could handle. Don't think that just because your company is big, they don't need any writers: my company doesn't have a single copywriter on staff! They farm everything out, were delighted to have an internal resource to help out, and I ended up writing brochures, newsletters, and poster copy.

"Frame it in the context of doing a 'stretch assignment' (one outside your normal job responsibilities that requires you to "stretch" by learning and applying new skills or knowledge) as that shows initiative – and a desire not just to pad your portfolio, but to become a more valuable employee. It's a good habit to get into. After all, a good freelancer isn't just after a paycheck, but actively looks for ways to add value to a client's business. If you want to do that as a freelancer, start doing it as an employee."

Consider the following strategies to build a portfolio from scratch...

PAST LIVES. Got 15- to 20-year-old samples? Use 'em. Sure, spiff 'em up by copying them onto glossy paper, or having a graphic designer friend drop the copy into a new, fresher layout. But, as a rule, good writing is good writing, whenever it was done.

PAST/PRESENT JOBS. Absolutely use any writing projects from a full-time position (past or present). Just be sure you're not violating any confidentiality agreements. If they *are* sensitive or proprietary in some way, simply purge the delicate information, replace with generic verbiage, and repackage it.

EXCERPTS. Got voluminous project samples too big or boring to make a good sample? Pull out and reformat some engaging chunks so prospects can *easily* get a sense of your skills—minus a 20-page slog. Even if that's precisely the kind of work you're seeking, excerpt it (while perhaps linking to the full text for those who want to read it).

JOURNALISM. Have a pile of news clips? While you can certainly use them and will no doubt boost your credibility in the eyes of your prospects for your writing ability and eye for the deadline, you'll still want to beef up your book with some more corporate samples like brochures, ads, newsletters (similar to articles), etc.

PRO BONO. A proven way to build a portfolio. It's a great strategy for boosting visibility, getting and keeping your name out in the community, building up goodwill, gathering the right kind of corporate-type samples (brochures, newsletters, press releases, ads, etc.) and, in many cases, positioning yourself nicely to land paying work from those same entities (which often have healthy budgets) down the road.

Below are a couple of links for the kinds of organizations that would likely be receptive to a "win-win" *pro bono* pitch. Try to find the local or regional branches of these often-nationwide organizations and approach them as you would any prospective client.

http://www.southarts.org/SAF_links.shtml

http://www.njnonprofits.org/linksNCNA.html

Here again is a great place to team with a newbie designer and make an attractive offer to a nonprofit or start-up: you'll create a brochure, for instance, at no charge for the copywriting or design in return for healthy creative latitude and plenty of samples. Remember, I didn't start out working for Fortune 500 companies. I worked up on the strength of projects done for smaller companies.

By all means, shoot high—especially if you can leverage past industry experience or contacts. And if you don't get hired, ask what it would take.

Mighty useful information. And sometimes, as happened so many times for me, you'll land work with the big boys by riding in the door on the coattails of a graphic designer, ad agency, PR firm or other "middleman." More on that coming up.

RE-PURPOSE. Try to leverage *any* past writing efforts, regardless of the circumstances, if you can honestly say *you* wrote it. Do whatever you need to do to—forgive this loathsome "corporatespeak"—*re-purpose* existing samples. Doing this, I assure you, will be far less of a hassle than having to land another sample from scratch.

CREATE A PORTFOLIO. How about teaming with a graphic designer to simply create some ads or brochures for fictitious companies? This is what arts school students do. They won't work on real jobs until they *get* a real job, so they build their "job interview" book by simply picking existing companies and making up stuff. Ideally, you'd land some *pro bono* work with real companies to build your book, but just know that tapping nothing more than your imagination and writing skills is a perfectly acceptable strategy.

A good source for a graphically-talented teammate is someone also starting out: a student at an art or design school (or a vocational/technical institute where they teach graphic design). Contact the professors and ask them to recommend talented students. Students always look for opportunities to build their portfolio with "real world" work. Consider swapping services and helping them with copy for their own marketing/promo pieces.

If they don't need copywriting, they'll want to be paid, which is only fair. You want your talents valued, even when starting out, and so do they. But, chances are good you'll be able to get them at low "starving artist" rates and they'll get a piece for their books.

"MOCK PIECES." This is sort of a cross between *pro bono* and creating a portfolio. Dayton, Ohio FLCW Jesse Reeves (**www.reeveswriting.com**) brought this one to my attention. A little background… Jesse struggled in the early days with a meager portfolio, before getting a solid foothold. He writes:

> *"If I had it to do over again, I would've made twenty or thirty 'mock pieces' for my online portfolio (mock pieces: those created for people who don't really need or want them). For instance, I did a brochure for a friend's dad who owned a print shop, but I wasn't paid.*

"When I first started calling, I only had six samples. Not nearly enough. Now, my online portfolio has the "scroll factor" —i.e., having to scroll down to see all I've done (translation: prospects say 'this guy's busy, people are hiring him.')."

"What Should My Portfolio Physically Look Like?"

Lorrie Lykins, an FLCW from Tampa Bay, shares this amusing tidbit about how *not* to present yourself and your work:

NOT a good idea to show up unannounced at a prospect's office expecting everyone to drop their phones and run over to ooh and ahh over your material. It's worse if you're clutching your son's long-rejected Beastie Boys three-ring notebook (true story) into which you've glue-sticked your PTA newsletters and pictures of your dog dressed in the PTA fundraising event T-shirt with snappy captions you wrote as samples of your professional ability.

Cringe. In seminars, I love showing my first portfolio: a mortifyingly unimpressive three-ring binder (I shudder at the memory), which, in terms of color, texture and variety of content, was the equivalent of unsweetened oatmeal. It had six black-and-white pieces in it, none of them in a nice layout, every one requiring constant accompanying chatter to pump it up into the distant outskirts of respectability. And I built my business on this near-disaster. It's a transcendent moment of relief for many seminar attendees.

Invest in a professional portfolio, available at good *art* supply (not *office* supply) stores. A typical portfolio is a large (at least 20 to 24 inches square) handled black case, zippered on three sides, with 15 to 20 plastic sleeves lined with black paper (allowing you to use both sides) and secured in a multi-ring binder. A decent one? $80–100+. Just do it. It's the cost of doing business. Dick Blick (**www.dickblick.com**; look under "Presentation Cases," not "Portfolios") has stores in many states, as well as online ordering.

Several colleagues (especially designers) take the portfolio one step further and mount their samples—angled stylishly—on loose pieces of stiff black cardboard (called mounting or matte board). They may use two copies of a brochure, opened and closed to showcase different sides of the piece. Perhaps they display several components of a larger campaign: pocket folder, brochure, insert sheets, etc. The separate boards are then stacked in a special large rectangular black suitcase. Very classy. Very optional.

Help Start-Ups, Build Your Book!

Atlanta FLCW Bobby Hickman (**www.blhickmaninc.com**) sent me these tidbits (used here with his permission) regarding four novel avenues he pursued when starting out. These kinds of events attract start-ups and small-business folks, so while not ideal for landing big jobs, they're great for portfolio building. And small firms do get big.

Four Business Roads Less Traveled

Business Expos I get a lot of leads here—not so much from visitors as other exhibitors. I get there early, set up my display and wander around. Exhibitors are usually start-ups or small concerns trying to expand, and all trying to get the word out. I did a free expo at a local Staples and got newsletter work from a chiropractor along with a brochure job from a computer provider. Staples said most stores try to hold one expo per year. Contact your nearby Staples and ask to be notified if/when the next one happens.

Business Seminars Attending Small Business Administration seminars can generate leads while improving business skills. Attendees are generally new entrepreneurs. I was hired by one to do a brochure and web copy for his new contracting firm, and have promises of work from a new bakery and a coffee service when they launch.

Pro Bono To build my portfolio, I volunteered to handle my local business association's newsletter. That led to several opportunities—all pro bono—and a seat on the board. But as my business grew, I had to curtail the free stuff. The board asked me how much I'd charge to keep doing the newsletter. I'm now being paid every month.

Coaches/Mentors Business/career coaches and professional mentors—folks also trying to expand their businesses—are a good source of leads. I used a coach to help me develop a marketing strategy; she's sent me several new clients and become my client. I'm helping her with publicity and I'll be ghostwriting her book this year.

"SHOULD I ADVERTISE?" As a rule, advertising just isn't a good bet in our business, except if the vehicle is laser-targeted to your audience. Translation? Skip the *Yellow Pages*, but buying some space in a publication serving your local creative services industry (or chamber newsletter) might be worth it.

In Atlanta, Oz (**www.ozonline.tv**), a local publication serving the creative industry, puts out their annual Creative Index (i.e., a one-year shelf life—an ideal scenario and one to look for). One business-card-sized ad a few years ago snagged a graphic designer who hooked me up with a client that put $9,000 in my pocket. Nothing in the 5–6 years after that so I stopped. But, that initial $150 investment paid off nicely.

Since then, my small copywriters group (**www.copyopolis.com**; more in Chapter Ten) advertised our entity for a few years in a regional creative publication and all got some business. Again, *targeted* works. *General* doesn't.

On Your Bookshelf

These four are mandatory. See Appendix A for a full roster of general writing resources.

1. *The American Heritage Dictionary*: lively, topical, fresh. The best dictionary out there.

2. *The Synonym Finder* (Rodale): hands down, the best thesaurus out there, and far and away the most frequently used reference on my shelf. Invaluable tool for copywriters—as we try to keep copy fresh on a subject we've written about dozens of times before. Forget the thesaurus on MS Word—doesn't come close to the detail this beauty offers.

3. *Woe Is I* (O'Conner): THE grammar guide gem. Covers all the ground *Elements of Style* (Strunk & White) does and a lot more, but with a fun, irreverent approach and tone that'll have you *wanting* to read it. Says a lot for a grammar guide.

4. *Bartlett's Familiar Quotations*: 25,000 famous utterings covering nearly 1,500 pages. Just the thing to spice up marketing copy and add an unusual touch to your work. Which can, in the mind of a client, separate decent copywriters from exceptional ones.

•   •   •

Okay, since sales and marketing are such foreign and frightening concepts to many, I think that's a wonderful place to head next. So, grab a plate and let's dig in…

Chapter 3

Me and my big mouth. I mention my sales and marketing background and suddenly a bunch of people without one decide they're hosed. Remember: *If you think you need that to succeed in this business, you're right. And if you think you don't, you're also right.*

Yes, I had 15 years of sales experience before starting my writing business. Yes, that helped me in the start-up phase. Yes, if you have a similar background, it will also help. But, the fact remains, most people in the business *don't* have sales experience.

Remember, I had no *writing* background, no paid professional *writing* experience, had never *written* anything for money, and was entering a professional *writing* field. I could have used those arguably more relevant shortcomings to talk myself out of it, but I didn't. While that background is an asset, I firmly assert the following. Read this carefully:

> *Success as a freelance commercial writer is far more about a **process** than a **personality**. It's far more about a lot of things you have to **do**, than some way you have to **be**.*

It's not about being a "salesperson" in the (likely negative) sense you have of the word. It's about following a blueprint. All that said, if I really believed that these opening words were enough to convince you, this would be a very short chapter. I understand that many of you, not having come from this world, might need a bit more TLC, so let's do it.

I received this email from a reader some time back—one of many in the same vein:

> You're succeeding in a business I've sort of ambled through for the past five years. Like many writers and other types of artists, I have the skills and the talent—but HATE MARKET-ING MYSELF. *[Caps his, not mine.]*

For many "creatives," SALES and MARKETING truly are *The Boogeymen.* It can keep them from pursuing the freelance life calling to them. Can't have that. But, things you fear you're not likely to do, so let's defang the beast. Along the way, we'll lay the foundation for marketing your writing skills and business and start a richer discussion about developing a marketing *mindset,* in order to write ever better marketing copy. Let me share a story that should provide a little comfort to the sales-averse out there…

FEASIBLE FREELANCING Some years back, I gave a talk to an Atlanta-based group of freelancers of which about 50 percent were writers. I asked the roughly 75 attendees how many of them had been successfully freelancing for at least three years. About 40 to 45 folks raised their hands. Next question: *Of those who raised their hands, how many market yourselves on a consistent basis?* Guess how many hands went up? Two.

Here was a group of successful freelancers who'd been paying their bills for three+ years, and less than five percent did any regular marketing. Yeah, yeah, anecdotal evidence and all that. Still, my personal experience has borne this out as well—once the machine's up and running and you've gotten into some good promotional habits, it's not some endless grueling battle to scratch out a tiny bit of market share.

SALES & MARKETING—DIFFERENT THINGS While both sales and marketing involve connecting with prospective customers, sales generally refers to *direct contact*—whether in person or on the phone. Marketing refers more to efforts to build awareness in less personal ways (email, direct mail, advertising) about who you are, what you're offering and why they should do business with you. But when building a small business, as we are, the two become a lot closer in function and the terms much more interchangeable than would be the case for a large corporation.

WHAT MARKETING IS I humbly offer up my simple definition of marketing:

Successful marketing of a freelance commercial writing business is simply letting prospective clients know you're out there —on a consistent basis, in a variety of ways, and with a message they can hear through the clutter.

Effectively reach enough people who give you as much work as you want, and then repeat the process whenever you don't, and I say you're a successful marketer. More good news? Once in the game, just follow the same proven strategies over and over again. Simple. Not easy, but simple (remember: earning $60–125+ an hour isn't going to be a breeze), and none of it beyond the capability of a reasonably intelligent human being. Oh, and add the Internet to dramatically streamline and simplify your marketing.

WHAT MARKETING ISN'T Marketing on this level isn't some arcane and wildly esoteric science decipherable only by Harvard or Wharton MBA's. *That* kind of marketing—replete with all the jargon: *demographics, psychographics, market share,* etc.—only really comes into play with big companies, not one-person writing shops. So, relax.

And FYI, you can likely gain all the marketing knowledge you need to succeed in this business by reading. Seriously. Check out the reading list in Appendix A.

In my 4/6/08 blog post (**www.wellfedwriter.com/blog**) Bay Area FLCW Kelly Parkinson echoed this sentiment: "Read every book on marketing, sales, and copywriting you can get your hands on. Then, if there is a faster, smarter way to do something, you'll be in a much better position to know what it is and to put it into action. But most likely, you'll end up knowing a ton of things your clients don't, and that will increase your value to them... You shorten the sales cycle and you charge more..."

YOU'RE DRIVING Read this very carefully:

There are enough components of the marketing process that you have complete control over, and they're more than enough to ensure your success.

You control the number of calls you make (both initial and follow-up), emails you send, and postcards you mail. Assuming you're targeting the right audiences, if you do all those things consistently, you'll succeed. That's powerful stuff. *Teaching-yourself-to-fish* stuff. And ponder this: For the most part, your prospects already know their lines. You just have to learn yours. Let me explain.

A GAME ALREADY IN PROGRESS Many years ago, I discovered the culinary adventure known as Dim Sum: the unusual and ultra-tasty Cantonese feast usually served on weekends in authentic Chinese restaurants (as opposed to the Chinese-American mutant joints most of us are familiar with). My first time was a revelation—a new and wonderful epicurean experience *and* the place was packed. Here was something I didn't even know existed and zillions of other people had been enjoying it for years!

It'll be similar when you start marketing this business. There you'll be, with all these fears: fear of failing, not being good enough, making an idiot of yourself, going broke, etc. All understandable, but if you're calling large corporations and creative "middlemen" (as we'll discuss later), one needless fear is that the people you call aren't going to "get" what you're offering. Marketing calls are commonplace to the folks you'll be calling.

You'll be all freaked and they'll be so matter-of-fact on the other end, because they *expect* to hear from copywriters. True, smaller firms may need more educating about your offering, but I've been pleasantly surprised at how savvy many small firms are about the need for professional writing assistance.

DARE TO BE SEEN As a single guy, I occasionally surf over to the online dating sites. The clichés are rampant. Here are zillions of people, looking for the most important relationship of their lives, and barely one in a hundred takes the time to craft a message even remotely creative and original.

Virtually every ad lists such unique gems as *I love moonlight walks on the beach...*(uh, that's "moonlit") *romantic, candlelight dinners...*(that's "candlelit"), *snuggling in front of a fire...* and, my favorite one to hate, *a man who's as comfortable in a tux as blue jeans* (finger down throat), just like *everyone* else's.

I want to ask: Do you think you'll attract the opposite sex by blending in with everything around you? That's called *camouflage*. People in the armed forces do this very thing when their lives depend on *not* being noticed.

If you want to be seen, you have to draw attention to yourself, and precious few commercial writers do regular marketing. Getting noticed isn't all that hard if you're one of the few who make the effort.

IT's NOT IMMODESTY I know—drawing attention to yourself is *immodest*. Listen: there's not a darned thing immodest about drawing attention to a legitimate, high-quality, professional offering in demand by virtually every successful business under the sun. You're enjoying your home, car, clothes, favorite restaurants and vacation spots because some company successfully marketed something to you. Or to the friend who made the recommendation to you. And you're probably glad it did.

A lot of companies in Atlanta are glad I made sure they knew I was out there. They acknowledge the difference I've made every time they call me for another job. You'd better be willing to draw attention to yourself or you'll need to find another line of work. You're not selling Veg-o-Munchers on late-night TV. You're not some smarmy car salesman. You're a professional writer marketing a service for which there's a huge need.

KEEP SHOWING UP Want to know the simple key to success in this business? Keep showing up. Assuming you're a competent, creative and reliable writer, it's all about multiple impressions. The writers who have built thriving businesses have just kept knocking on new doors. A *Last Man Standing* sort of thing. It's that simple.

And sometimes that process can literally take years. My friend and colleague Erick Dittus, an Atlanta-based speechwriter, echoed this sentiment:

> *In my business, on the first few calls [to prospects] I almost always hear 'there's no work here' or 'it's very rare that we hire outside.' It's the tone of how they say that—or the power of the brand—that makes me call them on a cycle (about every 2–5 months). Delta, Coke, and McDonald's all [became clients] after a couple years of calling.*

And while the speechwriting gestation period from contact to hiring may be longer than for copywriting, the point is nonetheless sound.

That "Icky Sales Thing"

When combined with marketing, sales completes, for many FLCW's, the "Panic Pair." Oh, the emails I've received: *I'm terrible at sales… I could never sell anything to anyone... The thought of selling is downright frightening to me...* and on and on. Such torment. Let's talk about what sales does—and doesn't—mean. Check out the end of this chapter, where several successful writers share what sales means to them. Not what you'd expect.

BAD ASSOCIATIONS Somewhere along the line, for many of us, "sales" of anything got wired to high-pressure techniques, pushy salespeople, slick sales practices, etc. We've all been the target of salespeople who embodied all the negative stereotypes. Maybe it was someone selling cars. Timeshares. Encyclopedias. Aluminum siding. Countless obnoxious telemarketers. It all added up to a bad taste about sales.

SALES: MEETING NEEDS Well, guess what? That's not what sales is. Sales is nothing more than matching your product or service with a prospect's needs. With this definition in mind, we can start seeing the potential for "sales" to morph into a more *consultative* function. Build a commercial writing business, one thing's certain: you sold something. Those clients *bought* you and your service because of who you are, how you presented yourself, what you had to offer, and a need they had. Over time, as we're about to discuss, you dismantled the barriers in the way of that client doing business with you.

B2B VS. B2C First, a few generalizations—but valid enough for our purposes. Sales happens in two main arenas: business-to-business (B2B) and business-to-consumer (B2C). A B2B sale (what we FLCW's do) is generally a "problem-solving" sale: selling a product or service to other professionals. Examples: mainframe computers, medical equipment, software, billing systems, pharmaceuticals, copywriting services, marketing consulting, graphic design, etc. You're helping a business address its challenges and your solution will enhance its position in the marketplace by making it more efficient, profitable, reputable, competitive, etc. So far, so good.

B2C is the other big arena and, as consumers, many of the bad sales experiences we've had in our lifetimes fall into this category. All door-to-door, in-home and telemarketing sales are B2C. Why are B2C sales usually the ones that bring out the "dark side" of sales and salespeople? Well, for a few inter-related reasons.

DISCRETIONARY VS. NON-DISCRETIONARY Many B2C sales involve discretionary purchases—items you don't actually *need* (e.g., a timeshare, encyclopedias, expensive jewelry, etc.). Yes, you need a car, but you don't need a $50,000 car. And when you don't need something, emotions play a much bigger role in your buying decision. Playing on those emotions, a B2C salesperson may resort to high-pressure and manipulative tactics. And you walk away with an icky taste in your mouth about sales in general.

B2B sales are generally more non-discretionary. Sure, an organization chooses to buy a product or service, but it's much more prosaic, yet crucial considerations like profitability, operational efficiency and competitive edge that typically carry the day. If a business wants to thrive, it doesn't often have a lot of choice about investing in certain things.

EMOTIONAL VS. UNEMOTIONAL Yes, emotion can play a slight role in B2B sales—i.e., a product carries with it the promise of success (or conversely, the fear of failure through non-action), increased competitive edge and the professional rewards that might accrue to a wise decision-maker. But we're still dealing with the primacy of largely *unemotional* business considerations. Hence, pressure and manipulation become non-issues.

Not that they're ever really appropriate, but when a juicy commission is on the line, many B2C salespeople will unhesitatingly exploit a customer's discretionary desires. In our business, high-pressure sales tactics aren't just inappropriate; they're irrelevant.

AN APROPOS ANALOGY Let's bring these discussions of marketing and sales together in an entertaining way—taking a closer look at the last job I held before starting my writing business, in the sales department of a video dating service (afraid so...).

This company's whole marketing approach nicely demonstrates what I'm talking about regarding the sales cycle: the importance idea of multiple impressions, an understanding of the limitations of each step of the sales process, and how everything works together to lead you to the final desired result. Here's how their sales process worked...

The company's telemarketing department would book appointments for people to come in and meet with a "member representative" (i.e., salesperson; my job). The member rep would explain the program, give them a tour and then try to "close" them on buying a membership—an investment of anywhere from one to three thousand dollars.

One of the first questions we'd ask them is, *What made you come in today?* Invariably, they'd reply with some version of, *Oh, I was just curious.* Ri-ight. Of course, we never really expected anyone to say, *Well frankly, my social life sucks*, or *I haven't had a date in two years*. But we'd ask anyway.

And when they invoked mere curiosity, we always smiled to ourselves, because we knew things they didn't know we knew. Lots of things.

For starters, we knew they were much more than just curious. In fact, they were quite serious about making a change in their social lives. The mere act of entering our doors proved they'd already jumped through multiple psychological hoops. Let me explain.

HOOP ONE This company was big on multiple impressions. They'd repeatedly send out direct mail questionnaires, knowing that most people would throw away the first eight to ten they'd receive. But then, one day, for whatever reason—a painful breakup, a string of bad dates, loneliness—a prospect would actually fill out a response card and send it in. That in itself was a huge long shot—and proof of the power of multiple impressions.

They sent in a card precisely *because* they'd received many others in the past—all of which had slowly built the company's credibility in their minds. By this point, they were quite familiar with this outfit, had probably read through several past flyers before tossing them, and knew the company was a reputable, nationwide organization. They probably even knew someone who'd joined and spoke well of the place. All bricks in the wall.

Each flyer they received affirmed the solidity of the organization (*they're still around*), and established a crucial trust level. Same with any ongoing marketing campaign you undertake. The mere repetition of it will boost your credibility. And yes, there would always be a percentage of people who'd never consider a dating service, just like there will always be prospects who will never consider using a freelancer, for any number of reasons. It's just the numbers.

HOOP TWO Prospects who'd sent in a flyer would get a call from the telemarketing department to go over the questionnaire and try to book them for an in-office appointment. Predictably, many dropped out at that point. Taking the next step proved they were serious about this, and many weren't prepared to admit that to themselves. Or, they'd explain, they'd filled out the survey in a moment of frustration or despair, which had since passed. Maybe since sending it in, they'd met someone promising.

But even if they did bail at that point—and the company counted on most doing just that—they were gathering still more information (*okay, so they call you when you send one in*) and becoming even more comfortable with it. And unless they did indeed suddenly meet the mate of their dreams, chances were good that the emotions that had spurred them to action before would resurface again. Which, in fact, was *precisely* why, at this stage of the cycle, a certain percentage of people did agree to an in-office appointment.

You'll likely communicate with prospects many times before you get work from them. Each time you do, if you're professional and share a bit more about yourself and your skills, you'll build a bit more rapport and legitimacy in the prospect's mind. And as you do, you'll be making it that much easier for that prospect to do business with you.

Hoop Three Oh, you thought that was it? They just show up for their appointment and we're done? Hah! Stop reading for a moment and take a guess as to what percentage of people who booked appointments actually showed up…

Try 15 to 20 percent. Roughly one out of six who'd booked would actually show. They'd book six times as many appointments as they could handle because they *knew* the average no-show rate was 80 to 85 percent. Etched in concrete. But every day, 15 to 20 percent showed up like clockwork and when they did, we knew what an incredible longshot that was. And so, whenever we heard, "Oh, just curious," it was hard not to chuckle.

Conclusions? Know the limits of any one contact. Think long-term. Keep showing up. Stay in the game and you can't help but win, eventually. Know it's all cumulative. *No* doesn't mean *not ever*—sometimes it means *maybe*, or *I need more information*. By the way, I'm talking about prospects who say they hire freelancers but haven't hired *you* yet, *not* those who've said they're not in the market for any writing services. There's little point in continuing to beat on the second group.

Dismantling Barriers Landing work with new clients is a process of gradually removing barriers in the way of them doing business with you. And before you start lamenting that all this "sales" stuff is just too much for your creative non-sales brain, remember, the ideas I'm discussing here are just part and parcel of any human interaction, whether it's finding a mate, landing a job, getting a promotion, etc.

Same goes for you when you're buying some big-ticket item—house, car, boat, etc. When you walk into that car dealership, you've got lots of barriers erected. If anyone asks, you're *just looking*. If you walk out two hours or two weeks later with the keys to a new car, then clearly those barriers got dismantled one by one.

When you call prospective "in-the-market" clients for the first time, you're on the ground floor with them. But over time, as you talk, and they learn your background, see a mesh with their needs, visit your site, connect with you in person, let you follow up, perhaps give you a small project that goes well, those barriers fall one by one.

8 Sales Tips For Non-Salespeople (from CEO of Sales Training Firm)

Atlanta-based Aslan Training and Development, one of my clients, is a sales training firm specializing in "inside sales." Translation: phone sales. A few of their clients? BellSouth, Xerox, FedEx, Apple Computer, Oracle, GE, HP and Russell Athletic. Given that Aslan specializes in transforming non-salespeople into effective phone marketers (your ears burning?), I asked CEO Tom Stanfill to contribute something to the book.

Unlearning Bad Habits In working with Tom, I realized many things I'd learned from my sales background—i.e., "ABC—Always Be Closing," asking for the order, and others—ran counter to what this guy, head of a top sales training organization, was saying.

At the same time, many ideas he was espousing were exactly what I've been saying about "sales" for a long time: that it's not about being slick, pushy or aggressive. It's not about "closing" hard. It's about taking the time to understand a client's needs, and exploring whether your product/service meets those needs. It's really about service, not sales. I asked Tom to offer up some tips, keeping in mind that he'd be talking to a lot of creative folk deathly afraid of "sales." Here are the gems he served up...

THE TIPS

1) **Clients Don't Want To Be Sold.** They want a partner, so adopt the voice of a partner: Someone who knows he or she can't be successful unless the client is successful.

2) Asking For The Order Doesn't Motivate People To Buy. What motivates people to buy is when they get that you "get" them—that you understand their world, and have shown how your product/service will impact their company in ways important to them. In most cases, the sales-person that wins the deal isn't the one with the best product or lowest price, but the one who best articulates the customer's point of view.

3) "Drop The Rope." Think about a tug-of-war. If two people are holding a rope and one pulls, the other will pull back. If prospects sense you have your sales hat on, they'll resist. They're not rejecting your solution, service, or product; they're rejecting you.

In the course of prospecting, if you get resistance from a prospect, regardless of your approach, "drop the rope" by saying, *Mr. Prospect, I'm not even sure my service is a fit for your company, but I'd certainly love the opportunity to learn more about what you do and see if there is some common ground.* Speaking of which…

4) Sell the Meeting, Not the Service. Don't sell writing services. Sell the idea of getting together—by phone or in person—for a "discovery meeting" and exploring, together, what they do, what you do and whether there's a fit. It's then you can evaluate the client's needs and determine how to position your services. Most importantly, you've built a relationship that will ensure, at the very least, your recommendation gets heard.

5) Sell the Process, Not the Service. Often salespeople rely too much on the client to determine the next steps. Every interaction with a customer should end with a specific event the customer agrees to (i.e., another meeting, a follow-up call at a set time, etc.). And the agreement is crucial. A planned action is much likely to happen than one left to chance. Just as importantly, you stay in your customer's field of vision.

6) Stop Trying To Be a Salesperson. Being aggressive and pushy is self-centered, and self-centered doesn't sell. *Motive is ultimately transparent.* If your motive is to do what's in the customer's best interest, that customer will sense it and respond positively. If it's to sell them something, *regardless* of need, the customer will avoid you. You don't need to be a salesperson; you need to be a passionate, competent copywriter unafraid to share your talents—not because you need the money, but because *they* need the help.

7) Calculate the Value Of Prospecting Time. Once you're established, figure out how much you've made up to a certain point divided by the number of hours you've "prospected" for that business. If 100 hours prospecting netted you $10,000 in work, then your prospecting time was worth $100 an hour. Might that motivate you a bit?

8) Answer the Question, "Why You?" How are you going to differentiate your services from the competition? There always exist multiple solutions: doing nothing, hiring a competitor or doing it themselves. Once you've determined your unique offering, make sure the client "gets" that difference, either by just telling them (or validating it through success stories), or, better yet, ensuring the customer experiences the difference through your actions—reliability, professionalism, creativity, etc.

•　•　•

Good stuff. So, if you run across a company that mentions the need for sales training, I'm not sure they could do better than Aslan. If more companies lived by these principles, the "customer experience" couldn't help but improve. **www.aslantraining.com** (770/690-9616). And ask for Tom. He'll leave the voice mail on for you (sorry).

Sales Redefined

Some time back, I was mentoring a budding LA FLCW named Rob Rutkowski, who was leveraging 15 years in software sales. He shared this great war story from his selling days—a really good example of a very different take on "sales." Keep the ideas in mind (not the specifics as much as the creativity) as you consider how to approach your clients. And yes, Rob knows he's good. Another lesson worth internalizing...

> *Three years ago, my sales team went through some outstanding sales training by one of the top firms in the country led by a Zig Ziglar type with amazing credentials. Now, in this room of 50 folks were the best salespeople in the company, 10- to 20-year veterans used to making $500K+. And me. The new guy. Who interrupted the class an hour after it started because his flight was delayed.*

> *The course leader hated me from minute one. Hated my questions. Hated my comments. I was a total pain. After the week of training, we were given an assignment: "mock" pitch the CEO of American Express on a specific project and secure a presentation to the board.*

That night, while everyone else went and got drunk at the hotel bar, I was scanning the Internet for articles, reading Amex's annual reports, digging into the business processes of the divisions and internalizing their vocabulary. The next day, armed with video clips of the chairman revealing operational problems our software solved; and CEO quotes from internal documents explaining challenges our software solved; and analyst reports trumpeting issues our software solved, I made a seven-minute presentation that landed like a single bullet assassination.

The audience paused when I finished, then erupted in applause. The course leader, with the reluctance of a dictator cooperating with U.N. inspectors, handed me the $100 prize for best presentation. He uses it in his training even today.

Now, THAT is sales. Potent. Focused. Thorough. Rob intimately got into the world of his prospect, discovered what was important to him, what challenges the company faced, and, using the prospect's own words, effectively showed how his product addressed those challenges. Pushy? High-pressure? Manipulative? None of the above.

Some time back, I contacted a bunch of experienced, successful FLCW's and asked them what "sales" (and by extension, "marketing") meant to them. What's interesting is that none of their responses fall into the typical negative stereotypes about sales. I've included several here, and a bunch more (including *Sales as Persistence and Suggestion; as Honesty; as Seizing Opportunities and Shifting Perspective*, and more) are posted at: **www.wellfedwriter.com/sidedishes.shtml** under "Sales Stories."

•   •   •

SALES AS STAYING IN TOUCH

Lisa Sparks
www.integritywriting.com
Ft. Myers, Florida

I send out an e-newsletter each month (discussed in Chapter Eight), and what a difference it's made. It generates at least a client per month. Sales, to me, is more about keeping in touch—even with people who don't seem like strong prospects.

When first starting out, I had a meeting with a prospect who was bent on keeping the conversation social, and I wrote him off as less than serious. But, I kept him on my email list. A few months later he referred someone to me, putting $1,500 in my pocket, then hired me himself for another $1,500 (and more to come). All because I kept in touch. I've found that the people you least expect to come through will reward your persistence.

Relationship building isn't about heavy sales pressure. It's just about staying in the game and presenting a strong and credible image to your potential clients.

●   ●   ●

SALES AS RAISING YOUR VALUE IN THE MARKETPLACE
Michele Lashley
www.karacomcreative.com
Raleigh, North Carolina

When I started my writing business (after 15 years in marketing communications and advertising), I contacted a local university about teaching an advertising course. While I thought it might just be fun to share some of my real life experiences with up-and-coming marketing communications folks, two wonderful surprises have come from it. First, I absolutely love working with the students in my classes. They're excited, eager to learn, and full of wonderful ideas and energy.

Secondly, because I'm constantly preparing lectures, keeping up on current advertising news and following marketing trends, I've developed a knowledgebase of information I can use in pitches to prospects and in my interactions with clients. It increases my value to them because I'm able to provide more than just copywriting services: I can help them look at their overall marketing picture and work with them to develop a plan that will help them accomplish their goals.

●   ●   ●

SALES AS BEING A TEAM MEMBER

Paul Glickstein

paulglick@mindspring.com

Atlanta, Georgia

I have a client—a marketing/design firm—that I've now worked with for more than a decade. For the first few years, the firm's principals considered me a contract service provider and not much more. But that perception changed immediately and irrevocably one Christmas Eve.

The firm had shut down for the holidays and the principals were traveling to distant states to spend time with relatives. One of their clients here called a meeting on the morning of December 24. Without hesitation, I volunteered to attend the meeting on their behalf, take notes and prepare a summary prior to their return. You'd have thought I'd hung the moon. My transformation from service provider to team member was immediate, and it's remained that way ever since.

The "sales message" here: It's certainly worth pushing the boundaries of roles and expectations with clients. Copy is only part of what we offer; service and support are no less critical. And the payoff can be tremendous.

• • •

Okay, now that we've reduced these not-so-ferocious critters from "SALES" and "MARKETING" to sales and marketing, let's start developing the mindset of the marketer...

Into the Mind of the Marketer

I saw a great series of billboards in Atlanta a few years back. It was for Apartments.com, an online clearinghouse for apartments that allows you to search for exactly what you want in any state. They could have devoted their billboard space to talking about themselves (like most companies do) and all the great things they offer: unmatched customer service, big selection, easy online access, etc. (I can picture big checked boxes, right?). They could have. But they didn't.

The first billboard had just one short sentence (their tag line) across the middle: *You want what you want.* Then, their logo and the Apartments.com name. Nothing more. A thing of simplicity and beauty. In one five-word sentence, they nailed THE hot button for their audience: personal choice in an apartment. Heck, they used "you want" twice in a five-word sentence!

IT'S ALL ABOUT ME People want to be acknowledged. Included. Talked to, not talked *at*. They want to know that what matters to them matters to whoever's addressing them (in any promo material). Remember that—it's key to cultivating the marketing mindset. And along the way, they disappeared from the process: it wasn't about them; it was about me and what I wanted. They were simply there as the vehicle to deliver that.

This example is a good way to segue into three fundamental principles of sales and marketing—principles that apply both to marketing yourself as well as to helping you write stronger marketing copy for your clients:

1) THE AUDIENCE The Apartment.com folks clearly understand the audience they're talking to and what's important to that audience.

2) THE FEATURES/BENEFITS EQUATION This company knows how to keep the interests of the audience ahead of their own.

3) THE UNIQUE SELLING PROPOSITION (USP) The fact that the search function on their web site delivers exactly what the audience wants sets them apart. OR, they're simply doing a better job than the competition of letting the world know what they're offering.

IT'S NOT THAT SCARY What follows won't be some exhaustive study of sales and marketing because, frankly, there's no need to turn you into experts in order to admirably serve your clients and promote your own business. By the time we're done, I'm hoping you'll see this arena not as some esoteric science, but rather as a predictable and intuitive reflection of human nature, and hence already familiar to you.

"WHY DO WE WRITE ANYTHING?" In my seminars, when I get to the topic of marketing, I start out with the question above. And I get all the usual answers: *To inform. Educate. Inspire. Motivate. Encourage. Entertain. Move. Touch.* All true. And yet, there's a far more basic reason why we write anything. Care to guess? How about this...

To have it be read. I know, you're rolling your eyes, but frankly, none of the others are even possible until you accomplish that. That's what this chapter is about—boosting the odds that your intended reader will actually read what you've written, whether designed to promote your own business or that of a client. It all starts there.

"Who's the Audience?"

THE absolute first question you ask at the start of every project. When you buy a product you heard about through some form of advertising, it's because something spoke to *you*. Someone knew what to say to make *you* sit up and take notice—exactly what will happen when a message is well crafted. You're no different from anyone else.

The really good news? As simple and logical as this formula is, it's amazing how much marketing material out there is poorly written and doesn't consider the intended audience. If you can get it right, you'll set yourself apart.

IT's LOGICAL   Do you talk to your friends the same way as you would a cop? Someone of the opposite sex you're trying to impress vs. someone who's trying to impress you? Somebody who really needs a favor from you vs. someone from whom you need a favor? Consciously or unconsciously, you're always thinking about audience.

Arguably, any project—technical documentation, corporate marketing brochures, or grandiose documentaries—requires the same *Who's the audience?* question in order to sell the audience on your point of view. And that first question leads to a bunch more:

What's important to people in this group?

What motivates them?

How do they think?

How do they talk?

What words and language will get through to them?

What's going to turn their heads and get them to pay attention?

Once they pay attention, what will it take to get them to take action?

"Take action" can mean buy the product, visit the store, take a test drive, make the call, order the bigger brochure, return the reply card, etc.

A GOOD EXAMPLE   A few years back, I landed a brochure (through a design firm) for a software company that specialized in doctor—patient communication. Combining the telephone and computer, their product would call patients automatically and remind them of upcoming appointments (in the doctor's voice), freeing front-office staff from those tasks. Another product allowed patients to retrieve lab results (with a PIN) after-hours, again taking tasks off the plates of admin staff.

A few simple questions revealed that while the final decision maker was the doctor, the primary user (*and* first audience) was *office managers.* If they liked the product, they'd recommend the doctor buy it. If they didn't, the doctor would never see it.

Tell me about these people, I said. *What are their demographics? What's their job description? What are they expected to accomplish?* Turns out they're mostly women, age 35 to 45, and with many crucial responsibilities: reduce no-shows, increase revenues, improve patient relations, reduce front-office workload, and boost overall efficiency.

I saw the firm's previous brochure—it looked like a million others of the "We-Do" model—*We do this, we do that, we do it all, we do it better, faster and more reliably—buy from us.* An occasional nod to the customer, but mostly focused on the company and its product. All *features.* No *benefits* (and *that* discussion's next).

Easy enough to improve. Once I'd gathered information about what an office manager's daily life was like, I knew how to talk to them to get their attention. I submitted copy, and a few hours later, the design firm writes, *They loved it! Didn't change a single word.* Whoa!

Open the brochure and the first page reads:

> *You have a simple job, right? Sure. Let's see…just increase practice revenues, decrease no-shows, reduce front-office workload and boost overall administrative efficiency. Oh, and build stronger relationships with patients. For starters.*
>
> *Well, imagine products that have been proven to do all that, while enjoying a 98 percent "thumbs-up" from patients and a remarkably high client referral rate. All from a company with a legendary industry reputation for customer service. Simply put, a company and product line with a mission to make your life easier and make you look good. Might be worth a look…*

I simply gave it all back to them. How hard is that? And by talking to the primary audience in language they could understand—*benefits*—the company got the attention of the folks with buying power and won them over. Now I could talk *features,* knowing they were listening. But even then, I made it interesting by not just *talking* about the product's features but telling stories that demonstrated how it worked. For example:

*After a cholesterol screening last week, Mr. Johnson left with a **LabCalls** reminder card, complete with "results available" date. At 10:15 p.m. on that date, he called the dedicated **LabCalls** line, and using a PIN, accessed his results, delivered in the voice of his favorite front-office manager. To double-check the numeric values, he pressed 2 to repeat and then 3 to leave a message for his doctor. **LabCalls** automatically generated a report entry confirming his successful retrieval of the results.*

GET INTO THEIR WORLD Another example. A few years back, I wrote a brochure for an importer who specialized in finding (or having manufactured) cosmetic-related products in the Far East: brushes, sponges, applicators, baskets, bags, etc., for the big cosmetic firms (for all the freebie packs women snag at cosmetic counters).

The primary audiences for the piece were product development managers (PD) and purchasing agents (PA), so I questioned both my client and the PD's and PA's themselves. *What pressures and demands do you face? What's a typical day? And most importantly, How has doing business with my client made your life easier?*

Turns out a PA's life is endless meetings, reports, and deadlines, plus constant pressure to deliver new products and the next "winner." They're also used to product vendors they have to track down for answers and status reports. They have no time to waste and no patience for problems. Through these little chats, I discovered all the ways my client simplified their lives: reliability, follow up, intimate knowledge of her clients' needs, and success in consistently bringing them new products or new designs.

These become the copy points designed to get the attention of prospects facing the same challenges and, as such, stood to reap the same benefits. The audience needs to see themselves in the copy for it to have any relevance to them (for a closer look, visit **www.writeinc.biz**, then *Portfolio*, then *Marketing Brochures*, then *Anisa International*).

Finally, a fun example of some headline concepting for a snack company. They needed a catchy slogan for a display going in a college cafeteria promoting snack products, and geared to the student market. In addition to a bunch of straightforward ones, I came up with these "tongue-in-cheek"-ers (note P.S. to my client).

Being Hungry Sucks.

Hunger Sucks.

P.S. Okay, so I'm kidding here, but if 18–24-year-olds are indeed your market, you'd sure sell a lot of snacks with these...

Of course they didn't go for them, though if they did, I'll bet they'd have been winners. If you understand your audience, you'll write copy they'll want to read. But it can't just be cute. It has to sell. It's fine to be clever, but ask yourself if your copy communicates to that audience. If it doesn't, start over.

A BAD EXAMPLE A good example of a company with zero grasp of audience. As mentioned, in Atlanta, we have an annual directory—the *OZ Creative Index*—put out by the local rag for the creative industry. In the back are business card-sized ads taken out by creative folks. One featured just a photograph of an object and a web address. Period. Nothing more. Nada. Photo and URL. Was this arrogance or just plain cluelessness?

Did they honestly think people were going to be so intrigued they'd just drop everything and go visit the site? Without so much as a clue as to what they did (*not* obvious from the URL). Amazing. Maybe they're drowning in work, though I'd never heard of them.

●   ●   ●

The Features/Benefits Equation

Had a meeting once with a client from a successful marketing company that needed some newsletter work. They'd just had a banner year and the future was looking bright. The client proudly handed me their brand new marketing brochure. While it was certainly slick-looking, you had to wade through half the copy before it stopped talking about how great, experienced, knowledgeable and successful the company was and got around to the things that truly matter to clients: bottom line, image, market share, etc.

The *Features/Benefits Equation* is an absolute cornerstone of sales and marketing. Yet, as you'll see in the coming pages, it's a concept we're already intimately familiar with.

Basic Definitions

Features are all about a product or service and the company selling it.

Benefits are about the customers—what's important to them
and how a product or service addresses those issues.
Always begin with benefits, follow with features.

A few years back, BellSouth, the Southern telecomm giant, had an epiphany. Till then, its marketing campaigns focused largely on *technology*. Ads (like those of many other high-tech companies) featured images of computers, keyboards, data streams, etc., all stylized and artsy, conferring a sexy patina over it all. Technology was cool. It was all about the latest fancy calling feature, network innovation, bell, whistle, etc. (i.e., *features*).

BENEFITS ARE KING   Then one day, someone woke up and said, *Guess what? People don't give a rat's heiney about technology.* Exactly. After all, what's so interesting about technology anyway, beyond the gee-wiz factor? Not much.

So, what *do* people care about? Simple. *How* technology can enhance the quality of their lives—free them from the confines of an office, give them more time for leisure, or help keep them in touch with family (i.e., *benefits*). And on some level, you know that.

People don't care about the speed of a DSL line. They care that that speed allows them to efficiently research their next vacation, find a date for the weekend, or get a great chocolate chip cookie recipe. *And* do it all so fast that they've got time to actually go on that date and make those cookies. They get to live their life, *not* deal with technology.

FEATURES DELIVER BENEFITS   People don't care that a cell phone is *this* slim or *that* stylish (*features*). Only that it gives them ultimate freedom and independence, while letting them stay connected (*benefits*). By the way, in case you're thinking, *You're wrong. I care very much that my cell phone is slim and stylish,* I disagree. You only care about that stuff because it makes you feel like One Cool Dude(ette), and *that* is a BIG *benefit*.

Soon after BellSouth had its realization, it launched a new ad campaign built around the tagline: ">>>connect>>>create something™." Perfect. All about benefits. The new TV ads were rich in touchy-feely images, graphically showcasing the *benefits* of technology: business success, family closeness, romantic connection, etc. And nary a feature in sight. They got what was important to people—their lives, *not* bits and bytes.

IBM GETS IT   Some years back, IBM moved in a new and very sensible direction: away from simply being a supplier of hardware and software and toward the realm of business consulting, acquiring a few companies in order to pull this off. This story echoes the teaming concept I've discussed *ad nauseum.*

When you team with a graphic designer (like IBM teamed with consulting and software entities), you're not offering writing services and design services. You're offering a complete solution to a business need. Customers don't want products and services (that's about you). They want complete solutions (that's about them).

CLASSIC FEATURES VS. BENEFITS   Before, IBM's approach had largely been about them (i.e., their hardware). *Features.* Now the company was all about its customers and what was important to them: profitability, market share and competitive advantage. *Benefits.*

STOP TALKING ABOUT YOURSELF   There's a big difference between what your client wants to tell a prospect in a marketing piece and what that prospect wants (and needs) to know. Most clients want to focus on *features*: years in business, excellent customer service, superior quality of products (with all the technical specs), the highly experienced staff, etc. Prospects want to know how a company's product will solve a problem they have and make a difference in their quality of life. That's *benefits.*

Just as importantly, it's unrealistic to think that someone will make a buying decision based on reading something. The goal is to get the prospect to take the next step—make the call, return the card, visit the showroom —and in effect, say, *Okay, I'm interested. Tell me more.* And you just don't need to tell all to get them to do that.

WHAT PROSPECTS WANT TO HEAR   A few years back, I came across an interesting article in *The New York Times* ("It's Not What You Say; It's How It Sounds" by Claudia H. Deutsch) about legendary image-meister Kevin Daley. In this brief snippet, he compares the approaches of two candidates for work:

> *Two copywriters applying for jobs at an advertising agency are asked what they would bring to the party. "Well, I'm very creative," one answered after a while. The winning applicant made no such claim but told of a successful and highly creative campaign he developed at another job. "A good presenter knows how to use a vignette to make a point without bragging," Mr. Daley said.*

The first copywriter, by describing himself as "creative," simply shared a *feature* about himself with the employer. The second, by discussing a success story, quantified the *benefit* to the agency of hiring him.

A "LOVE-LY" EXAMPLE   What's one of the most common complaints you hear from both women and men about the opposite sex on the first few dates? *They spent the whole time talking about themselves!* That's *features.* How can that other party feel special, important or even relevant to the first when he or she can't even enter the conversation? It's the equivalent of a company going on about itself and its products.

It's only when one party shows interest in the other—through appropriate body language, asking questions, and *listening* to the answers—that the other person feels acknowledged, important and included. And when that happens, that other person has seen the *benefits* to him or her of hanging out with this person, not just the *features* of this person. This is the equivalent of a company talking about what's important to a prospect.

POTENT PRESS RELEASES   In the course of promoting my self-published books, I've gotten a lot of practice writing press releases. Bottom line, if you're an unknown author, journalists couldn't care less that you've written a book. Stephen King, Tom Clancy, John Grisham? Sure. The rest of us? *Fuggedaboudit.* A release about a book and its author is...*features.*

That reporter wants benefits: *Tell me why that book is important to my readers/viewers, why they should care, why it addresses some trend or topical subject.* Not the book, but the *angle* represented by the book.

Same thing applies if you're sending releases to your local media about your copywriting business *or* writing ones for your clients' businesses. Unless you live in a town where the big news is the new dog catcher or the church steeple renovation, don't count on journalists to care that there's a new writer in town. In the case of releases written for clients, there's more wiggle room. While beat journalists (i.e., technology, business, lifestyle, etc.) may be okay with a release about new products related to their writing niche, even they appreciate the "bigger picture."

As such, in either case, ideally, focus your release instead on the *angle* represented by the business—the benefits, say, to the audience of hiring a copywriter: increased profitability, competitive advantage, enhanced industry reputation, etc. (perhaps illustrated with real-life client stories).

Even better, offer up short articles on marketing advice that can benefit business owners. Your demonstrated expertise (and contact info at the end) might just yield a few calls. In the case of client releases, focus on how the new product ties in with some topical trend that'll resonate with a larger audience. *Benefits*, not features.

LESSONS IN DRILL BITS   I like the old adage about the ½-inch drill bit. When you go to buy a ½-inch drill bit, you're not *really* buying a ½-inch drill bit. Think about it.

You're buying a ½-inch hole. A ½-inch drill bit is *features*. It's about the product. A ½-inch hole is *benefits*. Or, as my Brit friend and uber-marketer and copywriter Jon McCulloch (**www.jonmcculloch.com**) offers, "You're not buying the drill or the hole. No, you're buying the warm, fuzzy feeling you get from looking at your child's face in the photograph hanging from the screw. We buy on emotion, every time."

•   •   •

USP—The Unique Selling Proposition

Marketing copywriting guru Marcia Yudkin, in her 1/21/04 edition of *The Marketing Minute* (**http://www.yudkin.com/markmin.htm** to subscribe), underscores a wildly common error many companies make on their web sites (and often in their marketing materials as well):

> *In a five-year study of 901 new products performed by the Eureka! Ranch, those whose sales messages explicitly stated the product's point of difference were 52 percent more likely to survive than those that didn't. Don't expect readers of your web site to guess how you outshine the competition. Tell 'em!*

Every business entity is unique in some way. Once you determine the audience for a company's product or service, zero in on the *Unique Selling Proposition* (USP)—THE thing that sets that company apart in a marketplace full of competitors, and the reason to buy from them. Companies need to put their best foot forward, showcase their strengths, and build on the thing they do better than anyone else.

Marketing guru and author Jay Abraham (**www.abraham.com**), in his book *Getting Everything You Can Out Of All You've Got*, offers these useful guidelines, which you can use to drive the questions you ask a client to pinpoint that USP:

1) Ideally, the USP should address a clear need or void in the marketplace. When few (or none) are doing a particular thing, those who can will stand out.

2) Make sure you can deliver on the promise of your USP. If you're claiming, by way of a USP, that a company offers "the best in-stock selection and faster delivery than anyone else," it had better be true or that USP will end up doing more harm than good.

Most business owners don't have a USP, only a 'me too,' rudderless, nondescript, unappealing business that feeds solely upon the sheer momentum of the marketplace. Would you want to patronize a firm that's just 'there,' with no unique benefit, no incredible prices or selection, no especially comforting counsel, service or guarantee? Or would you prefer a firm that offers you the broadest selection in the country? Or one with every item marked up less than half the margin other competitors charge? Or one that sells the 'Rolls Royce' of the industry's products?

Once determined, put that USP to work as the focus of brochures, web copy, and ad/direct mail campaigns. Identifying a company's USP also provides more clarity as to what its mission is, what piece of the marketplace it's claiming, and how to protect it. By the way, a great way to bring all these ideas together when sitting down with a client is a "Discovery Questionnaire," which we'll discuss in Chapter Seven.

Are You Branded?

No, a one-person shop doesn't *need* to be branded to succeed (like a Fortune 500 might). That said, no one walking the earth has your particular combination of talents and abilities. How might you showcase that?

Branding expert Linda Travis (**www.brandrenovator.com**) has isolated five components of branding that anyone, in any size business, can practice to varying degrees in order to more effectively stand out in the marketplace.

1) **BE UNIQUE** Identify your authentic point of difference in the marketplace (and we'll discuss how in a moment) and work to highlight that in your marketing materials. Maybe you have a skill in transforming complex subjects into layman's terms. Perhaps you write marketing copy for one esoteric high-tech niche. Maybe you focus only on case studies and executive profiles.

2) **FOCUS YOUR MESSAGE** If you want to be remembered, stand for something specific. Linda discusses two brands of hand soap: Dove and Lava. As has been famously opined, *a brand is a promise*. Those two are textbook brands—each with their own culturally entrenched promise. Dove evokes soft, gentle moisturizing while Lava conjures up the power to clean really dirty hands. Similarly, if you want to earn the lion's share of your income as a copywriter, then don't present yourself as a writer, designer, photographer and illustrator, even if you can do it all.

3) **ADDRESS THE BUYER'S VALUES** What do your buyers value? Do they value what you do? Ask what your buyers see and value in you, and then make your marketing materials reflect this. If your clients value it, chances are others will, too.

4) **TELL OTHER PEOPLE** *What do you do?* You could just say, *I'm a freelance commercial writer* or you could figure out what's unique about you and translate that into a niche and a short, focused message. More on "verbal taglines" in Chapter 10.

5) **CONVEY CONSISTENCY** People experience your brand with every contact you make. Maintain consistency in your marketing brochures, web site, emails, letterhead, etc.

●   ●   ●

A bit more on #3 above. A client will usually hire you initially because you roughly match the general criteria they have for a copywriter: a certain level of relevant experience, a decent portfolio, confidence and enthusiasm, interpersonal skills, etc.

But if they *keep* hiring you, it's because there are certain things about you that have real specific value to them, whether *you* realize it or not. As discussed, ask what that value is. If something you're doing keeps clients coming back, you'll want to know what it is.

In a sense, it's like a consumer focus group designed to find out why people buy a product, like it, and continue to buy it. If the same things keep coming up, you can build those messages into marketing campaigns directed to the "not-yet-convinced" and turn one-time "snack" clients into long-term meal tickets.

●   ●   ●

Okay, now that we're a bit more comfortable in our marketing skin, it's time to talk about a most wondrous tool for business growth: the web site. Creating one for yourself can make your life (and marketing tasks) infinitely easier. Let's go clickin'…

Chapter 4

A prospect contacts two writers—#1 without a web site, #2 with one. #1 says, "I'll put a package together and get it right out." #2 says, "Check out my portfolio online." The sales cycle is moving MUCH faster now and, heck, by the time #1's package makes it to the client, #2 could already have sealed the deal. And given how relatively easy it is to put one together (and remember, we're writers; it doesn't have to be a work of art), why wouldn't you? I'm just sayin'…

I've got an online portfolio. Give me your email address and I'll send you the link. Two short sentences that not only represent a dramatic simplification of your marketing efforts, but enhance your legitimacy in the eyes of your clients and prospects (*and,* because you've removed a barrier, make it easier for them to hire you). I've become a web site convert, almost obnoxious in my religious fervor.

A COMPANY BROCHURE? In the original version of *TWFW,* I suggested creating a brochure to market your fledgling business. If you're wisely planning on creating a web site, it's just not necessary anymore (though if you feel better doing one, knock yourself out…*and* check out "Crash Course: Tri-fold Brochures" in Chapter Fourteen).

Reluctant "Web-Siter" Builds It and They Come...

A few years back, I got a coaching inquiry from a young woman in San Francisco. She wrote: "Been doing this part-time for a few years while juggling a crappy full-time job. I do have some clients, but not enough to go solo (my goal by next year)." She had a bunch of wonderful samples from her past—and current—professional lives. Put together a web site, I suggested (strongly), and show the world what you've done. "I don't want a web site," she whined, "they're so trite and passé. Everyone has one!"

A Tool, Not a Toy Ah. Like many people, she misunderstood the point of one for folks like us. It's NOT a vanity thing (like it is for non-biz folks); it's a "working smarter" thing. Plus, she'd look more professional, feel better about marketing herself, her marketing would be infinitely easier (no more copying, assembling, and mailing of samples to prospects), and it'd be promoting her, 24/7, while she was off doing something else. "There's no other way to build this business?" she asked. Not if she was serious about leaving the crappy job behind. She said she'd think about it.

Five days later, literally, I get this email: "TA-DA! **www.km-com.com**." She still wasn't happy that she had to do one, but she did it. All by herself. I was blown away. But what blew *her* away was what happened next. Some comments from the next few weeks: "It pains me greatly to say this, but you have a point with this web site business. I have been marketing like crazy and I have a bunch of good-to-very-good prospects. I hear a lot of, 'I looked at the samples on your site' when I follow up with people."

Other feedback? "One said, 'Your web site really nails it,' another, 'I've also perused your web site and am impressed with the range and quality of your work.' The latter one went on to say she has some work coming up that she'll consider me for. I *do* feel a lot better about things—including my goal of leaving my stupid job by the end of this year. I really had no idea that a site would make a big difference, given that I have the experience and the clips." And finally: "I just got the first piece of work from the site. A small editing job, but it's a start. Guess I'll have an apple martini with that crow."

Oh, and she *did* get to leave the crappy job, right on schedule.

P.S. I loved what she called her new marketing campaign: "market as if my life depends on it." Think about that. If you're in a job you hate, the life you wish you were living IS passing you by, and by busting her hump, she *is*, in fact, marketing like her life depends on it, because it does.

Your web site *is* your brochure, so use it to clarify your purpose, what services you offer, (are you a generalist or a specialist?), and just as importantly, your limitations—what you don't do. Until you do this, you may be operating with a vague direction, and "vague" won't move you forward like you want to.

In the original *TWFW*, I also described a systematic process for assembling packages of samples to send your prospects. Sure, you'll still want to occasionally send an actual sample as a way of continuing to stay visible to clients and prospects, but for both the initial and ongoing prospecting and business-building parts of your enterprise, few tools are as efficient and expeditious as a web site. The now-terminally overexposed expression *Work smarter, not harder* was referring to a web site.

The "before/after" prospecting scenario I painted in the first book went from 30–45 minutes to put together a marketing package for an interested prospect to 5–10 minutes. With a web site, we're talking about slashing that to about 60 seconds.

An interested prospect asks if you can send samples. You say, *Tell you what—give me your email address and I'll send you the link to my site.* You capture their email address, and by emailing a click-thru link, you boost the likelihood that they'll actually visit the site. Click. Instant samples. Instant credibility enhanced.

THE MAIN REASON   Someone visits a FLCW's site mainly to see samples. Sure, credentials are good (especially if you're a "niche" copywriter), and testimonials are always welcome, but those things come more into play *after* they see the caliber of your writing. No samples? Less reason to have a site. Unless, again, you're a "niche" copywriter, where background and experience count for everything. Regardless, remember this: how you craft the copy for other pages (especially the home page) will give prospects a taste of what you'd do for them. So make it good.

KEEP IT SIMPLE   Make it easy for prospects to get in and out. Keep the navigation simple and the links few. Dispense with fancy graphics and special effects. Makes sense for graphic/web design firms as a showcase for their creative talents, but we writers don't need to gunk things up. If you must open your site with some nifty-keeno Flash presentation, offer a prominently displayed *Skip Intro* option. Nothing will send prospects packing more quickly than being forced to sit through *your* creative vision on *their* time.

In addition to a home page and portfolio, consider including the following pages:

- *Terms (How you work)*
- *Client list*
- *Services list*
- *Testimonials (see section ahead)*
- *Contact information*

My web site (**www.writeinc.biz**) is one way to do this. Not necessarily the last word in sites and certainly not overly flashy, but I think it gets the job done.

(DON'T) SHOW THEM THE MONEY Many ask if their sites should include a rate sheet for different projects. Not a good idea. Include one, and I assert you might just appear a bit…green. Experienced writing-buyers know there's no such thing as a "typical" project. Even within a given category, like marketing brochures, for instance, every project is different. It's for that reason a client doesn't expect to see a rate sheet.

Even if you were able to provide a realistic fee range for, say, marketing brochures, you'd end up with one so broad as to render it virtually meaningless. Narrow those ranges to provide a more meaningful number, and you risk clients taking those numbers to the bank. What if their simple project would actually cost less than your low-end figure? You might be branded as too pricey and lose the deal. What if their complex project would exceed the upper end of your range? The client might be disappointed when your actual estimate comes in way higher.

Bottom line, there's virtually no upside to providing a rate sheet, and plenty of potential downsides. Use your site to showcase your competence, professionalism and reliability, and hash out finances later (See Chapter Nine for far more detail on pricing).

MULTIPLE SITES? A local FLCW colleague of mine realized that he had a ton of healthcare-related work. Why not create a site specifically geared to that specialty, in addition to his more general copywriting site? Good move. Prospects will be more receptive to a "specialist" in their industry, and given the relative ease and low expense of creating another site (*and* business cards), why not? It's all about perception, and my friend's site can easily and inexpensively ratchet up his perceived value in certain prospects' eyes. Just like creating multiple versions of a resume for different types of work.

DISPLAYING SAMPLES ONLINE   These are the three most common ways —with the pros and cons—I've come across for showing off your work on your site.

1) PDFs of Sample   PROS: It's always good to show the actual sample; just make sure they're large enough to read the actual copy. I've seen too many sites with too-small, and/or low-resolution images. CONS: Big images can take a long time to load, causing prospects to go bye-bye. Remember: Not everyone has the same browser as you.

2) Copy-Only Samples   PROS: Easy to put together and fast loading for visitors. CONS: Looks a bit amateurish and inexperienced.

3) Images/Copy Hybrid   I'm biased toward this one since it's how I do it. ☺ Small thumbnails (roughly 2½ x 3½) of several pages of the actual sample side-by-side with the copy—usually excerpted (see *Portfolio* link at **www.writeinc.biz** for a demo).

PROS: It's the best of both worlds: offers enough graphics to the visual folks, but if someone has a slow browser, at least the copy will load quickly. CONS: It'll take some web design skills beyond those of the layperson (certainly beyond those of *this* layperson). Here are the brief how-to details from my web guy, to pass on to you/yours:

> *The portfolio section was made using html frames. The body of the document and the graphic associated with it are located in different web frames so that they appear side by side. The main menu has a special link that, when selected, tells the server to load both the document and the associated graphic simultaneously in adjacent web frames.*

YOUR BEST STUFF   The big advantage of #2 or #3 above—and anyone in my field can *so* relate to this—is that you can show the copy you feel is your best, not just what ended up in the final piece. Because from time to time, a finished project will look beautiful from a design standpoint, but what the client does to your copy will make you sad.

In cases like that, if you've gone with #1 above, you can either not show it, even though it looks great and has a big-name logo on it; or show it and hope they don't read too closely. If you're going #3, and the copy is different from the thumbnail, while not a big deal, it's probably a good idea if the thumbnail isn't readable.

If you find yourself in a editing bloodbath, courtesy of a clueless client, save your pristine original copy under another name, to perhaps live on, on your web site, and then take up your hatchet and blowtorch and do the client's dirty work.

CREATING SAMPLE "FRAMES" If going options #2 or #3, you need to prep your samples before loading them up. First of all, keep copy samples short. Cull larger pieces down to a manageable size and include enough to give prospects a good sense of the logical flow of the piece. In the case of long, involved projects, include one particularly good representative sample, even if it doesn't tell the whole product story.

At the top of the page of text (whether by itself or to the right of the thumbnail), include an intro line that has the same font, point size, and style on all samples. In the examples below, note whether it's a *Sample Excerpt* or, in the case of a sales letter (where you can include the whole piece), just a *Sample*.

Sample Excerpt: Script for Junior Achievement Awards Ceremony and Dinner

Sample Excerpt: Product Brochure for Electronic Printing Software

Sample: UPS Marketing Letter Introducing Service Enhancements

PERMISSION TO POST, SIR? "Do I need to ask permission of clients before posting samples of work on my site?" I heard that question many times over the years and, finally, I addressed it in my blog (8/22/08 post at **www.wellfedwriter.com/blog**).

I say this is a non-issue. If I do a B2B or B2C project (virtually all my work) for a company—by definition, one created for public dissemination—I can display it online. Only once did I ever ask permission to use a piece. I was told I couldn't, and given no good reason (the pieces were part of a customer newsletter!). So what I took away from that unsatisfying encounter was *not* that I needed to ask each time, but rather that I'd *never* ask again. And in 15 years, I've never had a problem.

The only exception is an important one: if it's internal (i.e., proprietary and potentially sensitive), you shouldn't post it unless you "sanitize" the sample of all possibly problem language, but you'll know what those situations are. Not sure? Ask your client.

As I found out, if you ask permission, there'll be those clients whose anal legal departments have to justify their existences by saying no—and for no good or logical reason other than they can. Why bother, when chances are literally nil they'll ever know or care that you've posted them?

Worst-case scenario? They tell you to take it down. Think they'll slap you with a multi-million-dollar lawsuit for posting a sample thousands of people saw? Not a chance. If they decide to be jerks about it, they'll start with a simple "take it down" request. And you take it down. End of story.

THE $75 WEB SITE Low-cost avenues for personal web site creation abound on the Internet. One reader reported his success a few years back in creating a $75 web site (using **www.godaddy.com** and including domain name registration, hosting, site creation software licensing, etc.). Since then, Go Daddy has gone to a flat monthly fee that includes hosting, all site-building tools and a ton of extras. At press time, even their most expensive package—for unlimited pages—was, at most $13 a month (which you could easily pay for hosting alone). Here are a few resources that can dramatically simplify the process of creating your own site while keeping costs at mind-boggling lows.

www.homestead.com (has a kick-butt tutorial)

www.quickbizsites.com

www.godaddy.com

www.citymax.com

SALES BY TESTIMONIAL Get in the habit of asking for testimonials. If you suspect a client will be a regular, hold off until you've done three or four projects. You're likely to get a richer one at that point—one infused with detail and the now-warm feeling they have after recognizing the valuable contribution you're making to their company. If, on the other hand, you suspect a one-shot deal, angle for getting it then. There's nothing like a few compelling third-party references on your site to boost your credibility. For clients, after samples, testimonials are a close second on a web site.

Your Colleagues' Sites

Over the past several years, I asked commercial writers across the world to share their web sites for possible inclusion in the book. A nice list follows. You'll see a wide array of creative visions—things you'll like and things you won't. It's all about getting ideas.

Eileen Coale – Annapolis, Maryland: **www.thenaturalhealthcopywriter.com**

Andrew Hindes – Los Angeles, California: **www.theinhousewriter.com**

Jennifer Lewy – Boston, Massachusetts: **www.zenmarketing.net**

✝ Jake Poinier – Phoenix, Arizona: ~~www.mythreedots.com~~ boomvangcreative.com

Maria Rivera – Austin, Texas: ~~www.redwritingshop.com~~

✝Jeff Durosko – Pittsburgh, Pennsylvania: **www.duroskopr.com**

⌐ Jon McCulloch – County Cork, Ireland: **www.jonmcculloch.com**

✝ Casey Hibbard – Boulder, Colorado: **www.compelling-cases.com**

Pamela Beers – Rochester, New York: **www.freelancewritingetc.com**

Pete Savage – London, Ontario, Canada: **www.petesavage.com**

Bruce Lilly – Bloomington, Indiana: **www.BruceLilly.com**

Laura Wharton – Mt. Airy, North Carolina: **www.whartoncommunications.com**

Dianna Huff – Plaistow, New Hampshire: **www.dhcommunications.com**

Jim Meadows – Kansas City, Missouri: **www.jimfreelance.com**

Kristina Anderson – Seattle, Washington: **www.easyreadcopywriting.com**

Mary Guinane McNamara – Sioux City, Iowa: **www.twacopywriting.com**

John Barrett – Salt Lake City, Utah: **www.quillpro.com**

Patrick Leonard (a.k.a. Lp Camozzi) – Montreal, Canada: **www.camozzi.ca**

Kathy Steligo – San Carlos, California: **www.steligo.com**

Dave Riches – Prospect, Australia: **www.riches.com.au**

Michaele Charles – Centennial, Colorado: **www.voicecommunications.org**

Janice King – Sammamish, Washington: **www.writespark.com**

Julie Ann Waid – Dallas, Texas: **www.waidwrites.com**

Daniel Casciato – Pittsburgh, Pennsylvania: **www.danielcasciato.com**

Yvonne Perry – Nashville, Tennessee: **www.yvonneperry.net**

Kelly Parkinson – San Francisco, California: **www.copylicious.com**

Tracey Dooley – Brighton, United Kingdom: **www.mediaminister.co.uk**

Amy Lillard – Chicago, Illinois: **www.amylillard.com**

Nate Fredrickson – Fosston, Minnesota: **www.nmfredrickson.com**

Kristen King – Ruther Glen, Virginia: **www.inkthinkercommunications.com**

Ed Gandia – Marietta, Georgia: **www.edgandia.com**

Michael Stelzner – Poway, California: **www.stelzner.com**

Okay, now that we've got our web site set up and ready for action, who are we going to contact? What sorts of companies hire folks like us? Let's go find out…

Chapter 5

Ah, what a smorgasbord of juicy, well-paying projects awaits the ambitious commercial freelancer. That said, my experience is limited. While I haven't worked in every possible arena out there, I wanted to offer up a veritable buffet of options. That meant finding niche FLCW experts, who've generously shared their experience here.

We'll peek into the not-for-profit sector. Some rarely-tapped departments within corporations. Writing opportunities in colleges and universities. White papers. Direct response copywriting. Case Studies. Speechwriting. Writing for associations. A wonderful list of possible writing clients that underscores how much potential work may be sitting right under your nose. And more...

While the following offers a mighty good overview of where the work is, there's no way to cover it all in one chapter of one book. My goal here is to plant some seeds with basic overviews, steer you in the right direction, and let you check it out further.

B2C, B2B, AND INTERNAL There are three general categories of work into which most all of what follows falls. We've already discussed B2C (business-to-consumer; what we see mostly as consumers); B2B (business-to-business; a huge arena and what we see little of as consumers but more of as employees); and finally *internal communications* (IC).

IC—another enormous body of possible work—are all those projects that remain with the "four walls" of a company—i.e., internal newsletters, training materials and programs, employee benefits information (and other HR-related projects), intranet sites (internal web sites) creation, and much more. So, let's jump in…

WHO WILL HIRE YOU?

You'll either be writing for "end users" (EU's), the people ultimately using it; or for "middlemen" (MM's), the people producing the project for an EU. One or the other. Period. EU's means any company from small to Fortune 100, along with not-for-profits (NFP's), universities, and more. MM's include, but aren't limited to: ad agencies, graphic design firms, marketing companies, PR firms, event production companies, creative staffing agencies, and others. Think of MM's as "bird dogs" of sorts. As they hunt work for themselves, they'll find work for you while you're off doing other stuff.

END USERS: PROS AND CONS With smaller EU's relatively new to creating brochures, ads, or marketing campaigns, there's often a bit more educating necessary than with the MM's or larger EU's. Big EU's know the score—unless the person running the project is new, inexperienced, or newly reassigned from somewhere else.

The big advantage of dealing with EU's? One less layer of people saves time and frustration often inherent in working with MM's. And if EU's are used to dealing with MM's, that's a plus when dealing directly with an EU. Why? Because they're used to paying inflated rates for copywriting: a normal rate plus the MM's premium, commonly added on as a management fee. So, your rates won't scare them.

MIDDLEMEN: PROS AND CONS MM's know what they need, what it should cost, and what's fair. They know you need "concepting" time (those critical hours of noodling that precede your actual creative explosions), and they don't expect 27 rewrites at no extra charge.

The first MM downside is the "second layer" discussed above. More people = more egos and a greater chance your brilliant copy will get butchered (not always, but it happens). And often for no good reason other than to justify their existences and prove to higher-ups they can "take ownership" of a project. As one of my professional colleagues so elegantly put this phenomenon (which, incidentally, is just as common with EU's): "Everyone's got to pee on it."

In addition, you'll also have less control over the final product, and some MM's may restrict your contact with the EU (often a control issue), making it difficult to get questions answered and often jeopardizing the outcome. Bottom line, there's nothing like hearing it straight from the horse's mouth, so always push to have unfettered access to clients.

DON'T LOOK BACK When the copy has gotten to tweaking stage, the MM may often just say, "Go ahead and bill me. We can handle any minor edits ourselves." Just don't dwell on what they could still do to your copy —especially ad agencies—or you'll get sad. One of the few downsides to this business.

Another minus? MM's may try to beat you down on price. Cave quickly and you'll set a bad precedent and they'll always know you're easy. Stick to your guns and you'll probably get your rate. It shows that you're confident in your abilities, which people like to see. If they make a "take-it-or-leave-it" offer, then decide. If your reputation precedes you, don't give up a dime. If you're starting out, decide whether it's worth it as good on-the-job training and to help build the book. More on pricing in Chapter Nine.

DON'T GO "DIRECT" If you're working with an EU through an MM who's paying you, never, ever approach that big company directly for work unless you've received the blessing of your MM. Many won't mind, glad they were able to get you in the door. Try it with others, and you may never work with them again. Why? Because you're "their" copywriter and they're billing you out to the EU at a higher rate than you're charging them, and pocketing the difference. Standard operating procedure. It's also egg on their face because Biggie Corp. now gets you for, say, $75 an hour when before, they were paying your client $100 an hour for you. More detail on this in the "Well-Fed Do's and Don'ts" report in *The Deluxe Well-Fed Tool Box* .

END USERS (EU's)

End users include companies of all sizes and in all sectors. The larger the company, the more different types of work available. A Fortune 100 company has dozens of different departments, each with their own needs: ad copy, marketing brochures, POS (point-of-sale) signage, promo materials, training videos and manuals, product sheets, sales aids, CD training programs, proposals, internal publications, and the list goes on and on. Yes, some is done in-house, but downsizing has spawned a lot of outsourcing.

FIRST STOP—"MARCOM" Typically, your first stop in a big firm will be "marketing communications" (or "Marcom"; a.k.a. "corporate communications")—sort of an in-house creative agency for a corporation. Any time a division of that company needs, say, a brochure, sales sheet, web site, newsletter, PowerPoint presentation, etc., while they can and often do hire freelancers on their own, more commonly, they'll contact Marcom, which will tap in-house or outside resources to execute the project.

Marcom can be a great clearinghouse for lots of work, as well as connections to many other departments you might deal with directly. No Marcom (or corporate communications) department? Try the marketing department, sales department, or, when all else fails, human resources. HR is typically THE best way to make absolutely sure that your name and story get held up for the longest amount of time. It just makes more sense to ferret out the actual folks who have ultimate, specific, well-known needs—and the ability to hire you—than a department several times removed.

The BIG Small- to Medium-Sized Business Segment

One of the biggest EU segments is the small- to medium-sized business market. The owner of a graphic design firm (looking to add more copy-writing resources) I met with made an interesting comment about this sector: while he'd like to pursue them, the services he offered tended to be more than they really needed or could afford.

I commented that they sounded like an ideal client profile for a two-person freelance writer/designer team. Absolutely, he replied. While he might charge $15K to $20K (plus printing) for a brochure (given his market positioning and high overhead), the humble freelancers could likely deliver an appropriate product for roughly half that. His comments point to a large and largely ignored segment of the marketplace.

I've discovered tons of companies in this sector—firms with 25 to 200+ employees. They have a marketing budget, but with fewer employees (many already multi-tasking), they often lack the time or expertise to craft their own marketing materials. Even if they do have communications departments, it's usually one or two people—almost never enough to handle the workload. You'd be amazed at how many established, successful companies have virtually no formal marketing materials, or only bare-bones stuff.

THE UPSIDES Smaller companies make up a substantial market segment, and the work is often challenging and interesting (they can take creative risks that larger companies—with big 'n scary legal departments—can't). At smaller firms, you're more likely to be viewed as an expert, your opinions valued, and your work regarded as an important team effort. And with your help, today's small- to medium-sized companies can become the medium to large firms of tomorrow.

THE DOWNSIDES While, in a strictly relative sense, small companies aren't as financially flush as a Fortune 100 firm, in my experience they're usually just as reliable as the big boys, and typically pay faster. Do your due diligence, get your up-front deposits, etc. Smaller companies, by definition, have less work than a large firm would, though a medium-sized company can still keep a freelancer plenty busy with ongoing projects.

Often, smaller companies do their writing in-house, but often only because they don't know there are other options. Meaning, you'll need to educate these folks about the field and the writing process, which also means they'll tend to follow your lead: If you say a one-third deposit is standard, that's what you'll get. Speaking of educating…

DON'T ASK, DO TELL Ask smaller companies if they have any writing jobs, and they're likely to say no, either because they do it all in-house or because they haven't considered how communications materials could enhance their marketing message and strategies—both within their organization and with their client/prospect base. Remember, in smaller firms, people wear many hats and usually struggle to keep up with what they know they have to get done, without thinking up more projects to take on.

This is where a FLCW well-versed in the strategies discussed in Chapter Three—and with talented designer in tow—has the opportunity to become a valued marketing consultant, suggesting ways in which the client can improve profits, customer loyalty or in-house cohesion simply by creating the appropriate marketing materials.

No In-House Talent One question posed in a pre-teleseminar Q&A some time back was this: *Why are freelance writers in demand? What is it that companies are missing from their in-house talent that I, as a freelance writer, can bring to the table?* To which I replied, "What they're often missing *is* in-house talent. If they do have some, they don't have enough for the workload, or the right expertise."

Related to that, you'll often pick up jobs so simple you'll wonder why the clients didn't do it themselves. I'll tell you why: they don't have the *time* to do it themselves, but they have the budget to have someone else do it. Or they may've "hit the (creative) wall" and are looking for fresh thoughts and a new set of eyes.

Years back, I landed a trade show brochure—a rehash of an earlier piece with a few new sections. No reinventing the wheel, just a bit of writing and rearranging. I got the parameters, the old piece, the gist of the new sections, and off I went. Got it done in about 10–11 hours over the next two days, and with minimal revisions. Fee: $1,000. As the corporate world gets increasingly overworked, count on picking up more and more of these relative no-brainers.

Suggestive Selling Brian Konradt, founder of **www.freelancewriting.com**, wrote a piece about the smaller business segment for **www.writefromhome.com**. One excerpt discussed Atlanta FLCW Paul Murray and his "suggestive selling" success in landing a veterinary clinic as a client.

> *Murray discovered that his local veterinary hospital lacked a regular newsletter because the owner didn't understand how his hospital could benefit from one. "It wasn't because the owner couldn't afford a copywriter or he had other print materials that substituted for a newsletter," says Murray, "it was because he was uneducated as to how a newsletter could positively contribute to his business."*
>
> *Murray's selling strategy was simple: He showed the owner how hiring him to write and produce a monthly newsletter would convert initial customers into repeat clients, bring in more referrals, sell more products such as flea control and sprays, and enhance the hospital's image. The bottom line, says Murray, is "the newsletter would boost the hospital's sales; that's what the owner really wanted to hear." Murray got the job.*

What other business scenarios could you build from this kind of thinking?

Your Partners in Profit As a sidebar, your graphic design colleagues often cross paths with businesspeople who write their own copy. If it's lousy (more often than not), he or she can then suggest hiring a copywriter to improve the client's overall image. Designers hate designing around garbage, and ending up with a sample they don't want to show!

That said, if you're in a major metro with plenty of businesses, then stick to the clients already accustomed to using copywriters, as opposed to trying to convince others to begin outsourcing. As friend and fellow Atlanta FLCW Steve Marshall reminds, "If you're selling salad dressing, it's always easier to sell someone who already eats salad on buying your dressing than to convince someone who doesn't to start."

Remember, companies in this segment rarely have in-house creative resources of any kind, and an offer from a writer/designer team to deliver a "turnkey"—start-to-finish—solution (a true *benefit*: all about the customer) will likely get a warm reception, versus simply "writing services" (a *feature*: all about you).

•   •   •

Hidden Corporate Treasures

Let's venture a bit deeper down the corporate corridors, and see what else we can find. This tasty piece is from Mary Anne Hahn (used here with her permission), who comes from 15 years in corporate America. Mary Anne is the editor and publisher of *WriteSuccess*, a free biweekly ezine of ideas, information and inspiration for writers. To subscribe, visit **www.writesuccess.com**.

This opened my eyes to some avenues I'd never explored. While many of these folks aren't used to calling on writers, all corporate folk want to reduce stress and simplify their lives (*benefits*: about them and their lives). If you're already in the door of a corporation, ask for referrals to other departments—perhaps some outlined here.

•   •   •

CORPORATE ROADS LESS TRAVELED BY MARY ANNE HAHN

When targeting any corporation for work, most freelancers contact the communications department (i.e., "Marcom"). Logical—given that it's responsible for the majority of a company's external and internal communications.

But 15 years in a large insurance company taught me that the need for strong writers exists throughout the organization, not just in communications. And while the management folks in these other departments may realize that need, they probably won't think to seek out a freelancer unless you let them know you're out there and show them how you might help address their specific communications challenges.

This advice applies as well to utilities, banks, hospitals, brokerage firms, and many other organizations with similar departments and similar needs.

CUSTOMER SERVICE DEPARTMENTS

Having spent a good deal of my career in the customer service sector, I know firsthand what kind of writing needs exist there. A lot of customer service functions happen through form letters or more personalized responses from a representative to a customer. Often these letters could use a professional writer's touch or, at the very least, these representatives could use business writing training.

Some organizations might even hire a writer to assist them with correspondence backlogs or in creating new form letters. (*PB: This one struck a chord as I thought of all the atrociously written letters I've gotten from my HMO over the years. One of these days…*)

Why not offer a newsletter targeted to customer service department staff? It might include *Employee of the Month*, customer service tips and articles, motivational quotes and stress-reducing techniques and exercises. Those who've worked in customer service departments understand how valuable such a newsletter can be for employee morale.

HUMAN RESOURCES DEPARTMENTS

HR departments generate a large volume of written materials: company policy manuals, job descriptions, fliers announcing company events, employee benefits paperwork, and more. HR professionals (for whom writing may not come easily) need to constantly communicate to the rest of the company in writing. Can you help them get their messages out clearly and professionally? If so, freelance opportunities await.

MARKETING DEPARTMENTS

Next to communications, marketing departments probably produce the most written material: product brochures, business proposals, direct mail sales letters, etc. Outsourcing frees up the marketing/sales staff to study trends, identify potential new business and make sales calls. Have desktop publishing experience as well? Even better.

IT (INFORMATION TECHNOLOGY) DEPARTMENTS

The need for writers in this area is tremendous, and the gateway is IT department heads. Not only are technical writers needed to document system specifications or create system user guides, but also non-technical writers can assist IT with the creation of Internet site content for a company's customers, or Intranet content for its employees. People who excel in writing HTML appreciate those who excel in writing clear, crisp content.

TRAINING DEPARTMENTS

My current day job title is "Document Development Coordinator" for the training department: I support the trainers by creating and editing a wide variety of training manuals and procedure materials. These people have little time to research and update their materials. Writing needs include assembling industry-specific corporate glossaries of terms and acronyms, editing training and procedure docs to ensure they're user-friendly, and training the trainers themselves on how to write clearly and effectively.

Do your research. Make the phone calls to identify the people who head up these various departments. The effort could be well worth it in terms of uncovering dozens of "hidden markets" and new clients for freelance writing work.

•   •   •

Mary Anne's piece highlights the importance of letting clients know everything you do. Over time, we can get pigeon-holed: "Oh, he does brochures for us; Oh, she does case studies," because that's all we've done for them. Remember the age-old truism: *It's always easier to get more work out of an existing client than land a new one.*

WA-based Mike Klassen is a graphic designer (and ex-commercial writer). Mike wrote me recently about picking up a different kind of design work from a new client only because he happened to mention in casual conversation about finishing up such a project.

Mike says: "I assumed that since he hired me, he'd visited my web site. Nope. Turns out he thought I only did projects like the one we were working on. He had a company to run, so popping over to my site never made his priority list."

Dig Before You Call

Business networking sites www.Zoominfo.com, www.Spoke.com, www.Jigsaw.com, www.Xing.com, www.LinkedIn.com, www.Google.com and others (or in some cases, several in sequence) are good ways to search for info on specific companies and/or decision makers. Using these sites—and their "drill-down" functionality—is ideal for those with a specific writing niche (i.e., project type or industry), which might limit the pool of possible prospects, but make those prospects better bets.

In those cases, it's worth researching each prospect in more depth prior to contacting them, so you can speak intelligently to them (and *about* them to them), better understand their needs, and see how your skill set may mesh with those needs. (NOTE: For us generalists, whose potential prospecting base is far larger and less form-fitted to our skills, such in-depth research on any given prospect is likely not worth it, as we have to contact more prospects per job landed).

Erick Dittus, a speechwriter friend you'll meet later, uses these sites extensively to do pre-call research. He starts at Spoke.com, looking for certain job titles; a "premium" membership can buy you access to more specific contact info. He notes, "If you don't have a title, go to Zoominfo.com, drop in a name, and about half the time, you'll find a profile, maybe with articles, and sometimes a phone number or email addy. I then go to LinkedIn.com to verify the info. If none of that works, I'll go to Google and drop in the name and title." According to Erick, more established companies tend to be more transparent, with info easier to find, than newer ones.

NOTE: there are reports that some of the above sites will pull data from your own address book to populate their databases, making it difficult to have your own info removed from their site, etc. Just be aware.

NOT-FOR-PROFITS

While I've had limited experience with NFP's, it's all been positive. But aren't rates slashed to nothing when working with NFP's? Small, one-outlet entities like a theatre company, homeless shelter, or adult literacy organization will typically only pay sharply reduced rates, if anything at all (the latter's more likely, which is why they make wonderful *pro bono* portfolio-building clients).

But larger regional, national or global entities (and their local chapters on state or city levels) can be a whole different ballgame. These big boys remind us that, after all, "non-profit" is simply an accounting term. Many are downright flush with cash. Hefty salaries, impressive offices, and robust budgets can spell good freelance opportunities. At this level, they're no different from any large EU—they have tons of writing needs. Some handle them in-house, and many outsource.

But, good opportunities often lurk behind exceptionally modest exteriors as well. I had a most excellent adventure with the Atlanta chapter of a global religious-based charity I picked up teaming with a graphic designer—as a client in early 2006. Bottom line, unimpressive offices and hard-working, under-compensated staff belied a commitment to paying handsomely—nearly $14K in billings in a calendar year.

* * *

The following real-world piece on NFP opps comes from Bloomington, Indiana FLCW Kevin Klemme, and is used here with his permission.

WRITING FOR THE NOT-FOR-PROFIT (NFP) SECTOR

I spent six years as the primary writer for a consulting firm with a client base that was 90 percent NFP, and continue to serve that market on my own. Based on that experience, I'll list a few types of clients and discuss the needs, contact points and general revenue potential of each. The rates suggested reflect what I've seen in the Midwest.

SCHOOL DISTRICTS

I've often approached school districts through the superintendent's office and usually end up reporting to the assistant superintendent during the project. Most districts of any size have a community relations office serving a marketing function, and it's not unusual to work with them on a project. It's usually the superintendent's office, however, that makes the final decision and approves the spending.

School districts most often need help with grant proposals and planning documents. (If you have the background to help with strategic planning, they sometimes need that, too). The consulting firm I was with charged up to $150 per hour for my time on very large (eight figures) grant proposals from large districts. Rates for freelancers working on more common projects would be $75 per hour for big, urban districts, or $60 for smaller ones.

Local Economic Development Organizations (LEDOs)

"LEDO" can refer specifically to an economic development corporation, or to any organization with "economic development" as part of its mission: Chambers of Commerce, Workforce Industry Boards or other locally created business or workforce development committees.

LEDO's typically need writers to prepare white papers, grant proposals and planning documents. Usually, I've dealt with the organization's president or VP. Larger LEDO's, such as the Chamber in a large city, will have directors of education, legislative issues and others. I've worked for them as well. Rates can go as high as $100 per hour or more for big organizations, but $50 to $75 per hour is more common.

Trade Associations

Industry-specific councils, forums and associations (see sidebar below) are promising prospects for freelancers. Entities that lobby state or local governments have an ongoing need for white papers and reports on studies they've funded. Often, the experts conducting the study write in jargon, which the trade association needs translated into plain English for public use. Associations also produce educational materials for the general public or for distribution to schools. I've always worked for the president or vice president of these organizations. Rates are about the same as for LEDO's.

Community Service Organizations

From regional United Way chapters to small committees trying to meet local human needs, all need grant proposals written. CSO's of any size tend to have tight budgets: Larger ones pay, but smaller ones typically don't have much ready cash. If you're interested in the cause, decide whether to charge a small fee or do it *pro bono*. I've done paying work for United

Way chapters or affiliates conducting community needs assessments. In cases like that, it helps if you know how to design a good survey, because the same person or company will usually be expected to write the survey instrument and the report on the results.

FYI's ON NFP's:

- Most prefer flat rates to hourlies, because they usually have firm project budgets.

- Each has its own jargon (especially LEDO's). You'll need to know it or learn it, whether you have to write with it (for industry-specific jobs) or translate it (for public consumption).

- Brush up on potential clients before calling. No one will hire a writer ignorant of local events or industry trends. Check local papers for recent stories on school districts and CSO's. See if the national version of your local trade association publishes a journal. Many of the organizations above will have web sites with news sections.

Success "By Association"

Maryland FLCW and good friend Cecilia Sepp (**www.ceciliasepp.net**), whom I met through the great writers' organization *American Independent Writers* (**www.aiwriters.org**; formerly *Washington Independent Writers*), specializes in writing and consulting services for associations. I asked her to share the ins and outs of the field.

●   ●   ●

Associations and other types of nonprofit organizations are opportunities for freelance writers to build a long client list. While there are some big associations like the *American Medical Association* and the *American Chemical Society*, most associations are small—with small staffs *and* budgets (yes, rates paid to writers are generally a bit lower than for most commercial freelancing). Outsourcing is how associations stretch their two most important resources: time and money.

The reason most associations outsource is to get all the things accomplished that their members demand—always a challenge, given lean staffs. Hiring freelancers saves money by keeping staff small, thus reducing salary, employee tax, and benefits expenses.

Things to Know About Associations:

1. Nonprofit does not mean "non-revenue." Nonprofits are still businesses, even the ones organized as charities. The big difference? Unlike "for profits," nonprofits don't pay dividends or other profit sharing. All revenue goes back into the organization.

2. A *professional* association or society is an organization an individual joins to advance his or her career or to contribute to the good of the profession. A *trade* association represents an industry, and the members are companies within that industry.

3. Most nonprofits have two leadership tiers: the staff and the members elected to leadership positions (i.e., the board of directors). You'll be dealing with the staff, who answers to the members.

4. Be flexible. Association staff—overworked and underpaid—are pulled in many directions. Their schedules are usually in flux because of constant requests from members, and issues arising from their many projects. Deadlines may slip, but not because the project's not important; they're busy, and that's why they hired you.

5. Many nonprofits have gone "electronic" for membership outreach. Opportunities exist in the areas of blogs, web site content, email marketing, and e-newsletters.

6. Despite the electronic revolution, most nonprofit membership associations still have printed magazines. While these don't all pay for articles, it's a good area to investigate because, even without pay, a magazine article can be used for promoting your business.

Resources/Directories

Cecilia's Blog: www.associationpuzzle.typepad.com

www.ipl.org/div/aon

www.weddles.com/associations/index.htm

http://www.marketingsource.com/associations/ (Fee-based)

Buffalo, NY writer Paul Chimera writes: "I started teaching four years ago at Daemen College in Amherst, NY, as an adjunct in the English department. Once in the door, I got to know the editor of the alumni magazine. I got an assignment, he loved my work, and I've been the senior writer for the pub ever since, taking in $1,000–1,200 for one lead story and two smaller inside pieces. Probably spend about 10 hours on all of it."

Higher academia is an easy-to-overlook market. Big cities AND smaller markets are often home to colleges and universities. While it's a mixed bag, and not always with high wages, nonetheless, it's worth a look.

A few years back, I got a call from someone in marketing at Emory University here in Atlanta (referred by a too-busy colleague). Could I help revamp her web site copy? I was getting ready to leave town, so I had to steer her to yet another writing colleague (more on the power and potential of a writers group later). I asked her if we could huddle up when I returned. Her reply? *Absolutely. I have a constant need for freelancers.*

JUST LIKE A CORPORATION Okay, think about this. Emory University has a marketing department. Course they do. They're a business like any other and, as such, have to create brochures, newsletters, direct mail campaigns, web sites, orientation materials, educational CD's, tons of internal communications, etc. Just like any other business.

Next story. I was in Champaign, Illinois a few months after that first phone call, attending a luncheon for the local chapter of the Society for Technical Communication (**www.stc.org**). That area is home to the University of Illinois, and seated across from me was a woman who worked in publications for one of the big academic departments. I asked if she ever outsourced writing projects to freelancers. *I use freelancers all the time*, she replied. Interesting.

RESEARCH REVEALS... I contacted some universities around the country to see if they hired freelancers and if so, what they paid. A midwestern university's technical department said they hire freelancers to write articles for the department's magazine—both general interest and technical stories adapted for the layperson. $50 an hour. A possible avenue for those with a technical background (or a technical major in college).

A manager of editorial projects in the public affairs office of a southeastern school said she hires various freelancers to help with writing and designing publications and web projects. Alumni magazine articles, ad copy, brochures, web sites, etc. The 50 cents a word for articles isn't great, but not a bad portfolio-builder.

FORMAL COMMUNITY NETWORKS One institution had a network of writers it farmed out to the academic or local business communities needing copywriting services. Projects included internal communications, marketing, publications, web content design/creation, etc. Rates? $25 to $130 per hour. Now we're talking.

Interested writers would apply to become part of the network and provide a price list, either per project based on size, or based on an hourly rate. As my contact explained, *We want to provide competitive products to our clients. But we also seek to provide variety, which includes variety in pricing, experience in higher education, etc.*

Not surprisingly, they like to hire people with a proven track record (several rely heavily on referrals). One woman elaborated, *The people we use must meet deadlines, produce good, clean copy, be careful about fact-checking, be receptive to revisions requested by their client and be great to work with as a team member.* Imagine that. Pretty much true for any commercial writing arena.

WHERE TO LOOK Poke around on their web site. Good target departments: human resources, university relations, media relations, PR, public affairs, communications (NOT academic "communications"), marketing and others. Drill down within those departments and find the directors, assistant directors, managers or similar titles.

All in all, academia is a reasonably promising market. Sure, most universities won't pay the highest rates, but they're often competitive—and as a place to beef up the book, they can be great. For writers in smaller markets, where there are fewer large corporate entities and where cost of living is less, they can be an excellent direction.

•   •   •

Bringing "School Work" Home

Middletown, CT FLCW Adam Farrah (**www.technical-writer.net**) has had some juicy experiences working with universities. I adapted the following from a longer piece that appeared as a two-parter in my ezine.

•   •   •

While breaking into universities can be challenging, once inside, they can provide a nearly unlimited flow of work. Most institutions are understaffed and the employees overworked. A good copywriter who can skirt the bureaucracy has a lot of value.

University Project Work

Copy for program-specific web sites; graduate program brochures; conference brochures; ghostwritten blog posts; press releases for new programs/conferences; sales letters to accompany program brochures; promotional postcards, mailers and emails and more.

Challenges Faced by Universities

• *Creating high-impact marketing pieces*—Most university staff (even marketing faculty) don't know how to write effective marketing copy.

• *Getting good copy quickly at a fair price*—Some universities get hooked by big agencies charging exorbitant rates and delivering mediocre results.

• *Managing projects and keeping things on track*—University bureaucracies can really slow projects down. Writers need to keep projects on track.

Challenges Faced by Writers

• *Getting proposals approved quickly*—in academia, there is usually little sense of urgency, and proposals will likely pass through many hands before getting signed.

• *No single point of accountability*—This is the land of the committee, whether it's approving copy or getting things done. This can be frustrating for entrepreneurs.

• *Difficult access*—It took me four months to "get inside" the account, but once I did, the work was non-stop. Get to know professors and high-level administrators.

• *Disorganization*—I've experienced unanswered emails (including requests for copy review). False starts. Direction changes. "Is it worth it?" you may ask.

> **Success Suggestions**
>
> • *Make sure everything's in writing*—No matter how immediate a need seems, get a signed proposal before you spend time on anything.
>
> • *Track time carefully*—You'll often have to bill for time spent on a project that never goes to completion. To ensure you get paid, keep close track of your time.
>
> • *Get payment terms in writing*—Universities can be slow to pay, with invoices getting lost or held up. Know the rules in case you need to invoke them.

MIDDLEMEN (MM)

GRAPHIC DESIGN FIRMS

Graphic designers (GD's) aren't just "artsy creative types." The good ones are consummate marketers, able to create high-impact pieces that boost bottom lines (with the help of great copywriting). Just know they'll likely be drawn to the design of your portfolio pieces, not the writing—a bit frustrating if your portfolio is lean.

Very few graphic design firms have in-house copywriting talent. They outsource not only to stay lean, but because they work with a broad spectrum of industries with wide-ranging needs, and it's just smarter to cultivate a stable of writers, each with their own strengths and style, so they can fit the writer to the job.

Get to know the most talented staff designers within a design firm, marketing company or any other MM entity. Why? Because all the good ones eventually go solo. And when they do, they'll need writing resources. A by-product of this happy scenario is what happened to me: GD's (and other MM's) who liked me and my work got me in the door of some mighty big boys: Coca-Cola, Mercedes-Benz, BellSouth, UPS, DuPont, IBM, Cingular, Randstad, and others.

Teaming with graphic designers—some larger firms, mostly "lone rangers" —has been the single most profitable strategy in my arsenal from Day One. I've gotten more work from and through a handful of GD's than from any other source. And here's why: Become the "go-to" writer for a few busy GD's (or even one!), and every time they find work for themselves, they could be landing work for you as well. And then it truly becomes the proverbial "gift that keeps on giving."

LUCRATIVE "LONE RANGERS"   The solo designer (a "lone ranger") I've been working with since 1994 is one of my top three clients ever. For that whole time, barely a month has gone by without a job or two coming from her. It's a beautiful thing. And it's logical. One-person shops are likely to be much more stable (and profitable) accounts than ones with big corporations, where things always change (i.e., people leave, new people come in with their favorite copywriters, etc.).

Obviously, the best GD prospects to target are busy, successful folks—firms or individuals—who are always marketing, always hunting for new work. More work for them means more work for you. That's how it's unfolded for me. I'm off doing my thing, and the phone calls come out of the blue, and I've done nothing to land the work except pick up and say, "Hello?"

BECOMING THE "GO-TO" WRITER   Okay, so that's not completely accurate. In order to become that "go-to" writer, you've got to do a lot of things right. First off, remember this: a good copywriter will seriously enhance a GD's "value proposition"—what they can offer to their clients. GD's *love* good copywriters, because good writing makes their creations that much more powerful and effective. If you can help a GD make their clients wildly happy, make them—and their portfolio—look good, and make their lives easy, why would they go anywhere else?

Here's the thing: if a GD starts to realize your writing ratchets up the quality of their work a few notches, they're going to start lobbying their clients (especially those who want to write their own copy) to budget some money for a copywriter. They know the client will be that much happier with the final product, which in turn will reflect even better on them.

As for the "make-their-lives-easy" part of working with GD's, that means a lot of things: being easy to get along with (priceless; no one likes a whiner or a *prima donna*); being a quick study (i.e., getting up to speed fast); bringing marketing savvy to the table; never missing a deadline; asking enough questions—and the right ones—upfront so you "nail" your first drafts; and turning in work that's clean, error-free, and logically formatted (i.e., with copy clearly labeled as *Headline*, *Sub-head*, *Body Copy*, *Inside Left-Panel Copy*, etc., so there's no confusion and miscommunication).

Bonus attribute? You're able to engage with clients in an intelligent, professional, articulate manner. Remember: people buy people and if you "give good face-to-face," that counts for a lot. Not that you can't make it without that, but it'll help.

Teaming is ideal when dealing with the small- to medium-sized firms discussed earlier, which rarely have in-house "creative." Partnering with a designer turns both of you from "service providers" to *problem-solvers* for clients. Again, a turnkey (start-to-finish) solution from such a team (a true *benefit*: about the client and their needs) will likely get a warmer reception than just "writing services" (a *feature*: all about you).

But, keep in mind: unless you're specifically targeting just small- to medium-sized clients, only 20 to 25 percent of gigs will call for teaming. In most cases, the client will have the design side handled—either in-house or with their own freelancer.

The best part of a teaming scenario for a client? Given you're two freelancers with low overhead, they'll get that turnkey project for a fraction of what it'd cost them if they went with a bigger design firm, ad agency or marketing firm. Speaking of costs, and money, be sure to check out the sidebar in Chapter Nine about estimating and billing issues when working with GD's.

ADVERTISING AGENCIES

Ad agencies vary widely in size, scope, and specialty. With the BIG marquee agencies, the average freelancer is unlikely to land the juicier, high-end, and high-profile national campaigns, print ads, and TV spots (unless you've come out of an agency and are still plugged in). They'll be keeping that work for themselves.

CLEVER TRUMPS EFFECTIVE In cynical moments (a common state when discussing ad agencies), my colleagues assert an agency's real goal is to win awards. In the incestuous world of big-time advertising, it is often the cleverest stuff, not the most effective, that takes home the statuettes. While I have limited experience with larger agencies, agency-seasoned colleagues share far more negative than positive experiences. By most accounts, the bigger firms consider freelancers "the help"—simply cogs in the wheel.

Your best bet with the big boys is "collateral": brochures, internal campaigns, newsletters, web content, and other peripheral projects that are, by definition, less prestigious and less lucrative to them. Large agencies boast bigger supporting casts: the account executive (salesperson on the account), creative director, art director, and production people. By contrast, in smaller agencies, fewer people handle more jobs.

SMALLER AGENCIES, BIGGER OPPS Smaller agencies offer far more opportunities to get into the fun, creative concepting and headlining projects for, in all likelihood, small and local end users. But, it can be just as interesting and far more rewarding, because with smaller firms, you've got a much better chance of having your work see the light of day. That translates to more job satisfaction and creative fulfillment.

Friendly warning. From time to time, you might get calls/emails from design firms or agencies—some pretty prominent—saying they came across your info and are "beefing up their stable" or some similarly equine verbiage. Wow, they called *you*. Cool, huh? Don't get too excited. Sure, if it takes no more than steering them to your web site to make them happy, then do it. But, don't set up a meeting unless they mention *specific* projects and the *specific* skills you have that are a fit. If they're general inquiries, you'll likely never hear from them again in this life or the next. All hat, no cattle.

MARKETING FIRMS

While some marketing firms work with a broad spectrum of industries, many specialize in a particular industry (high-tech, healthcare, real estate, retail, etc.). These firms often help growing companies that have hit a certain point in their evolution: they've achieved some success by sheer hard work, but in order to take that success to the next level, they could benefit from some professional expertise—and can afford it.

SMALLER "OUTSOURCERS" Perhaps a high-tech firm has made its mark in a local market but is looking to have a national impact. A good marketing firm might come in and design a comprehensive strategy and campaign involving, perhaps, ad campaigns, public relations, direct mail, enhanced web presence, blog, etc. Many of these companies keep their staffs pretty lean, bringing in freelancers as needed. This allows them to be nimble and responsive to their clients—finding just the right person for the job.

PUBLIC RELATIONS FIRMS

PR firms are entrusted with fostering the best possible image of their clients in the eyes of the public. Because of the similarities and overlap between ad agencies and PR firms, you'll find many larger ad agencies have PR divisions and vice versa. PR firms can be heavily weighted to newspaper articles, print advertising, online, collateral, speeches, or any combination.

While MM's like design or marketing firms lean toward the smallish end, ad agencies and PR firms span the gamut, with a healthy number of huge ones in any large market. Like ad agencies, PR firms hang on to most of the high-profile work in a PR firm, but it's worth getting your name in front of them anyway.

If you come out of journalism (and haven't run off all the PR folks who contacted you over the years), this is an obvious direction to head in for work. In fact, a 6/20/08 *PR Week* article ("An Unstable Media Landscape Has Journalists Seeking PR Positions" by Frank Washkuch) chronicled this trend, stating, "While many journalists ultimately end up in PR, the media industry's troubles are causing some to do so earlier in their careers." If it's logical for those seeking jobs, ditto for freelancers.

DON'T IDOLIZE THE BIG BOYS Some years back, I did a marketing push to Atlanta PR firms, calling the top 50 firms (using *The Book of Lists* we'll discuss later). I sent info to about half of them and nothing happened. But a few months later, I got a call from one of the big boys (offices in 25–30 cities) who needed me to help rewrite a consumer presentation for a big local utility. Seems the first writer had missed the mark.

Several lessons here. First, lets things gestate. So you called 50 folks and nothing happened right away. So what? Plant seeds and eventually some will bloom. Second, don't assume that just because it's a HOUSEHOLD NAME PR firm, they know what they're doing. They knew something was off, but couldn't figure out what it was, even though it was glaringly obvious to me.

Don't put the big boys on a pedestal while discounting your own talents and ability to effectively address a company's—even a big one's—challenges. Never ceases to amaze me how much bad writing is out there, and attached to a lot of big-name firms—clunky, unfunny, obtuse, confusing, scattered, boring. That's good news if you're good.

EVENT PRODUCTION COMPANIES (EPC'S)

EPC's work with large corporations to produce conferences, trade shows, conventions, meetings, product launches—anything that's big, involved, and needs to be outstanding. Many handle the whole ball of wax: design and construction of all tradeshow exhibits, printed literature before, during, and after the show, conference signage, speaker support, meeting rooms, catering, entertainment, the gargantuan job of shipping every single piece necessary to pull off the above, often across the country, and much, much more.

WORK ACROSS THE SPECTRUM EPC's hire writers for a bunch of different work. Contact producers, creative directors or account executives (good-sized firms will have multiples of all three) for proposals (first step to landing contracts), treatments (mini-proposals outlining the EPC's ideas on executing program components), conference literature, speaker support (writing and editing speakers' comments), event scripting, and more.

SHOW UP REGULARLY One proven avenue to getting work with EPC's was regular face time. They operate in more or less constant crisis mode, and rarely have much time to think about where to find a writer (true for *most* clients, but even more so here). I found this out the hard way after I'd done several projects for one of these firms and then didn't hear from them again for about 15 months, at which point, I got several more.

In both cases, I got additional work after the initial jobs because I was around and visible. Both times, people stopped me in the hall and asked, "What's your availability in about a week or so?" Booked again. Once out of sight, I was out of mind. One creative director, only half-joking, said, "Heck, if you sit out in our lobby for an hour, you'll get work."

I did a little updated research on EPC's for this book, asking a marketing person with one of the big industry players to comment on the above. He wrote: "Yes, we still use writers regularly, and a great deal in our demand-generation activities for events. You touched on printed literature but it goes beyond that: email, web copy, telemarketing scripts, etc., require a great deal of our writers' attentions. Not to mention event education and breakout sessions, which require PowerPoint development and other writing.

"As far as landing work, as for walking the halls, maybe that works. For me, it's more about a regular email reminding me that someone's out there and showing me examples of what they have been working on.

We're always looking for fresh thinking and creative brilliance, of course!"

THE GATEWAYS TO WORK Check with area convention centers for the names of big EPC players ("EPC" is my acronym; they likely won't use that term). To quantify a given EPC's writing workload, why not angle an appointment with a decision-maker with something like this: "While I'm an excellent writer and confident I can be an asset to your firm, I'm unsure of your specific needs. I'd love to get a sense, in a 15–20 minute meeting, what exactly those needs are, and how you might best use my skills to make your job easier and make your company look good."

And by the way, geography isn't a big issue for these folks. When asked if he worked only with local writers, he said: "I don't work with any local writers, and while some other offices do, many don't. Location just isn't a critical determining factor anymore." Well, there you have it. Check it out.

CREATIVE TEMP AGENCIES

These entities typically work with larger EU's—placing creative talent on bigger projects. I wouldn't count on them for a lot of jobs, but it's always nice to land work you did little to generate. They often present a Catch-22: obviously, they want experienced, reliable, "no-surprise" vendors, but after taking their fee, they typically pay far less than that pro could make on his own.

Hence, they're ideal for the experienced pro who hates marketing, and is willing to give up a healthy slice in return for having work handed to them. Less of a fit if you want to maximize your hourly rate, or if you have little track record. To find the bigger players, ask creative folks in your area. If you have extensive industry-specific experience (definite plus), ask EU's in that arena who they use (though if you've gone as far as to contact them, do you need the middleman?).

TECHNICAL STAFFING COMPANIES

These firms generally service the technical writing (TW) arena, where huge software documentation manuals or user guides are the norm. Projects like those could take a writer six months and be worth $30–60K+ (hourly rates for TW are often considerably less than for commercial writing (CW), but 35–40 billable-hour weeks are far more common than with CW. The agency keeps a stable of writers, and matches the writer with the job, taking a commission of 10 to 30 percent of the total.

How Are You Being Represented? Some MM's, to look more established, may want to present you as "in-house creative." To avoid awkward moments, I prefer being introduced as outside talent—often spun as a positive: "We found just the right writer for this project" (vs. perhaps, an in-house writer unfamiliar with their business).

In most MM scenarios, the MM is your client and you'd bill them. And most MM's will mark you up, charging their client, say, $150 an hour for copywriting, when you're charging them, say, $100. Standard. Needless to say, when billing the MM, you don't utter Word One about any money issues to anyone but the MM.

GETTING TO THEM

A great way to quickly build prospect lists of both MM's and EU's for cold calling (*much* more on cold calling next chapter), broken down by city and category, is to use online phone directories like **www.superpages.com** or **www.switchboard.com.** Just enter categories like *Advertising Agencies, Public Relations Firms, Graphic Designers,* etc.

While you won't get contact names through the sites above, you *could* visit the company's site to gather that kind of info. That said, as a rule, it's not worth spending the time digging up a name at the preliminary stage until you know someone's a prospect. As discussed, that approach makes sense for writers with a niche and a limited pool of prospects, where you want to know more about who you're calling.

Free Library Resources LA FLCW Amy Sorkin suggests: "Your library's web site is home to some pretty extensive lists of companies under different sub headings…which can form the foundation for direct-mail or cold-calling efforts. And all without ever leaving your office. I've found that there are *many* more listed here than in a phone book. And if you're unsure of how to work the databases, just call your librarian for help."

Megan Tsai (**www.RedWagonWriting.com**), a FLCW in Minneapolis, shares her top pick for a free library database: *Dun & Bradstreet's Million Dollar Database.* It's accessible from home, exportable to a spreadsheet or contact management program (to create calling lists or do mail merges for postcard mailings) and will, according to Megan, "generate the kinds of lists people pay thousands of dollars for."

She continues: "To give you an idea of the power of this sucker, in five minutes, I built one spreadsheet of all the businesses within five miles of a zip code that have a marketing position and 20 to 250 employees. I built another of all the ad agencies with 15 miles of a zip code with annual sales of $500,000 or more. In many cases, they even list the name of the folks in the top-level sales and marketing positions. You can refine searches by number of employees, industry, annual sales, if they have a web site, even by employment trends (you could target rapidly growing companies)."

In Atlanta (and now in Charlotte, NC), we have something called *BusinessWise*—a fee-based database that lists companies in numerous ways and also provides contact names and information. For similar entities, check with your local Chamber of Commerce, which, incidentally, offers local business directories of their own.

P.S. **www.theultimates.com** is a cool site to do fee-based (usually a buck or two) searches for people, reverse phone or cell phone searches (when you have the number, not the name), email searches, or individual Yellow Pages business searches. **www.dogpile.com** collects all the different search engines in one place (including the ones above).

"THE BOOK OF LISTS" Another great source is the annual *Book of Lists*, put out by your city's local weekly business publication. In Atlanta, it's the *Atlanta Business Chronicle*, part of a nationwide family of business publications, most ending in *Business Journal* (e.g., *Los Angeles Business Journal, Philadelphia Business Journal*, etc.) Visit **www.amcity.com** for the complete listing.

In Atlanta, the *Chronicle's* BOL is an impressive 200+ page compilation of just about every industry category and the top 10, 25, 50, or 100 players in that business locally. The 2008 edition touts "127 lists—3036 businesses—5126 contacts." The print edition currently runs $60, a downloadable (and importable) version, $170. The print edition comes free with an annual subscription (currently $84), making subscribing a bargain.

Subscribing is a great way of staying on top of your market (many, including Atlanta, have free online editions, but then you'd pay for the *BOL*). Notes freelancer coach Melanie Rockett (**www.proofpositive.com**):

Local business publications can be a potential goldmine. An article about a company's newly hired PR or marketing director —a fresh face with fresh initiatives—might spell writing work…A story about a startup or expanding company might hint at a need for writing projects to support that growth. How about a story on a new hospital breaking ground? That could mean press releases, policies and procedures manuals and, most importantly, a communications department with ongoing needs for brochures, ads, direct mail, web sites, internal/external newsletters and magazines, and much more.

CREATIVE PUBLICATIONS Perhaps you've got a local publication dedicated to the creative industries—advertising, graphic design, photography, copywriting, video and multimedia production, etc. In Atlanta, as mentioned, ours is *Oz* (**www.ozonline.tv**), and annually, they publish their *Creative Index*, a listing of all the companies in all the above categories and more, along with more detail on names, specialties, etc.

LEVERAGE WHAT YOU KNOW If you have industry-specific expertise, go after that industry directly. Chances are good the big companies in your former industry are running leaner than ever, but the marketing show must go on. I've gotten tons of emails over the years—from ex-attorneys, engineers, software salespeople, healthcare managers, retail execs, and many others, all sharing stories of successfully leveraging a specific background—and often with very few writing credits.

In some cases, former in-house copywriters go freelance, often picking up work from former employers. But more often, these displaced souls end up in another full-time job. Those at their old firm now entrusted with getting the work done are happy to hear from anyone who can make their lives easier, especially if you speak their language.

CHANGE IS CONSTANT While I'd love to say your first clients will be loyal and lucrative for years to come, I'd be telling stories. I'm doing business with very few of my first customers. Clients change jobs, their replacements have their favorite copywriters and you're out. Companies tank, your clients join other firms with their own copywriters and you're out. Companies merge, one has in-house copywriters and you're out.

And the unthinkable: another copywriter contacts your clients, does better work, in the client's opinion (all that really matters) and you're out.

Sure, clients can make mistakes, and I've gotten several calls over the years to rescue projects. Always a great feeling, especially when you deliver. Bottom line, if you're a serious player in your market, then just as often, you'll be that *other* copywriter to whom a competitor loses out.

EASY TO OVERLOOK Waiting at the carwash one day, I picked up a home improvement magazine—little more than a thick ad circular for every home-related company under the sun. A cursory glance revealed half a dozen ads that looked like an office manager had written them, and a bunch of companies without web sites. Lots of possibilities.

Speaking of easy to overlook, in freelance writer Lucy V. Parker's great book, *How to Start a Home-based Writing Business* (5th edition; 2008; excerpt below used with her permission), she serves up this wonderful "thought-starting" list of possible writing clients. Yes, some are familiar, but most had never occurred to me, yet were there right under my nose. Use it to come up with even more ideas. Thanks, Lucy.

●   ●   ●

SIXTY POTENTIAL WRITING CLIENTS

BY LUCY V. PARKER

1. Accountants, attorneys
2. Advertising agencies
3. Art galleries, public and private
4. Associations
5. Athletic teams, sports promoters
6. Book publishers
7. Churches, denominations, religious organizations
8. City guide publishers
9. Colleges, universities, private schools
10. Concert promoters
11. Conference planners
12. Consultants
13. Convention centers
14. Corporate human services departments
15. Corporate marketing departments
16. Corporate public relations/communications departments
17. Corporate purchasing departments

18. Design firms, architects
19. Direct-marketing firms, especially direct mail
20. Directory publishers
21. Engineering firms
22. Fitness centers
23. Fund-raising departments and consulting firms
24. Government departments—federal, state, county, township, city
25. Government-funded special agencies, such as water districts, school districts, and libraries
26. Greeting card and gift companies
27. Health clubs
28. Health insurance firms, health maintenance organizations (HMO)
29. Hospitals, medical centers
30. Hotels, resorts, casinos
31. Importers, exporters
32. Individuals, families
33. Labor organizations
34. Laboratories
35. Magazines/Newsletters—business and trade
36. Magazines/Newsletters—consumer, including single-sponsor publications
37. Magazines/Newsletters—employees, alumni, organizations
38. Marketing agencies
39. Medical professionals, including physicians, dentists, psychologists, chiropractors, nutritionists and others
40. Museums, public and private
41. Newspapers—community and regional
42. Newspapers—business and trade
43. Performing arts centers, theaters, performing groups
44. Political parties and candidates
45. Private clubs—yachting, golf, etc.
46. Producers: industrial/educational/promotional films, video, broadcasts, CD-ROMs and DVDs
47. Public relations agencies
48. Research organizations
49. Restaurants
50. Resellers
51. Retail stores

52. Shopping centers, malls
53. Small businesses
54. Social service agencies
55. Software publishers
56. Theme parks, recreation centers
57. Transportation/shipping firms and agencies
58. Travel agencies
59. Web site developers
60. Wholesalers

•　　•　　•

"EVENT-FULL" MARKETING Melanie Rockett (**www.proofpositive.com**), mentioned earlier, coaches freelancers to generate more clients and jobs. In the category of rarely considered avenues for work, Melanie discussed the 2010 Winter Olympics, coming to her own Vancouver: "Millions of dollars will be spent on planning…This means tens of thousands of documents, illustrations and photographs. Hundreds of new web sites."

No upcoming Olympic games? Tap into local, city and state events by contacting Chambers, convention bureaus, city, regional and state tourism boards, and others. There may be needs for plenty of event-driven brochures, pamphlets, press releases, web sites and more. In addition, virtually all of these entities have business/marketing communications facets worth investigating.

Be sure to check out Chapter 14, "What Will We Be Writing?" for a pretty full-bodied look at the kinds of projects we'd be taking on, including sections on white papers, direct response copywriting, case studies and speechwriting—all penned by guest experts.

ONLINE JOB SITES

DEFINITE WASTE OR DECENT WAGE? DEPENDS… People flock to online job sites like elance.com, guru.com, monster.com and others because they require relatively little effort—no cold calling, driving to client meetings or other more threatening modes of direct client communication. But, as a rule, little effort = little results (sorta like life in general…). By and large, I think those sites are a waste of time *if* you're interested in maximizing writing income. It's a buyers' market, and too many writers and too few jobs can and typically *do* drive rates down to nothing.

That said, a number of no-nonsense writers charging $70 to $125 an hour are making a good living using these sites. You can still easily starve playing the price game like most writers do, but there is a way to earn top dollar IF you're aware of the realities upfront, IF you're willing to stand your ground, and IF you bring some unique value to the table.

Trish Lambert (**www.successinsweatpants.com**) and Heather Levin (**www.tfswriting.com**) are FLCW's who know their value in the marketplace and consistently get healthy rates on online job sites. In less than six months, they built full-time businesses by producing superior work and taking customer service seriously. They make a handsome living thanks to a steady stream of projects from clients across the globe. And quality of life? Trish splits her time between home, RV, and boat—as she puts it, "anywhere I can get a WiFi signal." Doesn't get much better than that.

Trish and Heather play the "Quality and Value" game and come out on top as a result. They're never the lowest bidders; in fact, they're often the highest. But their clients hire them for their talent and professionalism and come back again and again. It's *all* about setting yourself apart. Here are some of Trish's tips to making these sites work for you:

Influence the Buyer

Let your portfolio speak for itself. Include samples that match the types of projects you bid on. In a virtual setting, the buyer is blind: Your honest face, neat grooming, and clever business card won't matter. You have only your words to convey your professionalism and reliability.

Spend time crafting "generic" sales copy. Clearly and compellingly describe your expertise and qualifications. Open every bid with it—saving you from having to start each bid from scratch—then customize to match the need.

Focus your bid on the customer and how you will provide what they need. Benefits before features. Save terms and policies for the pre-acceptance phase after you've landed the project.

Write a good provider profile with complete contact information. Your profile is another opportunity to show potential clients you're professional and reliable. It's amazing how many providers don't list an email, phone number, or address—not a confidence builder.

Be responsive. If a prospect communicates with you during the bidding process (and any other time, actually), respond immediately. It will give you a competitive edge. I can't tell you how many times I've been thanked for my prompt responses.

Qualify the Buyer

Pay for the highest level subscription available. This way, you can bid on top tier projects.

Don't underbid. Stay competitive, but know what you're worth and stand firm on your price.

Convey clear terms and conditions. Manage client expectations, so they understand what you will and won't deliver. This includes communication policies. Get buyer approval before formally accepting a job, and create milestones and get them okayed before beginning work.

Don't start work until you receive a deposit. If you have payments tied to a milestone, don't continue past that point until you receive payment.

Below, Heather offers up a few pearls herself:

> *I never miss deadlines, I don't write crappy copy or cut corners, and I treat all my clients with honesty and respect…I made a pact from day one that I wasn't going to write for a pittance. I don't apologize for my rates or compromise my values by working for shady people…While there are plenty of people on those sites looking to pay writers a penny a word or less (avoid them like the plague!), plenty of others understand that you really get what you pay for, and those are the people I went after…I've made more money since I started a year ago than I've ever made in my life. I don't have to look for work anymore, because my clients come to me. They pass my name around and keep coming back to me with more work than I can handle.*

And get this: when Heather shared her story with me, she was 28, and had only been a commercial freelancer for a year. At press time, she was charging $70 an hour. She writes: "Because I get so many referrals and so much repeat business from my clients, I do very little with Elance anymore. I'm still a member, but 100% of my business now comes from clients, and colleagues of clients, I found from the site. Without a doubt Elance helped create the great business I have now (along with your amazing book!), but I've outgrown it for now."

Trish writes: "Elance (the only OL site I bother with) continues steady. There are always "diamonds in the rough" among the bottom-feeders and unrealistic buyers, and my feedback, longevity, and portfolio can't be ignored. Elance's policy and site changes have also begun to attract a higher class client. These days, my actual hourly rate ranges between $100 and $150, depending on job and client, though I go the fixed-price route whenever I can. Last year's revenue was $150K, and I expect to add $25K or so this year."

SHARING THE WEALTH Trish is such a fan of Elance as a viable source of freelance revenue that she wants to "share the wealth." She conducts an eight-week *Winning with Elance* course to help newbies or those who've tried the board with disappointing results get some serious financial traction for a change. She believes strongly in the site and takes a "more-the-merrier" view of her course: more high-quality providers on Elance will attract more high-quality buyers. Trish also makes this eyebrow-raising commitment to course participants: Work the course, and you'll at least triple the course fee within three months of completion or she'll keep working with you until you do. Sweet deal in my book. Check out the course details at **http://tinyurl.com/elancecourse**.

•   •   •

THE ANTIDOTE TO "COMMODITIZATION" These women have "un-commoditized" their writing (and this applies to *any* writer wanting to build a thriving commercial business). So many people struggle on online sites —and in writing careers in general—because what they bring to the table is something any number of other writers can deliver equally well. When that's the case, you've turned writing (or at least that kind of writing) into a commodity. Why would a buyer pay a lot for writing project A when he's got dozens, perhaps hundreds of writers lining up for the gig—all of relatively equal talent?

He wouldn't and doesn't. And don't blame clients, as many writers do (i.e., "They should be willing to pay decent rates for writing!"). It's not about the clients. It's about the writers. Clients are only doing what buyers have done since the beginning of time. These women have done well because they've attracted the attention of writing buyers looking for something beyond the "writing-in-a-box" they can get from anywhere. It's why *anyone* spends more than "the going rate" for *anything*.

You spend more for dinner at Chez Gilbert than Gil's Diner because the quality of your experience is higher at the former than the latter (or your *perception* is that it's higher). Same with cars, vacations, clothing, houses, etc. Check out the discussion on maximizing rates in Chapter Thirteen.

●   ●   ●

Now, that should keep us filled up for a while. Toothpick, anyone? Okay, we've put this off long enough, but now it's time to face the music: cold calling. But, trust me, it's not nearly as scary as it looks. And there's lots of good news along the way...

Chapter 6

Occasionally, readers send me articles with titles like, "Is Cold Calling Dead?" or "Cold Calling Doesn't Work Anymore" or other assorted nonsense. To say that cold calling doesn't work or that the practice is dead is tantamount to saying that the Law of Averages has been rescinded. Which, of course, is just as dumb. The LOA is ironclad. Make enough calls, and you'll get the business.

Sometimes, the focus of these articles is that no one answers their phone anymore. Well, as I recall, I sure got a lot of voice mail way back when I started 15+ years ago, too. All the talk strikes me as simply wanting to appear cutting edge and New Millennium-ish.

Now, is cold calling the only way to build a writing business? Of course not. Are you doomed to failure if you don't cold call? Nope (assuming you're aggressive in other arenas). If you put together a weak calling list, could cold calling end up a futile, fruitless exercise? Absolutely. None of which implies that cold calling isn't worth it. And after we demystify the process a bit, I promise you'll feel better about giving it a shot.

GET NOTICED This business—and life in general—is all about getting noticed. Figuratively (and sometimes literally) waving your arms around and yelling, "Hey! Over here!" The more effectively and consistently you tell the world who you are, what you do, and why they should hire you, the more money you'll make. Period.

Have I always been consistent in my own marketing efforts? No. When things have gone well, I've acted like most human beings: fat, happy, and complacent, and then when the phones got quiet later, I kicked myself.

KEEP SHOWING UP As discussed, most prospects are overworked and overextended, and don't want to spend a lot of time hunting for a copywriter. Show up in front of them by email, direct mail, phone, or in their face at the moment they're in the market for a writer, and you've got a decent chance of getting the nod (or at least being seriously considered), even if you've never been hired by them. It's happened to me.

Work for a client for a while, and you'll learn a lot about their business, which makes you valuable. There's minimal learning curve on new projects, and that makes your client's life easier, which is always their goal, and should be yours as well. This scenario is especially true in large corporations where, once you've done a good job, people talk.

If the first guy likes you, you'll get phone calls from their colleagues when they have projects. Just like with a good mechanic, hair stylist, or financial planner, the word spreads. Of course, if you're lousy, it works the other way, too, and probably faster. And don't wait for others to call; proactively ask for referrals to other departments.

Okay, let's assume you've now got some sort of portfolio to show, no matter how humble. It's time to go prospecting, and, as we'll see, that can take many forms. In my case, that form was cold calling. Don't run away...I promise it's not that scary.

LEVERAGING WHAT I KNEW When I started out, my past sales experience (starting with door-to-door book sales) allowed me to forge an intimate relationship with the Law of Averages and its business-building certainty. Coupled with a lack of a sprawling web of contacts and an aversion to meeting-based networking and its "mercenary" vibe, I decided to build my business by phone, something I did very successfully. As such, cold calling became the center-ring marketing strategy in the original *TWFW*. It's a powerful strategy, one used successfully by many readers.

Is cold calling the last word in business building strategies? Of course not. If you have a strong network of contacts, milk them for all they're worth and you might just avoid making *any* cold calls. We'll be exploring all this in more detail later.

All that said, cold calling should still be a cornerstone strategy—because it works. But regardless of how much of it you ultimately end up doing, there's enormous value in defanging the process. View it with fear and dread, and you'll avoid it like the plague, and such a mindset could hinder your progress. What if you're trying to penetrate an arena where you have few contacts? Cold calling (plus perhaps some targeted direct mail) would likely be the most expeditious way to make inroads.

The ultimate goal here is to have a quiver containing a broad array of marketing arrows—cold calling, direct mail, email prospecting, networking —all of which you feel equally comfortable employing, depending on the situation. That said, as a fellow Atlanta FLCW observed, "I don't know why people don't do more cold calling. A postcard or email by itself is just too easy to ignore."

While fearless cold-calling pros may find this chapter elementary, most of you will find some value here, regardless of your experience. As for the novice, the nervous, and the terrified, this chapter is definitely for you. And I promise you'll feel *much* better by the time we're done.

Incidentally, the other five members of my writers' group here in Atlanta—all in business an average of 20 to 25 years each—HATE to cold call. They smile indulgently at me when I sing its praises, comfortable in their firmly held contention that they'd rather be strip-searched in a very public place than call a business stranger who doesn't come by referral. All of them leveraged past experience to build their businesses.

Aluminum Siding, Anyone?

I was giving a seminar (I forget the city—not to sound like a rock star or anything) and we'd just gotten to cold calling. Someone raised her hand and said, very earnestly, *I just hate the idea of cold calling, because I don't appreciate telemarketers and I think most people feel the same way.* Whoa.

I gathered my thoughts, looked at her and asked, *Is that who you think you are? Just an obnoxious telemarketer—no different from the people who rudely interrupt your dinner to peddle aluminum siding, long-distance service, carpet cleaning, and a zillion other things you have no interest in?*

Get this or fail: Assuming you're a competent, reliable writer, if you pursue this business, you'll be a *professional* marketing a valuable and needed *professional* service to other *professionals*. Period. While the people you call may not need your services (80 percent won't) or even have the time to talk to you, I promise they will *not* be viewing you as an irritating telemarketer. So, don't view *yourself* this way.

Are you just a mouthpiece for someone else's business? Some interchangeable short-term worker? No. You have a skill vital to the success of any business—one that pays upwards of $125 an hour. Those who hire people like us will tell us how hard it is to find capable ones. Don't even *think* of putting yourself in the same category as a telemarketer.

And by the way, the big "Do Not Call" anti-telemarketing initiative of 2003 applies only to businesses calling consumers (B2C), not what we're doing—business-to-business (B2B) calling. Sorry, you're not getting off that easily.

•   •   •

DISSECTION TIME In typical human fashion, we make the marketing process dark, scary, and gnarly. Our imaginations paint bleak outcomes and one-way roads to destitution. We conjure up images of the process being unproductive, embarrassing and agonizing. So, let's take this thing apart. We'll start by establishing a few truths.

The cold-calling process is like a battle. Who's the enemy? Prospects, right? WRONG. We are. We will *always* be our own worst enemy in *every* aspect of our lives. It's never circumstances, lack of time, or other people. Or the government or the economy or our parents. When we put external reasons in control of the realization of our dreams, we put those dreams further out of reach. That's a lousy way to live. *Only you are responsible for your success.* And only you can allow someone or something to stop you.

WE CARE, THEY DON'T So, what's at the root of our fear of phone prospecting? *Our concern for what other people think.* When we know we're alone, we'll sing *Feelings* in the shower at the top of our lungs in a helium-balloon squeak. But then we'll freak out about making an entirely legitimate inquiry as a businessperson offering a professional service to another businessperson.

Just in case you're still harboring feelings of kinship with garden-variety telemarketers, why not take this test and put the issue to rest, once and for all?

You Might Be An Annoying Telemarketer IF...

1) When someone clearly answers his phone: "Peter Bowerman," you reply, "Can I speak to Peter Bowerman?" Or even better...

2) When someone clearly answers his phone: "Peter Bowerman," you reply, "Can I speak to...um...Peter...uh...Borman?"

3) You call prospective clients during dinner or on weekends.

4) You're just a hired gun, pitching consumer products (i.e., cellular service, home improvement, magazine subscriptions, cabinet refacing, home equity lines, etc.).

5) You were selling something completely different last month, and next month you'll be exploring another "challenging and rewarding" career direction.

6) Your job involves reading a script (with all the enthusiasm of a county tax clerk) and trying to get people to part with their money— then and there.

7) You use law enforcement-affiliated organizations to give yourself credibility.

8) You call the same people over and over even if they hung up on you the first eight times.

9) You offer people things like steak knives or a set of collapsible luggage to get them to do business with you.

10) Your only job is to get people interested enough to warrant turning them over to the next level of shysters...er, "sales professionals."

So, how'd you do? No matches? Gee, maybe you're not an *Annoying Telemarketer* after all. Whew! That's a relief. (Can we move on now?)

Here's a news flash: *Other people spend amazingly little time thinking about you.* You would be stunned at how little. Oh sure, your family and friends care about you. But when it comes to your business and the services you offer, it's really best to assume that people don't care at all—and that it's your job to make them care. But the fact that people don't care can work in your favor.

Let's imagine a worst-case scenario: You cold call someone and proceed to absolutely implode on the phone. We're talking main-core meltdown here, culminating in a virtually incoherent stream of babble. I promise you, the recipient of your call will spend no more than five seconds thinking about you after you hang up. Meanwhile, you're convinced a mass email has gone out to everyone in their universe, sharing the details of this catastrophic exchange along with strict orders to never, *ever* hire this gibbering idiot.

The truth? For all intents and purposes, you are a non-issue in the minds of your fellow human beings. And the day you finally get this will be your own personal Independence Day. After your "conversion," why not call back that client with whom you fell apart earlier on the phone? Chances are, they won't remember you anyway. Seriously.

CHUTZPAH PERSONIFIED   Reminds me of a true story from my door-to-door bookselling days in college. This bookman knocks on a door at 8:30 a.m. A guy answers the door and proceeds to ream him out: all soliciting should be outlawed, all salesmen should be shot, etc. He finishes his tirade and slams the door in our intrepid warrior's face.

The young bookman digests all this, makes a decision, runs around the house and knocks on the *back* door. The same guy answers that door, about to burst an aorta, when the kid earnestly exclaims, *I sure hope you're nicer than the guy who lives in the front of this house!* No doubt blown away by this audacious display of chutzpah, the guy bursts out laughing, invites the kid in and ends up buying a set of books.

Now, I never had the *cojones* to pull off a stunt like that, but just the fact that it really happened stuck in my mind as a sort of courage beacon. File it away.

GRIM EXPECTATIONS   So, what makes cold calling so tough in the beginning? You're nervous. Perhaps you've never done it before. Or you've done it, but with limited success. Add to that our expectations of the process, which are:

It'll be hard and unproductive

I'll get rejected (i.e., get my feelings hurt)

I won't have any fun

They'll know I'm inexperienced

But I say there's another reason that's crucial to get: on some fundamental level, *you don't really believe it will work.* I and a bunch of others in this book can tell you all day long that it works, but until you prove it to yourself, you won't believe it. And that's fine.

But a funny thing happens when you discover—lo and behold—that it *does* work. It ceases to be some unpleasant exercise in futility and morphs into a proven vehicle to success. You may never enjoy it—not required—but even that may change when you see the impact on your bank account. Would you approach the process differently if you *knew* you couldn't fail?

More importantly, cold calling will make you strong. It will be at the heart of your confidence and your sense of accomplishment. It's your battle—but one with yourself, your fears, your laziness and your fixed perceptions of your abilities. But, when you succeed, you will know that YOU have done it. Only you.

YOU'LL LIKE THIS   Some very good news: If your initial marketing push is big enough and thorough enough, *you only have to go through it once.* The Law of Averages in action. When I started, I made about 1000 calls in two months. Sounds unappealing, I'm sure, but it works. Make that many calls, and critical mass will make progress inevitable. Guaranteed.

After that initial 1000 calls, I *never* conducted a campaign even close to that magnitude again. Sure, I'd do 25 here or 50 there when things slowed down, but the machine was cranked up enough that even those few calls were enough to get something going. Of course, after a year in the business, word-of-mouth referrals started coming in, and that's what ultimately keeps you busy after a while.

How do you eat an elephant? One bite at a time. 50 calls a day for one month (or 25 a day for two months) = 1000. Can't think of a better way of kick-starting this business, especially if you have few contacts.

And it's critical to alter your definition of accomplishment. Let's say I make 50 calls one day and find virtually no one interested in my story. Wasted day? Au contraire. As the old sales axiom reminds, "Every *no* brings you closer to your next *yes*." Out of 50, you might have only spoken to 10, and gotten voice mail and over-protective secretaries on the rest. Nature of the beast. Keep calling.

I got this great email from FLCW Wendy Knerr, who built her business in Austin, Texas, making her first cold call, incidentally, on September 11, 2001.

> *I started out by making about 600 cold calls over several months and that yielded enough work to keep me really busy all of last year. Now, I occasionally have to make cold calls, but I rarely make even 50 calls before I land a project— either from someone I've just cold called or from a previous client who's calling ME to offer work. Even better is the fact that the cold calling is so much easier now because I know it pays off.*

ACTION OR RESULTS? In my seminars, I'll ask, *When you start cold calling, should you focus on action or results?* Many immediately yell out, *Results!* Why? Well, we're judged on results. I say *Action* is the right answer. Think about it. What's true of action that isn't true of results? If you answered, *You can control action, but you can't control results,* go to the head of the class.

You have no control over the results of any given phone call or email. Nor how that man or woman on the other end of the line will react to your contact or whether that individual will think your portfolio is good enough to consider hiring you.

Sure, you can improve your results by, say, getting more comfortable with your phone skills, choosing better prospects and beefing up your book. But still, fundamentally, the one thing you have control over is the actions you take. You can't wake up in the morning and say, *I'm going to land three new writing projects today,* or even *I'm going to find three hot prospects today,* and have control over those results. But you *can* control how many cold calls you make that day—your actions.

Focus on those actions, and the results—the hot prospects and the writing jobs—will come. Minus the anxiety. The Law of Averages is foolproof. I don't care how those calls turn out. Making 50 calls doesn't mean having 50 conversations (that's results again!). Just make the calls, and don't worry about the outcome (i.e., live contact, voice mail, message left with a secretary, appointment, dinner date, etc.).

Cold Calling Give You Cold Chills?

When you pick up the phone to call a prospect, does your heart start pounding? Do you have nightmares about what you'll say and the impression you'll make? Are your palms sweaty and is your mouth dry? If so, got a good book for you...

A few years back, I came across *Cold Calling for Women: Opening Doors & Closing Sales*, by Wendy Weiss (Guys, don't let the title fool you. Wendy tells me a third of her readers are men—hey, I found a lot of value in the book!). Easy to read, easy to implement, and it'll ease those oh-so-common fears, and help you have productive conversations with prospects.

I like how Wendy (a former professional ballet dancer who started in cold calling when she needed a day job) breaks down the process in a way that creative folk will totally understand. By book's end, you'll likely find yourself inspired and excited about the process (really!), and with concrete steps to take to build your business.

At **www.wendyweiss.com**, download her free report, *Getting in the Door: How to Write an Effective Cold-Calling Script*. The site's got a ton of tips and information about cold calling and new business development. And of course, you can order the book. If cold calling wigs you out, you owe it to yourself to visit...

ACTION, NOT RESULTS...AGAIN   When I sold door-to-door in college, our goal was 30 demos a day (the equivalent of phone calls made to prospects), a demo roughly defined as pulling the books out and beginning our pitch —either in the house or at the door—whether or not we got to finish it. Making sales the goal (i.e., results) would've introduced unnecessary anxiety into the process. They *knew* if we made 30 honest demos a day or close to it, the sales would come. And they did. Same here.

YOU'LL SEE IT WHEN YOU BELIEVE IT There were days as bookmen where we'd put in our honest 13½ hours (8:00 a.m. to 9:30 p.m., Monday through Saturday; insanity, yes, but character-building insanity) and come up with…bupkus. *Growth and Development Days*, we called them. Very, very rare. Our sales managers would congratulate us on having a G&D day, adding, *By the way, you do know that you'll sell the first three houses you visit tomorrow, don't you?*

And I'm telling you straight here, we always did, because, I'm convinced, we were, well…*convinced*. On my first call one morning following a G&D day, I remember approaching someone unlocking a car door in the driveway, about to head to work, and absolutely knowing that, despite the unpromising-looking circumstances, this person was going to buy a set of books (a $40 purchase, by the way). I guess he knew it too, because he did. Approach cold calling with that same bone-deep belief in the Law of Averages and you can't help but win.

THE ANTIDOTE FOR ATTACHMENT There's something almost mystical about the Law of Averages. Once I was established, within a few days of making, say, 50 cold calls, with eerie predictability, I'd get a few calls for jobs, yet *rarely* from the people on that recent calling list. It was almost always from somewhere else, as if the effort itself was the important thing. It's about an energy and flow that gets released when you reach out. This email from a mentoring client echoes this:

> *You really renewed my faith in the cold-calling process, too. Our discussion about how you need to believe that the energy you put out will come back to you—but not necessarily from the places you reached out directly to—was exactly what I needed to hear. It's really helped keep me from getting attached to direct results from the places I call, and instead just increasing the numbers. I'm focusing more on the process of calling itself and not spending so much time worrying about who I'm calling or more importantly, how any call or round of calling turns out.*

NOT BUSY ENOUGH In contacts with mentoring clients and budding FLCW's, I hear a lot of references to specific prospects, how they'd contacted this person or that company, how the conversation went, the types of projects this company did, whether it looked promising, etc.

There's always an earnestness about these descriptions, as if a lot of psychic energy was riding on the outcomes.

Whenever I hear this, my reaction is, *You're not making enough calls.* Or contacts of any kind. If you're focusing, in detail, on a few prospects you've called, you need more irons in the fire. Period. Sure, you've got a possible "live" one and you're nervous and excited. Completely understandable. I've been there.

You need to have a ton of things going on. When you do, a few things are inevitable. You can't even recall the specifics of any given situation without looking at your notes. When that happens, you don't care about any specific scenario, because it's one of many. There goes the attachment. Bub-bye. And finally, when you've got a bunch of things cooking, some will inevitably come through.

Other Common Concerns

What if I don't have experience writing for the client's industry?

A client's *ideal* candidate will always have multiple credits identical to the project at hand (understandable with technical topics). Yet clients rarely get just what they want. They'll state their ideal, but will certainly entertain candidates who are close. Remember, they want to get it done, not spend weeks looking for the perfect writer.

Say a prospect asks, *Do you have any experience writing brochures for rabbit production farms?* (Course, I'm tempted to ask, *Have you ever met anyone who did?*). Assuming you indeed have no such experience, your response should be something like:

> *Mr. Prospect, while I haven't had that specific experience, I have written brochures for many different industries and pride myself on being able to step into any new situation and quickly get up to speed. Writing is all about structuring the important information in a way that will have maximum impact. And I know how to do that.*
>
> *A good analogy is an ad agency that can promote staffing services one day and riding lawnmowers the next, without having much, if any, experience working in those fields. Unless it's a very technical subject requiring in-depth knowledge, I feel confident I can deliver for you.*

It'll either work or it won't. If not, move on and let them keep stalking their elusive rabbit-production-farm-brochure copywriter. When they get tired of hunting, you might just get a call down the line. Contact made. Next?

What if I run out of people to call?

I heard this once from someone in L.A. You're kidding, right? Even after being in the biz since 1994 in Atlanta, I still regularly run across established commercial writers I've never met—and with a whole different set of clients than me. There's plenty of work out there.

Tom Myer, a FLCW in Austin, Texas, with a healthy amount of high-tech writing experience under his belt, simply got the Fortune 1000 list of companies (found at **www.fortune.com**), started at the bottom and worked his way up. Between that and another list, he made about 350 calls before landing about $35,000 worth of work in four months.

I tried cold calling, and it didn't work for me.

To this I always ask, *How much of it have you done?* Not surprisingly, the answer is usually, *Not much.* Let's establish a few things. Cold calling *does* work. It may not be working for *you*, but you simply cannot even come to that *flawed* conclusion until you've done a TON of it. We're talking 500–600 calls, at *least*. If it's still not working for you (i.e., no bites, no nibbles), then something else is going on. Like…

1) Your portfolio consists of a few poems, an article for the neighborhood newsletter, and your own brochure. If you're in a good-size market, that's not enough. There *will* be other more experienced writers ahead of you in line. There were plenty in Atlanta when I started out. But if those ahead of you are getting work, then someone's hiring writers.

2) You still see yourself as an annoying telemarketer. Retake the earlier quiz. Period.

3) Let's say it: There's something abrasive, obnoxious or otherwise off-putting about your personality. If you're willing to entertain this idea (i.e., you're more committed to your success than your ego), find a mentor—whether an experienced commercial writer or successful salesperson—and have him or her critique your approach.

And maybe, you just haven't hit critical mass. Say you take some action and nothing happens. You take a lot more action and maybe get a little movement, but still not much. But stick with it a little longer and suddenly, the floodgates open. It happens all the time. People who've been hitting the phones steadily for three or four months with minimal results just hang in there a bit longer, then send me an email letting me know that (in one happy woman's words), "All heaven has broken loose."

Everyone I call already has freelancers they use.

I got the following brilliant answer to the above from Tacoma, Washington FLCW Spiros Psarris (**www.spiroswrites.com**), used here with his permission. While sometimes it pays (especially for those in smaller markets) to educate customers who don't currently use writers as to why they should, this is pretty much right on target.

> *Every company that already has a regular freelancer will need someone else later, **unless** all of the following are true:*
>
> *1) The company never has a spike in their workload or a last-minute project beyond what the regular freelancer can handle.*
>
> *2) The regular freelancer has no other clients, thus is never too busy with other work to accept every job this company needs to be done.*
>
> *3) The regular freelancer never gets sick or goes on vacation, thus is always available on a moment's notice when the client needs him/her.*
>
> *4) Every job the regular freelancer turns in is perfect, and never leaves the client dissatisfied or wondering if somebody else could do better.*
>
> *5) There will never be a personality conflict between the regular freelancer and the client, even as people change jobs within the client company and different people use the freelancer.*
>
> *6) The regular freelancer is expert in every possible area of writing, so that as the client needs brochures, radio scripts, speeches, direct mail, ghostwriting, PR, web copy, event scripts, etc., the freelancer can do EVERYTHING with documented expertise, leaving the client no need to look elsewhere.*

7) The regular freelancer is able to keep a fresh, "first-day-on-the-job" level of enthusiasm even after years of working on the same stuff—so the client never feels that new blood is required.

8) The regular freelancer will never move, quit, die, retire, change careers, decide to devote more time to family or cut back on workload.

If a prospect already has regular freelancers, say, "That's great! I'm glad you've found someone that you're happy with. Maybe I can just stop by and drop off some information for when your freelancers are maxed out and you need somebody in a hurry."

Or, "That's great! Are they also experts in [one of your specialties that you think this client might need]? If you ever need someone like that, I have [proof of expertise and results]. Maybe I could stop by and drop off some information, in case the situation ever arises."

I routinely hear things from clients like, *I've used this writer for years, but, 1) I'm getting tired of his prima donna ways, 2) she's great but just not creative enough, or 3) she's headed out on maternity leave.* Nothing stays the same.

The Cold-Calling Mechanics

Once you build your calling list using the strategies outlined in Chapter Five, it's (gulp) time to start calling. With a little planning and attention to detail, you can take this often daunting task and have a lot of productive fun with it—no drugs required. Just control the things you can, and manage the rest. Remember: your experience level and portfolio are what they are. Using the strategies discussed earlier, do what you need to do to get your "book" up to speed. And don't forget: if this were easy, everyone would be doing it and getting paid seven bucks an hour, not $50–125+. Let's take it step-by-step...

Dumb Down Step one? Check the analytical side of your brain at the door. Keep the rest; it might come in handy later. The analytical side is the one that alternately stares at the list and then out the window, asking a bunch of pointless questions beginning with, "Should I...", "Would they…" and "I wonder if…" (like I did, endlessly, when I started out). I promise you, there's no cheese down that tunnel.

REALITY CHECK Roughly 80% of those you call won't be interested in your service. It is what it is. Overwhelmingly, they'll be nice about it. Feel sorry for the few who aren't. Most importantly, don't take it personally. Just remember the high rates at stake here.

THE GOOD NEWS The *Law of Averages* is etched in stone. I'll never forget my sales manager's words during my summers of door-to-door book sales: *Tie an order book to a dog's tail, set him loose in the city, and eventually, someone will buy from him.* Keep calling and you'll find the business. Absolutely guaranteed.

YOUR SCRIPT Know exactly what you're going to say when your prospect answers the phone. It'll keep you focused and reduce your anxiety. Write it out on an index card and keep it in front of you. Always say it, and never say anything but. Keep it brief (15 seconds or less), simple, and to the point. It's a very powerful psychological anchor. If you hang up from a rude prospect, or lunch is calling, having something to zero in on will keep you from getting bummed out or distracted.

When the receptionist answers the phone, here are a few different opening salvos, depending upon the size and nature of the prospect:

(When calling larger corporations):
May I speak to the marketing (or corporate) communications department?

(When calling smaller companies):
May I speak to the marketing director?

(When calling agencies, graphic design firms, marketing companies):
May I speak to the creative director? (or assistant creative director—usually a better bet)

(If you're unsure who to ask for):
May I speak to the person in charge of hiring copywriters?

If they ask the nature of your call, you can then shift to the expanded version below (check out the wildly expanded cold-calling guide at the end of this chapter), but in most cases, you won't have to trot out the longer one until you're talking to the right person—or at least have left the administrative realm:

Good morning, my name is Peter Bowerman, and I'm a freelance copywriter, making contact with local banks (for instance) to determine whether you have any ongoing or occasional needs for a good freelance copywriter to help create marketing collateral material: brochures, newsletters, ads, etc. Who might be the best person to talk with?

Ideally, you'll have a name, but if not, this'll do, and it's always enough to get some reaction, which then drives the rest of the call. Hopefully, you know what to say if they respond, "Great! Your timing couldn't be better." It happens.

Dealing with Secretaries

Some prospects will have a formidable layer of barbed wire around them. While "marcom" folks are typically more accessible, creative directors for ad agencies, graphic design firms, and marketing companies, or the presidents of smaller firms, are often hard to pin down.

They're extremely busy, stressed, overworked, and fight a never-ending battle to get their work done and stay focused. They don't have time to waste, and for that reason, only phone calls immediately germane to their lives will typically get through. Absolutely not always the case, but be prepared for a not-uncommon scenario.

In response to your request to speak to Mr. Big Creative Cheese and Hirer of Unworthy Copywriters, when these admin types coldly and pointedly inquire, "And what's this regarding?" you will want to reach through the phone and strangle them. How dare they question you, when you're here to make their life a breeze?

If you're actually able to deal with that response in Zen-like fashion, good for you. Now, see how well you do when, after you tell them who you are and what you're up to, they reply, "I don't think we'd be interested in that." Gnash, gnash. All you can do is say thanks and hang up. Just know that most will need copywriters at some point.

FYI (RE BIG AD AGENCIES) I read an interesting article some time back in a creative services magazine about getting in the doors of ad agencies. One recommendation was *not* to cold call or even cold email the larger agencies. They're just too busy and won't reply if they don't know you. The best approach is a personal note (ideally steering them to your web site), followed up with a call some time after that. Makes sense. But before you get excited, I have not found that same paradigm to apply with other MM's (middlemen) and EU's (end-users). They're still fair game.

VOICE MAIL IS YOUR FRIEND While human contact is ideal *and* more promising, voice mail can be expeditious. Write out a slightly expanded version of your basic greeting script for voice mail (include your web site, spelled out slowly). In 30 seconds, you've thrown a line out. Keep track of the messages you've left, and if you hear nothing back, try once more, then move on. Some of those have panned out for me—often months later. Remember the "clients-don't-want-to-hunt-a-lot-for-a-writer" truism.

Speaking of voice mail, when a receptionist answers the phone and you tell her to whom you need to speak (ideally, you had a name going in), and she's about to connect you, why not ask, *In case I get her voice mail, can you give me Ms. Smith's email so I can send her a link to my site and not have to bother her anymore?*

It won't always work, but since those addresses are often on a company's site, they're not exactly state secrets. Then, if you do get voice mail, leave a brief message telling the prospect who you are and that you'll be emailing a link to your portfolio and will follow up in a week or so. It'll make the call that much more potentially productive, help your email stand out from the pile (try a subject line like: *Copywriter following up on VM*) and let your site work for you while you're off doing something else.

By the way, if you're trying to locate an email address for a prospect and you can find *any* address for that company (hint: try the "Media Relations" or "Press" link on their site), they almost always have the same formula, so if you know the person's name—Jill Jackson—and have another address —e.g., john.smith@abc.com—you're set.

HOW TO TALK Slowly, clearly, and evenly. Don't just chat away like you normally would. Adjust to accommodate people who don't know you, weren't expecting your call, and were busy doing something else (I'm just full of good news). You're asking them to turn on a dime. Make it easy for them to catch up.

GET YOUR MIND RIGHT Your goal? To simply have some nice conversations and ask a few questions. You want to come across as relaxed, easy-going, and confident and it's easier to do that when you feel there's less at stake. You both know why you're there: to drum up business, so don't come across as desperate or overanxious. Bottom line, people like to talk to people who make them feel comfortable, and will be more receptive to them and their message if they do.

What Not to Say Refrain from the ultra-cheerful, "How are you today!?" unless they ask you first. Coming from you, it fairly screams "Salesman Butter-Up Line!!" If they ask, it can be like a cool drink of water, especially if you've just crawled through a 25-call desert of voice mail, rude receptionists, and arrogant *artistes*.

Simply reply politely, "Very well, thank you. And yourself?" Resist the urge to jump all over them with dirty paws like a golden retriever greeting its master after a two-week absence. Often the nicest people are the ones in no position to help or hire you. When you're starved for a friendly, interested voice, it's only human to want to hang out with these people. But you'll just be wasting your time, unless they're your liaison to the top.

Are You Too Nice? If you're good on the phone, you can often develop such a good rapport with someone that he hates to say, "Gee, we just don't have any needs," which, believe me, is vastly preferable to "Well, we haven't used freelancers, but that could change" coming from someone who's never hired one and probably never will. Stay friendly but businesslike so people feel comfortable telling you the truth.

Better Bets Folks who say, "We have a few writers we're pretty happy with" are nearly as good as the "we-regularly-use-freelancers" set. After all, they definitely use writers *and*, nothing is forever. Follow up with regular calls (assuming that's cool with them), mailings, and occasional samples of the kinds of work that would resonate with them (something you should do from time to time even if you do have a web site). I've picked up several new clients because I was "waiting in the wings" when their regular writer moved on, moved away, or irritated them one too many times.

Try to meet clients as soon as you can, making it sound as breezy as a walk in the park. "I understand you're set right now, and that's great, but I'm going to be in your area next week, and wondered if I might stop in for five minutes and drop off a few things for your file." No big deal.

Keep a Log Track your calling. These days, an Excel spreadsheet is probably the more expeditious way to keep your efforts organized. Include columns for company name, contact person, address, phone, fax, email, along with date and results of first, second, and third contacts, info sent, etc.

For the long run, seriously consider investing in a good Contact Management (CM) program like *Act!*, *Goldmine*, or *Maximizer*. Programs like these will make the process of reaching out to (though mail merge), staying on top of (through "tickler" functions), and recording the results of all contacts with clients and prospects exponentially easier, and will simply make you more efficient and, hence, ultimately more profitable.

MAXIMIZING YOUR SUCCESS While you can convince yourself that any time of the day or week is a good time or lousy time to prospect, early morning (7:30–8:30 a.m.) and late afternoon (5:00–6:00 p.m.) are often the best times to reach decision makers. They got to that position by starting early and staying late. They'll be calmer and more receptive then.

Timothy Ferris, in *The 4-Hour Workweek*, echoes this strategy. He writes, "When I was in data storage sales…I realized that most cold calls didn't get to the intended person for one reason: gatekeepers. If I simply made all my calls from 8:00–8:30 a.m. and 6:00–6:30 p.m., for a total of one hour, I was able to avoid secretaries and book more than twice as many meetings as the senior sales executives who called from 9–5. In other words, I *got twice the results for ⅛th the time*." One man's opinion and experience, but worth a shot.

Monday—the "get-on-track" day—isn't a good phone day. Fridays can be good as things quiet down, but that can mean fewer people around. Tuesday through Thursday is best.

TELL THE TRUTH Some books on "guerrilla prospecting" suggest cute ploys to reach the decision makers. Like telling the receptionist you're returning your prospect's call, you have some info they requested, or some other tall tale. Don't do it. If they realize what you're doing, you'll irritate them and that's a lousy first impression. Just be honest.

GET OUT AND MEET YOUR MARKET When you generate some interest, always try to get a face-to-face appointment. For me, meeting clients in the flesh was key to the growth of my business. Early on in my career, a fellow writer shared the "1-in-10/1-in-3 Rule": *You'll get hired by one of ten prospects to whom you send information (or steer to your site) and one of three who meet you.* After hearing that, I made a point to put a face with at least one or two voices each week and my business took off.

Others disagree. Bob Bly thinks meetings are time-wasters. But he's also in demand—turning down far more work than he takes on. No question meetings are becoming less important these days, given phone and email. And if you're prospecting out of your geographic area, meetings are obviously a non-issue.

If someone agrees to meet you, you can safely assume that he's in the market for your services at some point, not bored, lonely, and starved for human contact. If they show interest, but won't meet, it usually just means they don't have anything right then. Just listen to how he answers, and judge his level of sincerity. If you're paying attention, people aren't that hard to decipher.

TIP: Working Smarter

In the wake of different prospecting outcomes, you'll want to follow up with a letter to prospects and new clients. As we'll discuss in the next chapter, if you've met with them in person, you'll likely want to send an actual snail-mail thank-you letter or card. And I provide samples of such letters in *The Deluxe Well-Fed Tool Box* .

Assuming you've got a Web site to which you want to steer prospects, you'll want to have a similar set of short two-paragraph notes to follow up on different types of contacts, by phone or otherwise (i.e., after leaving a voice mail, a phone conversation, a chat with an assistant, an actual meeting at a networking event, etc.) —all with links to your site. Once created, set them up in your email "stationery" feature.

Following up on these contacts then becomes a simple matter of clicking on a particular piece of stationery, which will populate an outgoing email screen with the appropriate message (which perhaps, you tailor to reference something you spoke about or a mutually agreed-upon next step), filling in their address, clicking "Send" and you're done.

•   •   •

The Expanded Cold-Calling Script

Sincere thanks to Brian Egeston of Atlanta (talented author; www.brianwrites.com), one of my first seminar grads from 2000, for volunteering the first version of this. They're designed to give you rough (vary/edit to suit) cold-calling talking points given certain prospect responses. As discussed, you'll generally only use the basic one below—and what follows—once you get to a decision maker, but not to the "gatekeepers."

•   •   •

The Basic Script:
Good morning, my name is Peter Bowerman and I'm a freelance writer, making contact with local banks to determine whether you have any on-going or occasional needs for a good freelance writer to help create marketing collateral material: brochures, manuals, etc. Who might be the best person to talk with?

Additional Prospect Responses/Writer Replies

WE DON'T USE FREELANCE WRITERS
Might you have any clients, associates or industry colleagues that come to mind who could use a good freelance writer?

I'M NOT THE RIGHT PERSON
I'm sorry to bother you. Might you be able to steer me to the individual who would handle folks like me?

HE'S NOT AVAILABLE RIGHT NOW
Not a problem. What might be a good time to check back with him? And who should I ask for? *(At this point, you might ask for an email address and send them a résumé/cover letter letting them know who you are and that you'll be in contact.)*

I'M THE RIGHT PERSON/THAT WOULD BE ME
Great! So, you do hire copywriters on a fairly regular basis? I'd love the opportunity to stop by, at your convenience, to drop off a résumé and some samples and perhaps discuss how I might help you out. Would that be okay? *(More Aggressive Approach)* Would sometime next week (later this week) work for you?

WHAT HAVE YOU WORKED ON? WHAT ARE YOUR SPECIALTIES?

I feel very confident handling a broad array of projects like: (*list your specialties: e.g., marketing brochures, newsletters, ads, direct mail, web content, etc.*) Currently, I'm working on a _____ for a _____ company. On what kinds of projects do you typically look for copywriting help?

DO YOU HAVE ANY SAMPLES OF YOUR WORK?

Certainly. I'd love to get them into your hands. I'm going to be out and about in (*the area of town where their office is*) in the next few days. Would it be possible to drop them off and introduce myself?

DO YOU HAVE ANY SAMPLES OF YOUR WORK?
(if you have a web site)

I sure do and I've actually got several loaded up to my web site. If you give me your email address, I'll send you the link. (*By doing it this way, you give them easy "click-thru" and don't rely on them to type in an address, which they may or may not do. AND you now have their email address.*)

NO, THE NEXT FEW DAYS AREN'T REALLY GOOD TO MEET

No problem. I could drop them in the mail. By the way, what types of work are you most interested in seeing?

SURE, THAT WOULD BE FINE.

Great! And in about a week or so, I'll follow up with you and if it makes sense at that point, perhaps I could swing by, show you some actual pieces, and we can explore how I might be of most use to you.

WE'RE NOT INTERESTED.

No problem, I appreciate your honesty. Might I mail or email you my résumé and a business card (*or the link to your site*) for your files?

NO! AND DON'T CALL ME EVER AGAIN, YOU MORON!
(NEVER happens...)

I'm sorry to have bothered you. Have a nice day. Goodbye.

Now, that wasn't so painful, was it? Remember, cold calling is just one way to reach potential clients, though it was a key one for me. Let's move on to some nuts 'n bolts...

Chapter 7

Letters, Meetings, Follow-Up, Phone Interviewing, Client Types and More...

Got one of those "catch-all" closets at home where you stick anything that doesn't have a logical place elsewhere? That's what this chapter is. A bunch of short but useful subjects that didn't really belong anywhere else, and fall roughly at this point in the sequence. Let's jump in...

SNAIL-MAIL FOLLOW-UP As discussed earlier, a web site is pretty much mandatory for the serious FLCW business-builder in the new millennium; it's become a baseline expectation of any serious business. And overwhelmingly, prospects like the web site approach better.

That said, snail mail has its place—especially as a first follow-up contact after a call, meeting, or networking meet 'n greet. In our all-wired world, actual written correspondence is a nice touch that'll make you stand out a bit—something that never hurts. So, make it easy on yourself by...

SYSTEMATIZING THE PROCESS Sit down and create the following form follow-up/cover letters 🧰. Each letter should be a separate file with its own distinctive name to be called up as needed, and should address the following situations:

129

1. You've met with a prospect and introduced yourself and your work. He's excited about working with you, but no work is immediately pending.

2. You've met with a new client and will shortly be starting work on a new job.

   2a. An expanded version of the above letter where you feel it's important to review a few key points about your skills that were discussed in your meeting as being particularly important to the client.

3. You've talked to a prospect who will probably be a long shot for work in the future, but you're sending out a letter, résumé, and business cards.

4. You've talked on the phone with a new prospect who hires freelancers on a regular basis, and this letter accompanies a résumé and samples (and mentions your web site).

5. You've received a call from an assistant to a creative director or communications manager with the request to send his/her boss information, and this letter directs them to your web site.

6. Slightly different versions of #4 above, steering prospects to your web site vs. sending them a package of samples.

SAMPLES PROVIDED As noted above, samples of these letters (as well as email versions with a link to your site) appear in the *The Deluxe Well-Fed Tool Box*. Check out the full contents in Appendix C.

As you'll recall, my standard letter opening is:

> *As a freelance writer, my goal is to enhance your image, improve your profit picture, and make your life easier. If it carries your name, shouldn't it be the best reflection of you?*

Please don't copy them verbatim. With a little thought, you can probably come up with different versions that are at least as effective, if not more, than mine. Try to customize them as much as possible, making a reference or two to specific points discussed in the meeting/conversation so it doesn't look too shamelessly boilerplate.

THE RIGHT GREETING Mr. Jones or Tom? Ms. Taylor or Mary? If you've connected nicely with a prospect, first names are usually safe, and will be appreciated. Clients want respect, but also appreciate the human touch. But when in doubt, stay formal.

RÉSUMÉS Another piece of the puzzle that, arguably, would be rendered unnecessary by a web site. While an optional step, it's never a bad idea to showcase industry- or project-specific expertise when a client is looking for just that. Having something ready to go could give you an edge in a competitive situation. Obviously, it's only over time that you'll have collected enough experience to generate multiple résumés.

I have different single-page résumés for ad copy writing, technical projects, brochure work, speeches, articles, PR work, as well as several general versions that show the scope of my abilities. None consist solely of projects in that genre, but if they lead off with two or three+ items in that arena, that's good for starters.

Want to skip that step? Then, at least consider an "Experience" link on your site, with broad categories of project types and/or industries, with one-line "who-and-what" descriptions under each heading to give visitors quick snapshots of specific skill sets. Ideally, if you have matching samples posted, link to them directly.

Create a client list to include with résumés. I update mine regularly and make it the second page of all my résumé files, and print it out on the back of the résumé. Only done one job with IBM several years ago? Include it. Here's my résumé format (minus the header):

SELECTED FREELANCE WRITING CREDITS

1) CLIENT: **ABC Corporation** – Atlanta, GA
PROJECT: Corporate Sales Brochure, Rate Book, and Customer Newsletter for Mexican Operation

2) CLIENT: **MegaPhone Corporation** – Atlanta, GA
PROJECTS: Monthly Internal Newsletter (CommTalk Online)
Eight-Page Small Business Division Newsletter
Descriptive Product Brochures (4) on calling features

Feel free to include several references on the résumé or client list: name, company name, title and phone number. They almost never check, but pretend they will.

Prospecting Without a Web Site?

Having a web site will save a boatload of sample-assembly-and-mailing hassle. Sending out piles of samples is decidedly old-world, but if that's all you can do in the short run, here are a few tips to streamline the process:

1) Originals are precious; unless you have dozens, send copies.

2) Do a "Copy Day": Look for copy-shop specials (two- or three-cent per page specials), make 25–30 copies of each of a dozen samples.

3) Excerpt a few eloquent pages from larger multiple-page pieces.

4) When possible, make double-sided copies, reducing weight and saving postage.

5) Keep samples in a rack unit with stacked sheet-sized compartments.

A Five-Minute Process When you've talked with a client interested in seeing a package, and know what type of work they want to see, just go to your rack, grab the appropriate samples, print out the right cover letter (after tailoring it to the conversation) and résumé/client list combo, add two business cards, and you're done.

And what can you do with all the time this system saves you? Build a web site and then watch the time (and money) savings *really* add up.

NOTE: Pre-web site, whenever possible, create project- or industry-specific files with résumé, client list, and Word samples all together. Or turn a particular résumé/client list combo into a PDF and merge that file with other PDF graphic files of relevant projects (requires Acrobat®) and then just email prospects the whole ball of wax.

Buyers Vs. Tire-Kickers Don't fall into the trap of sending out info to anyone who sounds remotely interested, because most will be just that—*remotely* interested. Many will take your information just to get you off the phone. In those cases, you'd do as well to shred it as mail it. I never ask prospects if I can send information. I wait for them to ask me for it, *and* listen to how it's asked for and what preceded the request.

More to the point, tier your mailings. For the hot-sounding ones ("Yes, we regularly use freelancers"), send out a full package (more on contents later). For the shaky ones ("Well, we occasionally use freelancers"), send a cover letter, résumé, and business card. Ask if you can follow up in a few weeks, and then do just that. Strongly suggest that what you're sending is a fraction of your portfolio ("So, let's get together for a meeting..."), and then keep following up until you can make that happen.

Don't Send It Unsolicited Let's say you're just not too stoked about hitting the phones (a stretch, I know...). You might be tempted to skip it altogether, assemble a big list of prospects, and just send out unsolicited sample packages. You might even convince yourself that enough of this will be just as effective as contacting them first. And you'd be wrong. Unless of course, you sent out, say, ten thousand or so; then, something would happen, if you didn't go broke first...

If people aren't expecting your correspondence, chances are excellent it'll go into the trash unopened (unless its design and packaging are pretty whiz-bang). You really need to establish a rapport *and* a potential need on their part before going through the time and expense of sending them something, so they'll know to expect it. Even then, there's no guarantee that it will turn into paying work.

Client Meetings

As discussed, Bob Bly says, "meetings are a waste of time." Doesn't believe in them. And I get it. Phone and email have eliminated the need for most meetings (definitely true for me), and if you're prospecting beyond your geographic area—common these days—by definition, all meetings will be "virtual."

All that said, if you plan on drawing business primarily from your local area (likely for big-city dwellers), it makes sense to get in front of prospects (remember: those who meet you are more likely to hire you). Especially if you know you "do good face-to-face." After you meet them, *then* you can push for a more remote working relationship.

A friend sent me this quote from uber-speaker, author, and consultant Alan Weiss (**www.contrarianconsulting.com**) that bolsters my gut feel about the validity of a face-to-face: "Persuading others is about building relationships, and that is best done in person, looking the other person in the eye, listening to what they say, and articulating your own position in such a way that they can see their self-interest being met. That's how you enable the buyer to buy in a solo consulting practice." I'm just sayin'…

MEETING TYPES The three outlined below obviously aren't all the scenarios you'll encounter, just the more common ones. *All* meetings are opportunities to demonstrate "P-C-O":

Professionalism: punctuality, appearance, physical portfolio, physical quality of samples, preparedness (i.e., visit their web site before meeting, ask relevant questions).

Competence: caliber of writing in samples; demonstrating you're a quick study; marketing savvy; "Discovery" questionnaire (coming up).

Ownership: Show—through attitude and sample stories—that you can "take ownership" of a project; show clients you can work autonomously, which makes their life easier (their #1 goal); discuss ability to team with designers to create turnkey solutions (i.e., one more thing client doesn't have to worry about).

The above is ideal. Don't fret if you're starting out and don't have beautiful samples, unparalleled marketing savvy, or oodles of take-charge stories. I sure didn't when I started out, and many clients gave me a shot. This is just the ultimate goal. Three basic meeting types are...

• *"The Introduction"* This kind of meeting is much more common when starting out. You've communicated with someone, steered them to your site (or snail-mailed samples if you're still in the Stone Age (sorry)…) and you've pushed for a meeting because your skills mesh with his needs. In many of these cases, there's no work immediately pending, but you're trying to capitalize on the "1-in-3-who-meet-you-will-hire-you" thing.

In these cases, be easy-breezy: "I'm going to be in your area this week (even if not) and if it makes sense, I'd love to stop by for five or ten minutes, put a face with the voice, and show you a few samples not on my site." Find out what projects he typically uses copywriters for and file that away. At the meeting, respect your 5–10 minute promise unless *they* extend it through their questions. Time and again, I've been hired or gotten into serious *unplanned* discussions by virtue of being there in person.

Goals of "The Introduction":

Showcase P-C-O (and likeability doesn't hurt)

Determine nature (frequency/type) of writing needs

Introduce writer/designer turnkey idea, if appropriate

Agree on timing of next contact (usually phone call/email).

• *"The Audition"* In this scenario, there *is* a specific project on the table and you're one of several possible candidates. Ideally, prepare a small array of samples similar to the one to be discussed. You may *think* they've studied your site in depth, but don't count on it.

• *"The Referral Audition"* In this case, you've been referred to a client. Obviously, these are stronger than just "Auditions," where you likely found them. Here, they either called you (the best) or someone suggested you call them. When they call you, in all likelihood, you're the only writer they're talking to, so it's yours to lose.

It's in both the above "Audition" meetings that you might introduce the "Discovery" questionnaire (below), but only questions 1–5; offering a taste of your competence and expertise, but not the whole enchilada. Only when they've officially hired you do you go through the entire questionnaire. No goodies for free.

THE DISCOVERY QUESTIONNAIRE A great tool to build client confidence (and reduce your own anxiety) *before* landing a job (only do questions 1–5), as well as getting a feel for the project, audience, messaging, and actual content *after* getting the green light (full questionnaire) is the "Discovery Questionnaire" 📋, suggested to me by Seattle FLCW Sonya Carmichael Jones. This piece, which can either be sent to a client prior to a meeting or filled out at the meeting, clarifies and quantifies the company's mission and project parameters. I adapted Sonya's version and came up with this. Tailor it to suit your specific situation:

1. *Who's the audience for this piece? Is it the same as your target customer?*

2. *What are their hot buttons? When it comes to considering a product like yours, what issues are important to this audience?*

3. *What makes your business, product, or service unique?*

4. *What do you do better than the competition?*

5. *What are your company's short- and long-term goals?*

6. *Who is your major competitor and where do you rank in the industry?*

7. *What's the purpose of this (brochure, direct mail piece, ad, etc.)? How will it be used?*

8. *How do you currently market your business, product, or services?*

9. *What are the main points you want to convey in this piece?*

10. *Do you have a company tagline or slogan? If not, have you considered creating one?*

11. *If money were not a factor, what would be your ideal marketing campaign?*

TALK MONEY BEFORE MEETINGS Financially qualify clients before investing a lot of time meeting with them. Ideally, you'd discuss it with them when you first determine they're a prospect for your services, but if you haven't done so before a meeting, do it. Last thing you need is to drive an hour round-trip only to discover the prospect thinks he can get a brochure for $150. No fun.

As we'll discuss in more detail in Chapter Nine, *don't* discuss hourly rates, which can be misleading and can scare clients. It's always best to talk money in the context of a specific fee for a specific project.

If you're meeting to discuss an actual project, say something like, "Mr. Prospect, just to make sure we're on the same page, money-wise, I recently did a ___ project (similar to the one at hand) and I charged $X. Does that sound about right?" If there is no specific project being discussed, bring up *any* recent project: "Mr. Prospect, I recently did a six-page brochure for a company that ran about $X. Does that sound reasonable?"

If he freaks out, better to know before burning gas. If there are no specific projects on deck (i.e., in "Introductions"), just pick *any* recent project (ideally, something this prospect might hire you to do) and explain it the same way.

Again, a lot of the above applies more in one's early career. Once you've made your mark, referrals are more the norm, meaning clients ready to get started on projects, wanting to work with *you*, and pay your rates. Nice place to be.

Bottom line, when it comes to meetings, it's a free country. You can do whatever you want. But, *The Las Vegas Rule* applies: Don't invest anything (time, gas, creative energy) you're not willing to lose.

Before the Meeting

1. Visit their web site; the more you know about who they are, what they do, and where you might fit into their needs, the more professional an impression you'll make.

2. Pick out five or six portfolio pieces to show, based on his stated copywriting needs. Better to be targeted than show everything, which will tire you and bore him.

3. Address and stamp a thank-you card, leaving the card itself blank and sitting on your desk so you'll see it first thing when you return.

4. Bring extra résumés; Chances are, there'll be someone else there who could use one.

Speaking of that, in addition to your main prospect—usually the creative director, communications director/manager, marketing director, etc.—it's common and preferable to meet with several people at once. Graphic designers, account executives, and executive assistants are typical support people who are good to know—and it's good if they know you. If your prospect doesn't mention it, suggest he assemble "the troops." He'll probably think it's a good idea, and you've just made your outing that much more productive.

CALL THE DAY BEFORE? Calling to remind prospects of a next-day meeting *is* the professional thing to do, *and* it could give them an easy way to cancel (it's happened). If you set the appointment just a few days earlier, you could get away without a call. A few weeks ago? Best bet is a voice mail or email after hours the night before. By the time they get it (on meeting day), it's usually too late to cancel. Sneaky, but effective.

On meeting day, allow an extra 10–15 minutes travel time, if traveling outside rush hour, and 20–30 during gridlock. I'm assuming that you wouldn't deliberately schedule a meeting before 10:00 a.m. or after 2:30 p.m. unless you couldn't avoid it (I'm not above fibbing to avoid it...), or could actually walk to their office from your house.

DRESS SAFELY Dress code depends some on the region of the country and the client. In the South—Atlanta in particular—it tends to be casual, and even more so in the beastly hot days of summer. Here, the "Southern Uniform" for men works for most any occasion—formal or casual: khakis, navy blazer, button down, tie (usually optional), loafers. The Northeast can be a little more starched.

Of course, casual is becoming increasingly the norm in most corporate settings. If you meet with creative folks—designers, ad agencies, etc.— wearing a suit and tie, they'll likely issue a mock threat to never hire you if you show up so attired in the future.

SHOW 'N TELL? Avoid interminable meetings with endless samples and "aren't-I-brilliant" banter. Certainly point out examples of work that matches client needs, using the half dozen or so you've set out in advance. If you haven't prepared samples, ask your prospect what project types would be likely assignments. Though, over time, most companies will have a wide variety of needs. Showing more comprehensive campaigns you've done for other clients shows you have the "big picture" mindset.

Some writers think samples should be the last thing you show, that you need to walk in, ask, "How can I help you?" and get them talking about their needs and challenges, segueing into how your skills can address those needs. I agree. Clients, like all other human beings, operate out of self-interest. As such, it makes far more sense to come in focused on *them* and what they need (*benefits*) than on you and your portfolio (*features*). More to the point, that prospect should already have seen samples of your work (right?) before you meet, so they know your work is a fit for what they're up to.

But I've had plenty of meetings—and many copywriters share the same story—where prospects never asked to see my portfolio. We just jumped into project discussions. If you're barking up the right trees, that'll happen more often than you might imagine. By the time most good prospects agree to meet with you, they're ready to get started.

ALL ABOUT CONTEXT All that said, in most meetings—especially with creative folks—you'll show some work. But, wait until you discuss needs— pending or otherwise. If you know what they need—on a general, ongoing basis, or a specific, immediate one—show the appropriate pieces. "Frame" your narration to highlight the benefits of your work: *how* what you created addressed a specific client need. *Not* the "museum tour."

Be alert to when a prospect's seen enough. It's easy to get on a roll and start giving the inside story on every piece in your book. Fascinating to you. Rarely for them.

As discussed, there will be pieces in your book that look nice, graphically, but that you don't like showing because the copy was edited into mediocrity. If it's a big name company (ideally, with logo prominent), point it out, without pulling it out, to show prospects the professional circles in which you're traveling.

"LEAVE-BEHINDS" & TWO BUSINESS CARDS Take a manila folder (preferably colored to stand out) and on the tab, affix a printed label with your name, "Freelance Copywriter" in big bold letters, phone number, email (and URL, if room). Great "leave-behind." Into the folder go a résumé/client list, three cards, and appropriate copied samples. All your stuff in one elegantly conspicuous "file-cabinet-ready" folder. They'll be impressed, I promise.

Keep plenty of cards handy, and in any business setting, give at least two to each person: one for them and one to give away. This is especially important in meetings where others in a position to hire you aren't present.

At the end of the meeting, get business cards along with a feel for the next step, upcoming projects, etc. If no work is immediately pending, find out if it's okay to follow up, and how often to do so. FIRST thing when you get home, before even going to the bathroom—okay, go do that—is to write out and mail the thank-you note you prepped earlier. It's a simple way to show your professionalism and get your name in front of the prospect yet again. Log the agreed-upon follow-up date and do it.

THE QUADRUPLE WHAMMY Any promotion you do—cold calling, networking, direct mail, a targeted ad—will likely generate some interest. Many will be a waste of time (companies "updating their files," never to call you again in this lifetime), but some will pan out. Respond quickly and thoroughly, and you've got a great shot at the business. Here's an example of such a response (works whether they're coming to you or vice versa).

Imagine you're a prospect who's called a writer to get a quote on a project (yes, avoid "pricing-on-command," but sometimes it's hard; in Chapter Nine, we'll address how to best deal with it). Said writer offers up a quote, but not being a crack marketer (true for *most* of your competition), sits back, hoping to receive a call back.

The same prospect calls me. We talk, I ask for his email, and five minutes later, I've sent him a link to my site along with a client list and résumé—either tailored to the project I've just quoted, to the kind of work he says he typically needs, or just a general one if he's been less specific. I call the next day and ask if I can drop off samples. If he says yes, I get in front of him, upping my chances of being hired. Even if he can't meet, I can confirm his receipt of my email.

If we do meet, my thank-you note puts me in front of him again several days later. I've shown up three or four times in as many days *and* ways, and, between the information he now has, and my professionalism, I've made it easy for him to hire me confidently. Assuming my quote is competitive (though professionalism like this could keep me in the running even with a higher quote), if you were him, who would you hire? Separate yourself from the pack. A little extra effort, big potential payoff.

Top 10 Ways to Stay in Touch with Clients (Without Asking for Work!)

Got this great little list from Toronto-based FLCW Elizabeth Cockle (www.ecwriting.com) of creative reasons to show up in front of prospects besides just a "Hey-got-any-work-for-me?" call.

1) Notify them of upcoming vacations 30–60 days in advance. Email a reminder a week before departure, letting them know you'll be in touch when you return.

2) Ask for a testimonial, or provide a draft testimonial for their approval.

3) Send a regular ezine. Invite comments and acknowledge responders in the next issue.

4) If you do a blog that's relevant to clients, invite them to subscribe.

5) Notify them of new published reports on your site that might interest them.

6) Send articles of interest by snail mail with a short note.

7) Let them know when you're featured in the media (and send a link if available).

8) Send "Thank-you-for-your-business" cards to celebrate business anniversaries, thank-you cards for successful referrals, and off-season holiday cards.

9) Pass on referrals for services they may need (or provide).

10) Suggest job candidates for full-time positions.

Google Alerts

A little elaboration on #6 above. Let's say you service clients in residential mortgages, construction and healthcare. Through Google Alerts (http://www.google.com/alerts), you can sign up to receive news feeds—links to any new articles that appear on the web on those subjects. If you get one that you feel a client would appreciate, just forward on the link with a quick note: "Hey Jack, saw this and thought of you..."

For a good article on this subject, check out, "Don't 'Throw Away' Your Prospects," from Atlanta FLCW Ed Gandia on his site (www.theprofitablefreelancer.com). And while there, sign up for his newsletter and grab a copy of an excellent free report, "7 Steps to Landing More (and Better-Paying!) Freelance Projects." Ed made $163K in his first full-time year in the biz—we'll visit him in Chapter Eleven—so he's worth listening to.

Phone Interviewing—The Basics

Phone interviews are something you should get good at and offer as a service. The most common reasons you'd conduct a phone interview would be content-gathering (e.g., for brochures, newsletters, speeches, case studies, etc.) or to collect customer testimonials. Let's touch on some basics of *any* phone interviewing, and then look at suggestions specific to testimonial and content-gathering phone interviews (and know there'll be some overlap between the two).

Successful phone interviewing is a combination of preparation and flexibility. Use your questions to stay on track. If you get a cold fish—someone who's hard to draw out into conversation—it's usually not going to work to just ask your questions, take what he says, and be done with it. You won't end up with much.

TEASE IT OUT With tough nuts like these, keep encouraging them with "That's great...just what I'm looking for..." Or probe for more detail with, "Say more about that," or "That's interesting, can you elaborate?" Make them feel special—like they're really delivering the goods—and believe me, they'll open up and give you good strong material. And remember: you represent the company you're working for, and that's important, whether your interviewee is a customer or an employee of that company.

Don't be rigid, or too sure you know what someone's going to say, or even of what you need. Use your question list as a guide, and to stay on track, but the more open you are to interesting, *relevant* diversions along the way, the richer and juicier your copy will be.

MAKING CONTACT   Whether you reach them in person or get voice mail, variations on this script should work with most interviews (*low-key, professional*): "Hi, Mr. Smith, this is Joe Bleaux, the writer who's working with ABC Company on their new marketing brochure. I'm sure Bill Brown from ABC has already contacted you to let you know that I'd be in touch with you to grab you for just ___ minutes to get a few comments about (how you like dealing with ABC) (the new branding initiative) (the Smith–Jones case study). My phone number is 770-555-6543 and I look forward to speaking with you soon."

(Note: As for how much time you tell Mr. Smith you'll need, say five minutes for testimonials, and 15–60 on longer interviews, depending on the scope of questions. The shorter the time, the more receptive they'll be. But, be straight. If you think it'll be 45, say 30–45, not 15, so they don't book a meeting 20 minutes after your start time. That said, within reason, if you're cool to deal with, most clients are flexible.)

If Bill Brown never made the contact, Mr. Smith knows with whom to check with questions. Give Mr. Smith a few days to call back, then try again. Count on making several calls. Usually, they're glad you called because now it'll get done. You're the one on deadline, so take responsibility. Make it happen by being "intentional," not pushy.

THE PROCESS   When you finally connect with Mr. Smith, start out by reiterating how much time you need, and confirming he's got it. Setting the time parameters at the outset will relax him. Ask him if you can put him on speakerphone (if you don't have a headset; you do have one or the other, right?) so you can type while you talk.

Don't get too buddy-buddy. Walk a fine line between friendliness and professionalism. Suppress your incandescent personality or you risk inhibiting their eloquent inclinations. You want to disappear from the process, except as a facilitator of their thoughts.

RELIABLE BACKUP With my list of questions onscreen, I'm always typing during an interview (the steady clicking assures subjects they're saying stuff worth capturing), but before starting, I have a recording device cued up and ready to go (i.e., a phone recorder—try Radio Shack—or a mini-cassette/digital recorder placed next to the phone's speaker). Make sure whatever you use has a counter—crucial for noting a place where your subject is sharing key info but you're not getting it all with your typing.

(TIP: Denver FLCW Joe Coplans uses **www.Recordmycalls.com**, where you dial an 800 number, enter a PIN, and the call is recorded and archived on their site for easy reply/retrieval. Might be more than you need, but it's a cool option to consider. Mac user? *Garage Band* recording software—standard with all Macs—allows you to record all conversations via the built-in mike, and archive them as mp3 files.)

Explain to Mr. Smith: "No one speaks in perfect sound bites, so don't worry about providing perfect answers. I'll put a quote together from your comments, and email you what I come up with to make sure you're okay with it." For all you ex-journos or magazine writers, you're in a different sandbox now—one where you run things like this past the interviewee. This isn't journalism. It's still about accuracy, but the different approval structures and money dynamics in our world render the journalistic model moot.

Once you've got what you need, let him go. You've got the recording to fill in any blanks. Thank him sincerely for his time, and especially effusively if you went over the promised time limit (which you should always acknowledge and apologize for).

PERMISSION TO RECORD? I did an ezine piece about **www.Record MyCalls.com** (discussed above), and several ex-journos wrote in that you always had to ask permission of clients to record them since that's the law in many states. Sigh. Okay, technically, they're right, so *For The Record*, you should ask.

That said, I don't. Gasp! Why not? As I see it, it's about *intent*. I'm not surreptitiously recording someone I'm interviewing for some investigative report, trying to catch them in an embarrassing "gotcha." I'm simply ensuring I've captured all they said to save their time and my sanity—*and* they're going to approve the final product. Once done, I'll be recording right over their words the next time I tape a call.

Since 1994, it's never gotten any more eventful than that. It's an efficiency-enhancing tool. Period. If *they* ask if I'm recording, I'll say yes. Rarely ever happens, and usually they're fine with it, but why ask and risk having them say no simply because it *sounds* vaguely suspicious?

"Testimonial" Interviews

Third-party testimonials are always a good call for any marketing piece; they're far more credible, and will sell far more product than a stack of brochures. If the client's hip to the idea, offer to conduct them yourself. Why? Three reasons. First, it's one less thing for him to mess with. Clients remember people who make their life easier.

Second, it's always easier for an outsider to get good, positive feedback from a customer than it is for their vendor (that "bare-your-soul-to-a-stranger" dynamic). Plus, customers often fear that too many direct compliments will lead to swelled heads and complacency. Third? It's more billable time (note: if testimonials weren't part of your original estimate, make sure your client understands they'd be additional, but well worth the extra investment, since, given the above, you'll get better results than they would).

Once you get the green light, have your client contact her clients to ask them if they'd be willing to provide a testimonial for their new marketing material and, if so, to let them know that Joe Bleaux will be in contact with them shortly. Then follow the steps already discussed.

Typical "Testimonial" Questions to Ask:

What do you like about dealing with ABC Company?

Why do you do business with them and not the competition?

Any stories come to mind of "service-above-and-beyond"?

FACTS & FIGURES, NOT FEELINGS While it's not always possible, shoot for testimonials that quantify success (e.g., "Our qualified leads/sales/orders have risen X%"). At the least, go for a quote that points to a tangible benefit (e.g., time savings, industry reputation enhanced, competitiveness boosted, etc.). As opposed to, "I really like working with ABC. Great people and always helpful and cooperative." Which means what?

After you hang up, put your quotes together and run it by the client for an OK. Discuss with the graphic designer in advance how much space will be allotted to testimonials, and how many they want (I suggest three or four), and hence, how long they should be. Quotes can vary in length, but should fall somewhere in the range of these:

"With ABC, I can place an order and not worry about it. Great follow-up and great follow-through. I don't have time to babysit orders, and with ABC, I never have to."

"GHI makes it their business to understand our company culture, and they're very good at being able to tell whether a job candidate will fit into that culture—far better than competitors of theirs with whom I've worked. In three years, GHI has never brought me a candidate who I felt was a waste of time, and that, to me, is the single most important benefit of working with them."

"XYZ places a lot of emphasis on the personal relationship with me, and works hard to grasp my needs. They understand my business, are good at quantifying what I need, and what systems would be the best fit for my situations. They've been very successful in anticipating my growth and recommending the right solutions to keep me running at maximum production and make best use of my resources. Results are everything. And ever since we've started using XYZ, we've consistently surpassed our previous numbers. XYZ helps me be successful in what I do."

FYI, I recently did a series of 10 testimonial-gathering interviews for a client. And even though the calls themselves only lasted 10 minutes or so, the entire process of crafting each one into its final form took about an hour apiece. That included the initial call, transcribing the recording to catch anything I missed, and then editing it down to the right length. Just as a rule of thumb.

"A-Mile-In-Their-Moccasins" Interviews

In the sales and marketing chapter, when we discussed "audience," we looked at a project example where I contacted my client's clients to get a sense of their world so my copy could better speak to that audience. Just so you know, that's not typical; you'll usually get what you need from *your* clients, not *theirs*. That said, if you feel a piece would benefit by digging a bit further, by all means lobby for it.

If you've made a positive and professional impression up till now (and, even better, can show them examples of phone interview content from your portfolio), they'll probably agree to it. But if it's a new client, understand they're thinking: "Will this person handle himself professionally with my customers?" After all, they'll be picking their best and most satisfied customers, and all they need is for somebody to screw up that goodwill.

Assure them it's pretty standard in the industry and that you'll represent their company with complete professionalism and integrity. If they're not crazy about the idea, don't push it; just get what you need from them directly.

Content-Gathering Interviews

Most phone interviews won't be five minutes long. If you're doing a trade article for an industry publication, or a case study for a company's web site, you might need to interview four or more different people. Some of them may be providing a good chunk of input to your piece, in the form of source material about the company—processes, procedures, products—or they may simply be providing a few quotes.

SET APPOINTMENTS If you just have a few folks to contact, or it's just for a testimonial or quick comment, the way discussed above for tracking them down will work fine. If, however, you've got to reach a larger number of people for longer interviews, set phone appointments. Ideally, have your client help nail down a schedule.

I recall once working on a 12-page newsletter involving nine one-hour interviews with a bunch of senior execs. My client set up all the appointments for me, so I knew that on Tuesday, October 27 at 10:00 a.m., I'd be talking to Harry Schmoe.

Sure, even with such planning, you'll still have people cancel and then reschedule, but it's still light years better than tracking them down haphazardly. I've done it that way and if you've got a lot of people to reach, it'll make you crazy. Endless phone tag. Sneaky returned calls at 7:25 a.m. Tons of wasted time.

Too Many Cooks? (i.e., Multiple Content Contributors)

A potentially crazy-making situation is where you're getting input for one project from a half-dozen or more people. The challenge is not having it turn into a free-for-all. In such a scenario, they'll likely want to bombard you with their respective content and feedback—often contradictory—for you to sort out. Can you say "nightmare"? Endless emails, "who-trumps-whom" calculations, tons of extra time. Who needs it? Preserve your sanity, and insist—bullying them, if necessary—they designate a point person on their side, through whom all suggestions, revisions, and feedback flow. That person will process it all *before* sending on the final content to you. Ignore this one at your peril.

And here's a solid strategy for content generation with a gang-up situation like above. Sometime back, I did a brochure for eight nonprofits with similar missions who decided to collaborate on a marketing piece. Instead of every group dumping a stack of stuff on me, from which I'd ultimately generate about one paragraph, I created one questionnaire for all of them, where they provided facts, statistics, and a few sentences about the brochure, what it should accomplish, who it should speak to, etc. My total source material? Eight two-pagers. That's working smarter. Speaking of which...

ADVANCE WORK? A tip to streamline the process with multiple longer interviews: get your proposed questions approved by your contact, who then gets them into the hands of your interviewees prior to the call. Some will actually fill them out before the interview, but at least being familiar with them will have the process go more smoothly.

Take it a step further and attach a cover letter 📁 to the questions, emailed "from" your contact to her colleagues, telling them what to expect, and reminding them of the importance of the project, so they're less likely to treat you and the time slot cavalierly. Providing such a letter to your client (inviting her to "edit to suit") will earn life-simplifying brownie points, while underscoring your professionalism—in *all* senses, but especially in the "no-time-to-screw-around" department.

"HIT-THE-MARK" INSURANCE Your sources won't always share information in a logical "most-to-least-important" hierarchy. If you have one main content source (often called a "SME"—Subject Matter Expert) for a project, at the end of your interview, ask him what three things he's going to want to see front and center in the finished piece.

It's a great way to summarize the interview, and ensure that you've been paying attention and have captured what he feels is most important. I promise, he'll be glad you're taking the time to make sure he's gotten his points across. The best part? It's nearly surefire insurance against "missing the mark."

Working Smarter

As you build your business, you may come to realize you could make a LOT more money with an assistant whose hourly rate was a fraction of yours. Plenty of freelancers have done just that. One FLCW—anonymous by request—wrote to me a few years back:

> *I've found that the internal administrative tasks—including database calling, various forms of marketing, web site updates, etc.—can really pull energy and focus away from jobs I'm working on and new work coming in. By chance, I found a fantastic intern who came to work with such enthusiasm and willingness to learn, I can't imagine how I got along without her before.*
>
> *She manages my contacts (using a script similar to the one I borrowed from TWFW). She writes the headlines and copy for my postcard mailers. She has written several ads for my business and placed them in a local media newspaper, plus she tracks all my marketing efforts. She even re-wrote my web content and developed my new tagline. I've also made a point of giving her opportunities to write articles for one of my clients, for example. Her contribution is invaluable and I recently hired her for eight hours a week (she was previously unpaid). We're both delighted.*

Three Tips For Maximizing Work Efficiency

Use Project Folders Get some legal size "reinforced file jackets," which look like manila folders except they're closed on the sides and accordion-like, to accommodate a stack of papers. Get a wire rack with 8–10 slots. When you start a project, grab a folder, scratch out the last project name on the front of the folder, write the new name on it, and keep everything related to that job in the folder, so you'll always know where everything is. When the job is done and billed, unless you *know* you'll be needing some of it again, toss or recycle the contents. Be ruthless about this, or paper will take over your office.

Organize Your Computer Perhaps a "duh," but set up your computer into a main directory for your business work (mine is WriteInc.) and sub-directories for each of your regular clients. You'll always know where to find any project you've done for XYZ Corp. If you pick up a new client you suspect might be a one-shot deal, keep their project in another sub-directory called Misc. If they become steady, give them their own. Create a second main directory for your other writing—the creative stuff that your dreams are made of. I call mine Soulfood.

Get Google™ Desktop Way cool resource. We've all been in that situation of trying to remember which file contained a certain passage, phrase, etc. And, the sniffing-dog search function in Microsoft *Word*® is pretty useless. But load up Google™ *Desktop* and it tags everything on your hard drive (*and* new things as they're added). Yes, it can take 12 hours (they say four, but not so), during which time your system is slower. Just start it some day after you finish working, and by morning, it's done.

Now, when you want to find something, just pull up a regular Google search box, type in what you're looking for, click Google Search, and the first things that come up (next to the Google Desktop icon) are the first few references on your own computer. Or click the actual *Desktop* link, and voila! In the time it takes you to say "Uh"(mazing), up pops every reference on your computer. It's fairly miraculous. For us "Mac-kies," the *Spotlight* feature does the same thing.

And who says you've got to keep it stateside? I ran an intriguing tip from CT FLCW Mary Shaw in the Well-Fed E-PUB about spanning the globe to get low-priced admin help. THIS is truly working smarter. Here's what she wrote:

1. Outsourcing Idea #1: **Get Friday** (**www.getfriday.com**) is a service in India that provides virtual personal assistants (PA) starting at $15/hr. The price goes down as hours increase. My PA does online research, all of my admin work, and formats Word docs. He's on a $10 monthly retainer and I only pay hourly fees when I assign projects to him.

2. Outsourcing Idea #2: **Brickwork** (**www.b2kcorp.com**), also based in India, has helped me develop my prospect database. They do all the painful legwork of identifying companies and qualifying appropriate contacts (name, email, phone number) so I can stay focused on my paying clients. Pricing is very reasonable and worth the investment.

SUBCONTRACTING? Related to the above is the whole idea of subcontracting: hiring other writers to execute projects you've landed through your marketing efforts. You pay them less than you're charging clients and pocket the difference—in return for providing steady work that they've done nothing to land (except answer their phone). Check out a great primer on the subject at the end of Chapter Twelve.

The Ebb and Flow of Work

FEAST AND FAMINE At times, it'll seem like all your clients have plotted together to all call you at once, and then *not* call you at all for a month. And repeat that cycle until you've gone stark raving mad. The feast/famine dichotomy, while common, isn't inevitable. If you're disciplined about marketing yourself consistently (few of us are), you should have a steady flow of work. Getting to a point where you can pick and choose among many jobs is a nice problem.

Unfortunately, in most cases, human nature usually prevails: we market a bunch, get work, stop marketing, only to resume after the job's done. The result? Alternating periods of being swamped and dead in the water. C'est la vie…

NORMAL PATTERNS When work is flowing, you'll likely have three or four overlapping jobs. No need to finish one before starting another. Think about it. If you've bid a job out at $1,200 (i.e., 16 hours @ $75 an hour), and it's due in a week, that leaves a pile of potentially billable hours. Take what comes. You never know when it'll get really quiet.

That said, get a handle on how long projects take you, to better gauge what else you can comfortably add to the mix. In the beginning, bite off less than you think you can chew. Better to regret taking a job than miss a deadline because you're overextended. But realize it's all relative. Going from no work to just two projects may seem like a lot, since you're comparing it to nothing. I've turned down jobs thinking I was swamped, only to find I could've done it by working a little harder for a few days.

And what if a new client calls? Then it's not just another job. It's a key audition, which, if it goes well, could lead to lots more work. Not like he'll never call again if you turn it down (he may even be impressed you're that busy), but say yes, work a little harder, and come through for him, and the next time, he'll think of you—not the writer he used when you couldn't do it.

Call me crazy, but I say the feast/famine thing is what makes this life so great. If you've just had three straight $1,500–2,000+ weeks, a two-week dry spell can be a gift. Sleep late, work out at noon, meet friends for lunch, catch up on errands, hit the beach mid-week, do a little marketing, etc. In short, take a breather and smell the flowers (or the ocean). One taste of the freelance life, and you'll be hooked.

THE BIG KAHUNA What about long-term (three+ weeks), full-time assignments? Sure, they sound great, but I better be getting paid well to offset the significant "opportunity cost" in lost business when I cut myself off from my network for that long.

Not saying you shouldn't. Big jobs are awfully tempting—especially when sporting $5–10K fees, or when they're in an arena you've been trying to break into. Just make sure you couldn't make just as much in the same period with a normal work load, doing multiple jobs and staying plugged in to your network.

SEASONAL SWINGS January can start out slowly in our business—a great reason to do a mailing that'll land on people's desks right after the holidays. Things start picking up as winter turns to spring and companies get back into their marketing groove, and can continue all the way to the summer.

July and August are generally slow. Ends of fiscal years (June 30 for many companies) plus summer vacations can mean projects on hold and new ones not yet started. Do a late-June mailing to get an extra boost during a traditional lull. Right after Labor Day, there's usually a burst of activity, which can extend through the year's end. Don't count on a quiet December, as many clients are scrambling to get it done before the champagne corks pop. But look on the bright side. You'll have a very happy holiday.

THE TEASE Never ever turn down real work in your hands for a *promise* of a bigger job from someone else. I've had this happen often over the years. Typically starts with a prospect who calls and says, "We've got a lot of projects coming up and we've heard good things about you." Sounds great, right? Not so fast.

In one such case, I went in, met everyone, they liked my work, were excited about working with me, I followed up regularly, and...nothing happened. Never a return call—much less a job—for six months, at which point, they actually called me about a project. I met with her, discussed the project and a timetable...and waited.

Nothing. I called. Nothing. Called again. Nothing. They never took one minute to call me and say the project got scrapped, we found another writer, you remind me of my ex-husband...nothing. Tacky and unprofessional, but it happens. Moral: Have so many irons in the fire that you don't care about what happens with any one particular client or job. Remember: Calls are just calls. Meetings are just meetings. Both can be mirages. Only assigned, "let's get moving" work with (ideally) a deposit check is work.

DAY IN THE LIFE "How can you sit in front of a computer all day long and just type?" I hear that a lot. Well, in truth, there are precious few "just-sitting-and-typing" days in this job. It's a mixed bag. Some days, I'll be "concepting" (i.e., brainstorming) on a project with notes and legal pad in a comfy chair at home or in my local coffee shop. Or marking up the latest round of edits on a project. Or, yes, just sitting down and typing.

Speaking of "concepting," this process is just as important as the actual copywriting. It's when you're coming up with ideas. Clients who've got a clue understand you need some hours for brainstorming. How *you* end up doing it is very personal.

For some, it could be as simple as taking a legal pad and pen to a quiet, comfortable chair—minus all interruptions and distractions. Others may need to take a walk in a nice setting with a mini-recorder—one of my favorite strategies. Or maybe for you, it's "The "Beer Barrel Polka" cranked up to ten, while you sit in the lotus position in your college sweatshirt, madras shorts and Mardi Gras beads. Whatever yanks your creative crank.

Speaking of individual tastes, we all have a unique work style. Figuring out your M.O. will not only ease the transition to self-employment, but will have you see that there's no *one* right way to do it.

Clients and Other Fascinating Species

Okay, so what would **The Perfect Client** look like? Someone who…

- *Understands the creative process*
- *Is knowledgeable about copywriting and what it involves*
- *Is reasonable as to timeframes and budgets*
- *Is helpful in providing, at the first (and only) meeting, everything you need to do your job, or the contact info on people who can get it for you*
- *Knows their subject and doesn't waste time going off on tangents*
- *Is organized and goes out of her way to facilitate the process*
- *Doesn't micro-manage, actually letting you do your job*
- *Gives you lots of referrals and hires you again and again*
- *Pays you in ten days*

I've actually had several clients over the years that have come awfully close to the above description. When we find them, it's great. In the meantime, be aware of those of the less-than-perfect variety…

CLIENTS LOOKING FOR A "MASSAGE"   This client introduces a project you've been told you'll write from scratch by saying, "We've pretty much written the copy, and just need you to *massage* it a little." Other red flag terms? *Tweak, polish, spruce, jazz, spice, etc.* Translation? "I don't want to pay much, so I'm making it sound like a minor job."

If he then tries to pin you down on price, politely tell him you'll need to see what they've done before you can provide a firm quote. Point being, good copywriting is a lot more than just wordsmithing. The structure and flow of the piece is as important as the words you choose. If a client's written their own copy, just "massaging" it may not be enough. Of course, if editing is all he wants, then give it to him.

Clients With Limited Budgets When starting out, you'll likely be working for some clients with little money (though, hopefully, growing reputation and "book" willing, not for long). As in most businesses, the smallest customers are usually the most demanding. While it's important with any client to get specific about project parameters, it's even more crucial with the less-than-well-heeled. These folks are often new to hiring writers, and may not realize they can't change their mind daily or revise their copy endlessly for the same price.

Editing for the Frugal, Skeptical or Technical In cases where the project and budget are small, why not suggest they write it and you edit it? Have them put down what they're trying to say—even if it's badly written—and in what they feel is the proper sequence for optimal flow. It'll be a fraction of the cost of doing the whole piece from scratch.

Ditto with the client who's not convinced they need a writer. In such cases, it could be the foot in the door. Once he sees what a difference your talents can make, the next time, you might just get the whole job. Converting skeptics is great fun. Finally, over the years, I've had a handful of high-tech clients with low budgets who, rather than pay for many hours to get up to speed on how their widget works, write the piece, give me a quick and dirty technical overview (enough to grasp the overall concepts) and then I edit the piece. By distancing myself from the technical complexity, I avoid getting frustrated, and they get their copy prettied up nicely at a low cost. Win-win.

Clients Who Want You To Take Dictation Sometimes you'll feel like little more than a stenographer, as the client essentially spoon-feeds you what he wants to say. Of course, if you're getting $75–100+ an hour, you soldier on. From time to time, a juicy "yes-sir-no-sir-whatever-you-say-sir-I-have-no-independent-thoughts-except-to-think-up-new-and-creative-ways-to-serve-you-sir" project can be most welcome.

CLIENTS WHO SAY THEY WANT CREATIVITY *Bring me something different,* they say (after years of safe stuff). *Let's push the envelope.* So you do. Then, when they see what you've done, they get nervous. Ah, not so brave after all. Then it starts. Why don't we say *this* instead of *that.* Let's *soften* this and *smooth out* that. Pretty soon, you've created something indistinguishable from everything they've done before. C'est la vie. Goes with the territory. Not always (and the smaller the company, the better the chance your creativity will survive), but it happens enough to have become a cliché in the field.

MICRO-MANAGERS WHO THINK THEY'RE WRITERS These folks are easy to spot: they'll adopt a pleased-with-themselves tone, as they say, "Well, I dabble a little bit in writing myself." Be afraid. Be very afraid. In the eyes of many, copywriting is viewed as something anyone can do. It's amazing how many people think they can write, and how few of those actually can. Fortunately, many others know they're not writers, know the profound difference a good copywriter can make, and are smart enough to not spend money to massage their own ego, but rather to get the job done right.

I have one such client, a wonderfully evolved human being, who sends me these comically bad pieces for rewriting/editing, but, because I know his business and him, I know precisely what he's trying to say. When I'm done and he sees my work, you'd think I had a halo and wings. People like him make it all worthwhile.

COPING STRATEGIES The challenge with "writers-in-their-own-mind" is how to be diplomatic when they *repeatedly* foist their version of "how I think it should be written" when it reflects skills, at best, a notch or two above the average sixth-grader. You could just suck it up, give 'em what they want, collect your money, and split.

Or instead, driven by a commitment to the quality of the end result, you could shoot straight: "I'm assuming you hired me because you felt I had a particular skill you don't possess, just as you have talents in areas I'd be lost in (stroke, stroke…). But, I'm feeling like I'm not really being given the opportunity to show you the difference a professional copywriter can make. I want to do a good job and create an effective piece, but if you don't trust that I know what I'm doing, then maybe I don't need to be here."

Not snarky, just firm. And pick your battles. A word here and there? Let it go. However, if the comprehension, clarity, or flow of the copy is being compromised, speak up. If they're smart and honest, they'll appreciate your outspokenness. It shows you're more committed to the success of the project than to protecting their ego.

THE IGNORANT CLIENT #1: OUT OF THEIR DEPTH When someone's entrusted with a project beyond the scope of his normal responsibilities, you can end up educating him tactfully as to how it all works: project phases, typical hours, timeframes, edits, fees, etc. And that means adding a few hours to your quote if you suspect that's what you're getting into. Do a good job of working with him, covering for him, and making him look good, and you'll create a friend for life. If he's the one approving hours and budgets…you get the picture.

THE IGNORANT CLIENT #2: NEW TO THE GAME These folks, having never done any literature for their company, are simply unfamiliar with the process. Again, just cover the bases: set project parameters, costs, and timeframes in writing. Make their life easier by offering to perhaps bring in your graphic designer ally to do a turnkey project. If you can ease their "overwhelm," demystify the process, and deliver finished product for a reasonable cost (far less than what an ad agency, marketing company, or large design firm would charge), that's a beleaguered project manager's dream come true.

●　　●　　●

Okay, so now that we've got a few nuts and bolts out of the way, let's go take a look at some powerful and intriguing strategies for direct mail and email marketing…

Chapter 8

Got this from Philly FLCW Kennerly Clay:

> *As my database grew, I started mailing out purple postcards (my logo color) each quarter to clients and prospects to announce site updates, new partnerships (with designers, printers, etc.), or to simply flex my creative muscles.*
>
> *Ideally, I call everyone in my database a few weeks before to confirm contact info. I've landed a few appointments this way, but from others who don't yet have a need for my services, I often hear, "I have your purple card right here in front of me."*
>
> *After my last mailing, I got a call from an IT consulting company that ended up hiring me to re-do their web content, brochure and possibly more. My new client said he'd decided he'd call me the next time he received one of my cards.*

Bottom line, direct mail is a solid strategy for staying in touch with your contact base of clients and prospects. And incidentally, given the tighter reins being put on the telemarketing industry (which doesn't affect our business-to-business phone prospecting efforts), direct mail will undoubtedly increase in prevalence as companies turn to other proven —and legal!—ways of reaching their target audience. Keep that in mind when pitching work with prospects.

DIRECT MAIL KEYS With any direct mail campaign, the three catchwords are *consistency, clarity,* and *frequency.* Show up regularly in front of your target audience, make sure your message is simple, clear and uncluttered, and do it often.

As you prospect and network for work, you build a list of contacts who've said that yes, they do have ongoing or occasional needs for copy-writers. This growing list becomes your target list for postcard direct mailings. And over time, a list of 200 to 300 can be more than enough to yield steady work.

Most importantly, always consider the larger picture and the bigger goal. Remember the story of the dating service marketing campaign earlier in the book. The point is simply to move your prospects along the sales cycle until you reach the point where they either tell you they're not in the market for your services OR they hire you.

And there's no one right way to move someone along that cycle. Some send letters, postcards or emails first, follow up with a phone call, and stay in touch with more letters, cards, etc. Others skip the first step, go straight to the phone, and then keep in touch with the other correspon-dence. Whatever you're most comfortable with. Just make those multi-ple impressions. While chances are good you'll do some cold calling along the way, it isn't necessarily the order that's key, it's the process.

TIPS FROM A PRO At a recent BMA meeting (Business Marketing Association —**www.marketing.org**; a nationwide organization worth checking out), the speaker was Chris Coleman, marketing industry veteran and Chief Marketing Officer of Atlanta-based Secureworks. Echoing the ideas above, Chris made these points about direct mail:

TARGET. The more targeted your audience, the better. List quality is more important than quantity. (Chris's most targeted mailing had a ten percent response, mind-blowing, incidentally, given that good response rates are two percent.)

FREQUENCY. Response drops over time, but the more "touches" you can make to your customer, the better the response. Chris's goal in year one was eight touch points (direct mail, calls, releases, etc.). Year two: 12. Year three: 18. Probably more than FLCW's need to do, but I can cer-tainly see half that number spread across different approaches.

Frequency Trumps Nice Creative. Good creative in combination with a good list is ideal, but a fairly plain mailer sent often can do the job with a good list. It's all about continuing to show up on the radar.

For FLCW's, along with frequency, there's a lot to be said for a consistent look (like Kennerly's purple cards), design or logo that allows clients and prospects to recognize your mailings. If you choose one of the postcard houses I mention below, this might mean sticking with one design and message—cheaper, for sure.

Follow-Up. Following up will always boost response. The mailer with the ten percent response was repeated four times. Everyone on the list of 800 was called after each mailing. Leaving a voice mail was considered acceptable.

Postcard Houses In the original *TWFW*, I detailed a process for creating your own direct mail postcards using *Microsoft Publisher*, some bright-colored card stock and your friendly quick copy shop down the street. You'd design the cards in *Publisher*, lay them four-up on an 8.5" x 11" sheet (or oversized versions at two-up on the same page), print out clean laser copies, copy them onto the colored stock and cut them up with a paper cutter. And all for roughly $60 for 250 cards including paper, copying, and postage.

It's still a great strategy, and limited only by your imagination and creativity. Since then, many online postcard houses have popped up. They're more expensive given that the price doesn't include postage, but the convenience and aesthetics factors are high. The company I keep hearing about is **www.modernpostcard.com** (a few others: **www.amazing mail.com**, **www.purepostcards.com**, and **www.postcardsplus.net**).

The drill: You choose from literally thousands of slick graphic and photographic images. You craft your card copy—typically, headline on the front and headline/body copy on the back. At **www.modernpost card.com**, they'll print up 1,000 cards with your message for roughly $180–280 depending on postcard size (prices at press time). You get a slick-looking (in a good way) card at about a quarter a pop and leave the designing to someone else. If you're doing targeted mailings, 1,000 cards can be plenty for two to four mailings. And every time your prospect and client base sees that card, it reinforces your image.

"NEWSETTES" Another intriguing direct mail possibility is what's known as a "newsette"—a hybrid between a newsletter and a direct mail piece, with colorful graphics and two short 150- to 200-word articles on topics of interest to your audience, one on each side. Not only a possibility for your own personal marketing but something to suggest to clients. I did a bunch for a local mortgage company with a fun, friendly tone— all designed to demystify the loan process, present different financing scenarios, and, of course, think of my client once they were ready to move on something. Check out a few at **www.writeinc.biz**, then *Portfolio, Direct Mail,* and *Family Mortgage "Newsettes."*

TIMING IS EVERYTHING Doing just two mailings a year? Try January and June. Four or more? Make sure two of them are around those months. A mailing right after New Year's makes you one of the first names they think of when they need a writer. June? As mentioned, summers are often slower for various reasons. Hence, a reminder to your market will ensure you get your share of a somewhat reduced industry workload in summer.

GET CREATIVE In addition to using direct mail to make general intro and "don't-forget-me" contacts, why not create mailings targeting a certain industry? Or to remind your market of a specific type of work they may not realize you do. Or if you've decided to focus on a particular industry or project type you find you enjoy. In all cases, focus on *benefits* to the client—why doing business with you will address one or more of their hot buttons—not just all about you and your services (*features*).

Invariably, within a few days of sending out a mailing, I'll get a few calls and at least a job or two, sometimes off of the mailing, sometimes not. It's called synchronicity. Someone who forgot about me just had a need arise for copywriting when my postcard crossed their desk and their regular copywriter wasn't available. Bingo! I get the call. If I do a good job, guess who they're going to think of the next time they need a writer?

"The Free Report" Strategy

An exceptionally powerful lead-generating direct-mail strategy. Simple concept: you send a sales letter to a targeted group of prospects (as you'll see in the sidebar below, if you've got a good list, less than 100 names can be more than enough to yield a lot of business) offering a free report (or white paper) just for responding. Whole idea is to demonstrate your expertise in an area of value to a client.

The report addresses a key client challenge and offers true "how-to" value, not fluff—information a client can act on, regardless of whether they choose to contact you further. Now, some recipients will be "D-I-Y" types. They'll snag the report and put the ideas to work on their own. Others though—and this is the real power of this approach—will say, "Don't have time to do it myself. This guy obviously knows what he's doing. I'll call him."

The free report approach is deal for "niche" practitioners talking to clients with industry-specific issues and challenges—often in high-tech. A few years back, I coached a writer working in a specific high-tech realm, where the clients' big hot button is simplifying complicated subjects. She planned on doing a free "how-to" report along these lines. Prospects could adopt her suggestions on their own or, better yet for her, hire her to make their tedious copy sing.

THE MAGIC WHITE PAPER Good friend Michael Stelzner, the white-paper guru (**www.whitepapersource.com**), completely turned his business around a few years back using this strategy. He wrote a white paper on how to write a white paper and offered it free as a download. He had more than 60,000 prospects take him up on it over three years or so and ended up with more white paper business than he could handle.

Check this out. You sitting down? Mike shared with me that he's got the white paper drill down to where it takes him roughly 18 hours to do a 6–10 page white paper. His fee? $7,500 each, and he does four monthly. That's where this can go. Check out the whole cool story of how it unfolded at **www.marketingwhitepapers.net**.

The Free Report That Earned a Canadian FLCW $80K (and Counting...)

Great story. Seems Pete Savage (**www.petesavage.com**), a B2B (business-to-business) software/technology copywriter near Toronto was frustrated—tired of dealing with too many small-ticket, time-sucking, tire-kicking clients, and decided to go after the steady, low-hassle, high-dollar ones he really wanted. He put together a free report with a sales letter, sent it to just 77 people, and it generated $64,000 in new business in 12 months (80K+ in 15 months).

As Pete explains, "No direct mail package is complete without an offer—something of value for your readers to entice them to respond to your sales letter. For copywriters, a well-targeted complimentary report is a great way to generate interest in your services."

What should the report be about? Asks Pete, "What's on the mind of your target audience? What are their biggest challenges? Responsibilities? Goals? To find out, visit the online forums/sites where your audience gathers, read their industry pubs, and do research.

"For one report, I visited the web sites of hundreds of companies in my industry, making observations about the home page, then publishing my findings in the report."

Speaking of reports—though not a free one—Pete's put together a 60-pager outlining all the how-to detail of this $80K+ promotional coup. Pete's a no-BS, no-hype guy, and this is a solid blueprint. Details: **http://tinyurl.com/savagesuccess**.

Atlanta FLCW Ed Gandia took a similar approach in building a $163K income in his first full year as a FLCW. He writes, "The best use of direct mail? Create a free report with valuable and relevant information for your target market. Then, make *that* the offer, not a "hard" offer in a direct mail letter (such as selling your services directly)." We'll take a closer look at Ed in the chapter ahead on part-time biz-building.

DIRECT MAIL TO NEW PROSPECTS If you're planning on mailing to "cold" prospects—those who've never heard from you—a simple postcard mailing that steers them to your site is fine, but do NOT send out big packages in cold mailings. If people aren't expecting it, chances are excellent they'll end up in the trash, unopened. This warning is really for those without a site who want to blanket their market with a full package. Not smart.

LINING UP A LIST To reach new cold prospects, obviously you need to get a list. Remember resources discussed earlier like the *Dun & Bradstreet Million Dollar Database*, available through your library, and *The Book of Lists*.

A NOVEL APPROACH One FLCW (who wished to remain anonymous) generated enough business with her unique marketing approach to keep a small stable of writers busy. She got the idea for the strategy from Gill Cargill, a top sales pro (**www.cargillsells.com**).

Step 1: She bought a list of prospects from a list broker—potential buyers for her different writing services, which include commercial, ghostwriting books and articles, and others. You could create your own list from your prospecting and networking efforts, though the beauty of this approach is that it "warms up" totally cold prospects.

With list in hand, she makes just 25 contacts a week, five each day. She put together four letters, and each week for four weeks, she sends one letter to each contact. Each letter is written in a different style—funny, serious, upbeat, etc.—and focuses on a different writing service she offers.

FROM COLD TO WARM She comments: "Over four weeks, I showcase a broad range of talent. They're getting to know me, so that by the time I call, in most cases, it isn't a cold call any more. More often than not, they recognize me." Of 25 contacts, she books three to five face-to-face appointments—always the goal. Many of the rest remain on the list for future contacts.

She figures you could do the same thing with direct mail postcards, using different writing approaches for different cards. In her case, letter copy lent itself better to the types of writing she wanted to do for her clients. To boost the odds that her letters actually get read, she hand-writes the addresses and uses stamps (ink-jetted labels and metered postage screams 'JUNK MAIL!').

Follow up? She buys lists in a format importable into *ACT* (*the* contact management program). She loads her four letters into the program, picks her five contacts a day and generates the letters. The system's "tickler" function reminds her daily of what letter she needs to send to whom, and the phone follow-ups she needs to make that day.

I like it. Targeted. Innovative. Not terribly labor-intensive. And your eventual calls will be a lot easier and more fun. Most importantly, you can't argue with the results.

Is it a DM Postcard? A Case Study? Both!

There's a kick-butt graphic design firm in Atlanta called *Design That Works* (slogan: "It's not creative unless it works!" Amen to that…). Consummate pro Linda McCulloch and crew turn particularly successful projects into direct mail pieces masquerading as compelling mini-case study/ testimonials with the following sections: *The Challenge, Our Solution, The Outstanding Results,* and *The* (gushing client) *Quote*.

For examples, visit the *Side Dishes* link at **www.wellfedwriter.com/ sidedishes.shtml** and look for *"Case-study-style direct mail pieces."* And at **www.greatdesignthatworks.com** then *Success Stories,* you'll see the same basic success stories, but adapted for the web.

She sends one out two or three times a year to roughly 400–500 people: current clients as well as warm, medium, and hot prospects. While she can't claim that each mailing yields X# of projects, she's been in business for 20+ years and, according to her, "Other than the odd recession, depression, or loss of a client out of no fault of our own (e.g., the company being sold), we've pretty much had as much business as we can handle."

She also hands them out at talks and conferences—as a sort of seriously enhanced business card. What better to give prospects than a quick snapshot of what you could actually do for them? We writers could do this, and even team with a designer whose work we were showcasing, while splitting the cost and promoting both of us.

FREE USPS DM!? Free direct mail. No catch. No kidding. The folks at USPS have developed a cool program called *NetPost,* an online automated direct mail program offering postage-inclusive postcards, letters, flyers, newsletters, etc. Get this: for their B&W, 4x6 postcard program, you pay ONLY the postage (the card is free).

With no minimum quantity, it's perfect for "onesies" like welcome notes to new clients and post-project thank-you's—all automatically personalized to recipients. For details, visit **www.usps.com**, and click "Create Your Own cards" under *"Would you like to…?"* Once there, scroll down to the *Click2Mail* and *PremiumPostcard* programs.

FOLLOW-UP IS YOUR JOB   I'm amazed at how often I hear, *I sent out a bunch of direct mail cards (or packages) and I haven't heard back from anyone.* For starters, never send a full-blown marketing package to anyone who isn't expecting it. It'll be a waste of time and money. But once you do a mailing, it's your job to follow up, not theirs.

In fact, you're doing them a favor by following up. How many times have I called clients and heard, *I'm glad you called. I've been meaning to call you but I've just been so busy.* You just made their life easier *and* moved the project that much closer to paying work. If they're not in the market, you'll find out quickly and painlessly and move on.

HOW MUCH MARKETING?   I assert that in typical markets, if you follow the marketing steps I've laid out here—web site, prospecting, regular (and simple) direct mail campaigns, networking, etc.—you'll be plenty busy. Just figure out how much marketing is enough to keep one person steadily working, and then do a little more.

By the way, do all that and, at times, you'll probably have to turn down work. A better strategy (discussed in Chapter Ten) is to develop a network of trusted fellow writers. You steer overflow work to them and they'll do the same when the tables turn. Everyone wins.

•   •   •

The ABC's of Email Marketing

The Five Basic Rules

1. **Don't Spam**. Sure, the law of averages could work in your favor in one sense, but you could blow your reputation at the same time.

2. **Personalize**. The more you can send your email to specific, named individuals, the better your hit rate will be.

3. **Keep It Simple**. Use fancy graphics *only* if sending to those expecting them (i.e., regular ezine subscribers). If emailing cold prospects, using text only (fancy graphics scream, "Spam!!") ratchets up the personal touch.

4. **Cross-Market**. Do a mix of marketing by snail mail, email and phone. Be everywhere your prospects are—a recurring presence with a friendly, helpful, upbeat vibe.

5. **Keep It Brief**. Your audience gets too much email (just like you!). Make whatever you send worth their while. Keep your message brief, link them to a web site, and let them know you'll be following up by phone (and then do it).

Sunny Email Success

It was 2002 when I first met Florida FLCW Lisa Sparks, an extraordinarily impressive then-27-year-old African-American woman who, through persistence, resourcefulness, ingenuity, and plain hard work, was building a thriving writing business (**www.integritywriting.com**) in the small and predominantly white Ft. Myers, Florida market area (population: 50,000).

Lisa's since moved into some new business directions, but her initial strategy of email marketing made all the difference.

FOCUSED ON WHAT WORKS For Lisa, email marketing (specifically, a monthly ezine) became THE focal point of her overall marketing strategy. Yes, she still networked, made cold calls, and did postcard mailings, but all contacts from those efforts were added to her ezine subscriber base. Within two years of starting this strategy, Lisa's business doubled —all coming from her ezine. Some email marketing applications?

MARKETING TO EXISTING CLIENTS/PROSPECTS In this scenario, use email addresses collected over time through prospecting or networking. *Always* get permission to email someone. If you've created a quality ezine —focused on subjects of relevance to your audience—subscribers will come to respect your expertise as you build the case for hiring you. Lisa suggests, Make it easy to say yes: *'Mr. Prospect, I put together a great monthly ezine with good business-building tips, success stories and more. Can I add you to the distribution list? I think you'd enjoy it.'*

MAKE IT GOOD, OR ELSE Fact is, most recipients won't read much of your ezine, so grab their attention with bold, snappy headlines that speak to the things near to their heart: increased profits, enhanced reputation, competitive advantage, etc. That said, make *all* the content good. As Lisa points out, some *will* read it, and if it's lousy, self-serving, or self-promotional, they'll unsubscribe. Poof! You've just lost your monthly "access." While you want them to read every word, it's the *regular* monthly "I'm-still-here-and-ready-to-serve-you" message that makes it a powerful strategy.

THE RIGHT HEADLINE For a regular newsletter, stay with the same subject line. People come to expect it, and won't confuse it with spam. For cold prospects, be more bold with your headlines, *and* make them relevant. Experiment.

If you're sending, say, an ezine to people who are expecting it, you can be more graphically creative. There are tons of inexpensive, easy-to-use programs to help you look good, allow you to import your list (which yields personalized "Hi John" results), and provides tracking information on your campaigns—i.e., how often different links in the email have been clicked, and hence what interests your audience and causes them to take action.

Some examples of email marketing programs: **www.cooleremail.com, www.constantcontact.com, www.verticalresponse.com, www.imakenews.com, www.ezinedirector.com** and **www.topica.com.**

MARKETING TO COLD PROSPECTS One strategy is to harvest targeted email addresses from relevant company web sites. Just make sure you *personalize* it—by name *and* some specific detail about their company, their web site, an article about them, etc. Time-intensive, yes, but the personal touch works, and won't backfire like spamming will.

Should you buy or rent an email list? Not recommended unless you plan to personalize each note, which sort of defeats the purpose.

With cold prospects, because you don't yet have a relationship built, you need to grab their attention in a *relevant* way. As Lisa says, *Make it brief, concise and meaningful. It has to pass the test: 'What's in it for me?' and if the answer is, 'Nothing,' it's gone.*

Remember: plain text messages for cold prospects, as slick graphics usually mean spam.

INEXPENSIVE, TARGETED ADS Lisa echoes the "Free Report" strategy: Buy an ad in an industry ezine (every industry has them) with a big subscriber base, offering, say a free special report (that addresses a key audience issue) for subscribing to yours. Ad rates are usually reasonable. You should see a huge increase in subscribers. Translation? *Access.*

"Should I Do a Blog?"

Not necessarily. In 2008, I launched mine (**www.wellfedwriter.com/ blog**) and it's been great. I had a platform and a following, so I knew I'd get visitors (I average 20+ comments on each post). Because my blog has a narrow focus—commercial freelancing—I had the potential to be an industry "thought leader." I also liked the idea of boosting site traffic— an oft-cited blog by-product. Plus, I have products to sell, so there's a tangible bottom-line benefit to that higher traffic.

Should you do one? If you, too, had a narrow niche, a following, and products or expertise to sell, it might be worth it. None of the above? I'm not sure I'd bother. Ninety-nine percent of blogs out there have virtually no traffic, so you end up talking to yourself.

If you're seriously considering one, here are a few things I've learned…

1. **Be a Discussion Catalyst**—Many bloggers post to pontificate, not to stimulate discussion. My posts always wrap up with 3–4 questions, inviting readers to weigh in. And they do.

2. **Be Relevant**—People don't care what you think unless it's relevant to them. Look at my blog. The topics are directly germane to FLCW's. Between the posts and the commentary, we end up with a mini-knowledgebase on each subject (as evidenced by the many references in this book to specific posts and the ensuing discussion). And when visitors see bottom-line value in participating, they come back.

3. **Once Every 1–2 Weeks Is Plenty**—Conventional wisdom says you need to post 2–3 times a week. Bunk. I post once every 10–14 days. Why? 1) It usually takes that long for the commentary to wind down, and 2) people are too busy to keep up with 2–3 posts a week on multiple blogs.

•   •   •

Okay, now on to a subject near and dear to our hearts: money! Specifically, "What do I charge?" and the nitty-gritty of getting paid…

Chapter 9

Early in my career, I was hired to write a seven-minute video script. Should've earned me $700–800+ (plus a 25% rush fee, since I had 36 hours to do it). I did it for $300. Was I glad to have the work? You bet. Since I turned it around in 24 hours, I made $300 for a day's work. Not bad for starting out. So what that I fell far short of my $50 per hour rate at the time? I did good work, impressed the heck out of the client, ended up with a great sample, and picked up a bunch more work at more fitting rates.

There are two philosophies for those starting out. First one says, within reason, be flexible on your fees. Down the road, get righteously indignant at clients who don't have a clue what good copywriting costs...*when* you're backed up with work for the next four months. In the beginning, think of it as *paid* on-the-job-training. Second one says set your rate and don't deviate. Jim Meadows, a part-timer in Kansas City who we'll meet in Chapter Eleven, started at $75 an hour and refused to take less. Worked for him.

As a rule, #1 makes more sense for those with little to show and a lot to prove: small or non-existent portfolio and little experience. #2 is logical for those with strong expertise and a decent collection of relevant samples—two things Jim had going for him.

169

Flat's Where It's At When you first talk money with a client, typically, they'll ask, "How do you price your services—by the hour or by the job?" Unless a client demands to know your hourly rate (rare), talk only in terms of flat fees. Rule of thumb: Don't get into hard numbers until you're talking about a specific project.

A $100 an hour rate could freak out a client ("Times how many hours??"). But, if you work fast, and you figure the job you're discussing would take eight hours, and $800 is within your client's budget, then bringing up the hourly serves no useful purpose. Keep it to yourself for your own internal fee calculations.

As mentioned in Chapter Seven ("Talk Money Before Meetings"), discuss money before meeting with clients to ensure everyone's in the same financial neighborhood.

Flat fees are how you'll price 95% of your work. As a rule, clients will only let you bill by the hour if the project parameters are fluid and shifting, *and* they've worked with you enough to build a trust level, knowing that it never turns into a runaway train.

"Bonus" Bucks A clarification. Say you quote $900 for a brochure (you've mentally calculated 12 hours @ $75 an hour) and the client signs off. Or, you've been given a $900 budget, which, after crunching the numbers, works for you. What if the job only takes you nine hours? No, you don't have to charge $675 now (nine times $75).

Once you agree on a flat fee (even though calculated using your hourly rate), that fee trumps the hourly. Of course, if that 12-hour job ends up taking 15, you eat three hours. The only time you'd bill them $675 is if you agreed to quote by the hour, and you only used nine hours, even if you told them you *thought* it'd take 12. That's different.

Flat Favors the Fast Do you work fast? If your hourly is $75 and a fair market price for X project is $750, and you can knock it out in seven hours (vs. 10 for someone else), you've just effectively bumped up your hourly rate to nearly $110. Sweet.

Some years back, I did a four-page quarterly newsletter for a client for several years. For the first one, I bid $1,500, based on X hours. Over time, they got easier, until they took a little over half the time the first one did. But I was still making the same fee—virtually doubling my hourly. That's where the job gets fun. Develop long-term relationships with clients, and this'll happen more and more.

YOUR HOURLY RATE For marketing-oriented work such as brochures, ads, newsletters, direct mail, web content, and the like, hourly rates range roughly from $50 to $125+. Hourlies for technical writing run lower: $35 to $60 (though projects are much bigger).

I started at $50 an hour in 1994 with no writing experience, background or track record, and a pretty pathetic portfolio. In most good-sized metros, no serious businessperson will flinch at $50 unless they've never hired a writer before. In fact, $50 will have seasoned copywriting buyers wondering how good you really are. No kidding.

To determine *your* right hourly rate, do your homework, find out what the local market will bear for your type of writing and level of experience (contact other writers or ad agencies/design firms for the local rate scoop). AND check out the sidebar below…

By the way, before you get euphoric and multiply $50 or $75 an hour times 40 hours a week, it doesn't quite work that way. Billing 15 to 20 hours a week is actually typical for most FLCW's. In a few years, depending on your market (and your ambition), when you're at $75–85 an hour, 20 hours looks even better.

For a most enlightening discussion on hourly vs. flat rates, visit the post from 12/15/08 on *The Well-Fed Writer Blog* at **www.wellfedwriter.com/blog**.

Debunking the Myth of "Standard" Writers Rates…

Some time back, I had an email exchange with a few FLCW's in a chat room. Someone had posed a question about rates, and someone else responded thusly (excerpted): "Here's what I've seen experientially: junior copywriters can start out at anywhere from $20 to $28 per hour (will vary by region); mid-level copywriters often charge from $29 to $50 an hour, and senior copywriters often charge from $55 to $150 an hour."

While the upper end of her senior range was correct, I took major issue with the rest. Of course, getting paid more is predicated on being a *good* writer. Here's what I wrote:

> While I don't dispute such rates exist, I've never seen $20 as the norm in OUR field for those starting out; $50 should be the lowest. Are there plenty of junior and mid-level copywriters making the rates you quote? No doubt. And plenty of clients who'll confirm those rates are about right for those groups?

No question. Does that mean that's all a copywriter can hope to earn at those levels? Absolutely not. ALL it means is that there are bunches of copywriters making those rates, and plenty of clients unwilling to pay more. Sure, many clients think $50 an hour is too much to pay even a pro, but there are also plenty who won't flinch at $125 an hour. And I'm working for a bunch of them.

Sure, when starting out, maybe you work for those only willing to pay less, in order to make a few bucks, learn the ropes, and build your book. Fine. But, at some point, you need to move on and make room for those willing to pay more. And they're out there.

What's sad is that tons of talented writers are making pathetically low hourly rates for NO other reason than that's what some guide told them they can expect to make at their experience level, and because they're working for clients who pay no more than that. Meanwhile, other writers who never got that memo (like me when I started out, and perhaps those who read my books), and don't realize that they shouldn't be able to command higher rates, are doing just that. All because they looked in different places, believed different people, and found those willing to pay more.

THE "WOO-WOO" FACTOR The day you decide to upgrade the quality of your clients and stop working for $25, $30, $35 an hour is the day that you'll start getting better clients who truly value what you bring to the table—and will pay you well. It's weird how it works, but it works. It's as if your new belief in yourself informs the universe of your intentions, and it responds.

Annapolis, Maryland FLCW Eileen Coale seconds this: "I am not one prone to 'woo-woo' metaphysical philosophy; I'm about as pragmatic as they come. Yet, I have seen this proven out in my own career, and in all my copywriter friends' careers as well. It's as if your fist is clenched so tightly holding on to those low-paying gigs (because you fear not having enough income) that your hand isn't open to any better. Refuse the low-paying jobs. Step out in faith and market to prospects a rung or two higher on the ladder than you think you're ready for. When I hung out my shingle in 2002, my effective hourly rate was $50. Today, it's at least $125, and sometimes a lot more."

Mike Klassen in Washington state offers up this interesting insight: "A not-often-realized negative aspect of accepting low-paying jobs is that those clients typically refer similar types of clients who expect to pay a low price. By contrast, I once got a referral from a colleague who charged a healthy amount for her services. So the person getting the referral and calling me was used to more realistic prices. When that person referred me to someone else, he also expected to pay a higher fee."

"HOW DO I ESTIMATE A JOB?" There's no magic formula for accurate estimating; it's simply something that gets easier with experience. Put simply, break a job down into its component parts: research, background reading, travel, meetings, brainstorming (a.k.a. "concepting"), interviewing, writing, and editing (you won't have all these in every job). Then assign a time figure (i.e., X hours) to each category.

"But how am I supposed to know what any given project will entail?" ASK. I'm amazed at how often writers email me about getting into trouble on a project because it turned out to be much bigger than they thought, and it turns out they never asked the necessary questions to establish the parameters. Clients don't always know how it works (especially if they're new to hiring writers). They're taking their lead from *you.* So, ask LOTS of questions to cover the above bases before giving a quote:

How many meetings do you plan to have? (Push for one, max.)

How will I get my source material to write the piece? Interviews? Background reading? Meeting with data dump from SME's (subject matter experts)? (It's usually a combination, and often, they want you to tell them how it'll work.)

If interviews, how many? (See Chapter Seven for interviewing how-to detail.)

If background reading, how much? (Again, if they hand you a foot-high stack, get them to distinguish between "source"—what you'll use to write the piece —and "background"—what you'll read to steep yourself in their world.)

Then multiply the total number of hours calculated by your hourly rate to get a flat fee estimate (which can be a range that varies by 10 to 15 percent—e.g., $1,500–$1,700, $3,600–$4,100, etc.). Avoid "premature estimation" (i.e., "on-the-spot" estimating). Ask questions, then go away and crunch the numbers before getting back to them. Over time, you'll develop a sixth sense about the process.

What's the Budget? The second way fees are often determined, more common with experienced clients, is simply telling you what the budget is for a job. Again, find out specifically what's expected for that fee, then go away and do the numbers. If they work, go for it. If it's lower than what you think it'll take, say, "With all due respect, that seems a little low. Typically, a job with these parameters will fall into a fee range of ___ to ___."

If they're inexperienced or were just trying to see how low they could get you, they may simply agree, and you move on. If their reply is, "Well, that's all we have," then you need to decide. If it's too low, walk. Who knows? They might counteroffer. If they do, and you accept it, again, make sure you're on the same page as to parameters.

With a BIG Grain of Salt I once met with a client who, up till then, was writing copy in-house, but had decided to outsource the task to free up his staff (increasingly common). At the first meeting, he told me that, based on their experience writing a similar-sized project to the one we were discussing, it should take about 30 hours.

Careful. My ego was now involved: as a "professional writer," it should take me less time than it took an "amateur," right? But how did he arrive at that figure? Did it include time for meetings, brainstorming (a.k.a. "concepting"), travel, and other intangibles? Were they experienced enough to be able to estimate competently? Might he be low-balling me, thinking a pro would balk at estimating higher than them?

Regardless of how sinister or innocent you judge their motives to be, use their "estimate" *only* as a mildly interesting but essentially irrelevant piece of information. Rely on your own tried-and-true estimating guidelines, and keep your ego out of it. More to the point, what's ultimately most important is that the professional writer does a *better* job, not necessarily a faster or cheaper one.

"You Go First...No, After You" Ideally, I want the client to speak first, so I'll ask, like a casual afterthought, "Do you have an idea of what you'd like to keep this to, money-wise?" In response, they might just give you a number, or say something like, "Well, the last time we did a similar project, we paid the writer $___." Again, use your own guidelines. If it's too low, respond as above.

If their number is higher than you figured, pause, visibly ponder, and then say, unemotionally, "That number should work." If you quickly blurt out, "Works for me!" they'll know they shot too high. And that can set up all sorts of little unconscious resentments and raised expectations on their part, and make them more difficult to deal with.

NOTE: That said, resist the urge to pillage and plunder. Say you're thinking it's a $1,000 job, and the client says their budget is $2,000. If you accept that, and then he hears from another writer and discovers he can get the same quality (if that's the case) for a lot less, then you could be out. Better to perhaps earn a bit more than you expected, but a lot less than the client was willing to pay. That can translate to client loyalty.

THE BOOMERANG Of course, asking them what figure they had in mind could elicit, "Well, what do you think it'll take?" Back in your court. If forced to quote on the spot, shoot high. You can always come down. In certain respects, it's a game, and the better you get at playing it, the more money you can make. You can go in assuming people are honest because you are (*and* you hate playing games), but the fact remains that business-people will try to get the most for the least and will often bluff their way to the best possible outcome. You'd probably do the same. Nothing malicious. Just business.

All the above notwithstanding, don't get the idea that fee discussions are always white-knuckled psychological warfare. I can't remember the last time I had to negotiate a fee. I tell them what it is, and they say yes or no. If no, maybe we alter the parameters a bit so it works. Or, they tell me their budget and I decide if that's acceptable.

PICK SOME BRAINS Not sure what to charge for a project? Find a friendly, seasoned writing colleague and ask about these and other issues. I found such a 'simpatico' guy early on, and rang him up every few months, mostly about estimating. Most won't mind at all, and will probably be flattered. He's now a valued member of my writers group. By the way, even after an average of 20+ years in the business, the members of my group still regularly canvas each other about specific estimating issues.

ALWAYS INCLUDE MEETING TIME When preparing an estimate, find out how many meetings the client expects and how long they'll be. At most, there should be one—at the beginning—and barring a dramatic change in creative direction, everything else can be done by phone, fax and email.

As discussed, many freelancers hate meetings ("time-wasters!"). I get it. *And* I like to launch big projects with an initial meeting. In addition to giving you a chance to connect personally with a client (which can lead to more work), going face-to-face is more productive in my experience (*and* gives you insights into relevant office politics).

Should they want an additional unplanned meeting, politely inform them that you'll have to bill them for it (at your hourly rate). If it's a big project, and they've been generous, maybe you don't. No hard and fast rules; just know an extra charge is standard. Also mentally figure on a certain amount of phone time to review edits and generally discuss the project. You'll learn by doing. Remember the "paid training" thing.

By the way, if you incur miscellaneous project charges (e.g., long distance calls, copying, etc.), try NOT to itemize them on an invoice. It looks nickel-and-dimey. Just use a bit of your fee range to absorb those costs. If they're $100+ (unlikely), and you're already at your fee ceiling, then bill it.

Don't Write That Proposal
Until You Ask The 'Magic Question'!

Australian sales trainer Tessa Stowe (visit **www.salesconversation.com** *to sign up for her newsletter) says, "I teach small-business owners and recovering salespeople 10 simple steps to turn conversations into clients without being sales-y or pushy." Sounds pretty useful. The following piece addresses a common time-wasting mistake made by many FLCW's. While her advice is more fitting for salespeople submitting more elaborate proposals, her basic thinking is sound and applies nicely to us as well. Read and heed.*

• • •

Ever had a prospect ask for a proposal or presentation only to respond with "Thank you for doing this and we'll get back to you at some time in the future if we decide to do something"? If you knew that'd be their response, would you have bothered? Unlikely. So, how do you find out where they stand? Simple. Ask them "The Magic Question"…

And it's magical for two reasons: 1) It transports you both into the future (after they've received the proposal you have yet to write) and, 2) often, the need for writing the proposal will vanish after you have asked it. So what's "The Magic Question"?

"Imagine that you've read my proposal and, without a doubt, the solution proposed is a perfect fit for what you want. What would happen next?"

Let's suppose their response is one of the following:

"I'd discuss it with my manager (partner, etc.) to see if they want to move ahead."

"We'd assess it along with everything else we're doing and decide on our priorities."

"I'd need to make sure the costs are within our budget."

What do any of these tell us? That writing a proposal isn't the next best step and may, in fact, not be necessary at all. So, the need for writing a proposal has vanished (magical!).

Instead, the next best steps could be:

1) Determine any and all decision makers and meet with them.

2) Ask a lot more questions to discover a compelling reason why they should solve this problem now. If you can't find one, chances are good they won't be doing anything.

3) Discuss your pricing for the project in question to confirm it's within their budget.

Depending on the outcome of the above steps, it may become obvious this isn't a qualified prospect. Make it a rule that you only write proposals if you know in advance what they are going to say after they've read it and are happy with the proposed solution, and you're satisfied with this answer.

© 2007 Tessa Stowe, Sales Conversation.

BIG JOBS? GIVE 'EM A BREAK Now and then, you'll land jobs billing 30–40 hours a week for many weeks. We love those. They're more typical in technical writing, but not uncommon in our world (e.g. huge web sites, big marketing campaigns, major event speaker support, etc.). If a 100-hour job's on the line, the client *might* ask for a 10 to 15 percent break, and I'll probably give it to him (if not asked, I won't offer). To work with people, you gotta work with people.

VIDEO MAY BE DIFFERENT   When doing video scripts, some clients might ask for a "per finished minute" (pfm) rate, which can range anywhere from $80–200. New writer and/or simple project = low end. More experience and more complex project = upper end. Straightforward "talking head" type training videos will be less, while more creativity will boost cost. But remember, *it's still time.* When pricing, use your hourly rate, figure out how many hours it'll take, and then convert it to a pfm rate.

THE "LOW FIGURE" LAW OF NATURE   Let's say you've quoted a prospect a fee range of about $1,000–1,200 prior to getting all the details on a project (Mistake #1), because he insisted. Now, no matter how much you qualify that range (e.g., "Now, this could change…please don't take it to the bank, etc., and, of course he'll agree, "Oh sure, just trying to get a ballpark…"), he will *only* remember the low end of the range.

Come back with a higher number and he'll likely say, "Gee, I thought you said you could do it for $1,000…" And you'll curse and gnash your teeth, swearing you'll never do it again. And, of course, you will. If a client insists you estimate on the spot, add 25% to what you think it'll take. Yes, you could overprice yourself, but if he goes for it and it comes out lower, you'll have made his day.

NO WHINERS ALLOWED   You don't do anyone any favors by agreeing to a figure lower than you want. As soon as it starts getting a little sticky or more complicated than you pictured, you'll start resenting it, and it'll show (a lesser-known corollary of Murphy's Law states: *The likelihood that a writing job will turn into a nightmare is inversely proportional to the amount of the fee*).

But whenever you decide on a fee, live with it, even if it ends up taking longer. That's being a professional. If you took the job for less because business was slow, tough. Suck it up and be a pro. Remember, the client couldn't care less that you miscalculated. She just wants the job done well, on time, and for the agreed-upon amount. Period.

Got "Aggravation Fees"?

FLCW Devon Ellington (**www.fearlessink.com**) writes, "I add 'aggravation fees' to my quotes when I run across these scenarios:

1) In initial talks, clients make red-flag statements like, 'This is a short, easy project; shouldn't take much time,' or 'I'd do it myself if I had the time.' It clues you in that the job will take much more time and effort than they claim.

2) Clients with no clear of idea of what they want, meaning they'll constantly change course during the project, which adds up to more time.

3) Projects which will be vetted by a committee. I always ask for a single 'point person,' but that's not always the reality. And if it isn't, it'll always mean more time.

If I decide to take on the job anyway, adding an 'aggravation fee' addresses the question: *How much is it worth to me to work for this person, still be fair to the client, but also make sure I'm being paid enough so I won't resent the project?'*

DIRECTION CHANGES = FEE CHANGES   Say you're writing a brochure for ABC Company. You agree on a concept and direction and get to work. You write all this beautiful copy, and then he says, "We decided we want to scrap that concept and do this one instead." Or, "We'd like to add these three new sections." *No problem, Mr. Client. Of course, we'll need to recalculate the fee.* And then you dust off your estimating formula. This is *non-negotiable*. And frankly, 99.9% of clients will get this.

If it's just a small addition on a big juicy project, maybe you cut them a break. If you do, make sure they know that. Otherwise, they might get the idea it's S.O.P., which it most certainly is not. But, in the interest of long-term work, and making a good impression, I've often eaten a few hours, and the goodwill it can engender pays dividends.

REVISIONS NOT ALL INCLUDED   Mentally factor in time for revisions, and note on your estimate (see "Bid Letter" ahead) the number of revisions you've included. Consider how long revisions may take and add that number of hours to your quote. Count on 10–15% of what it took you to get that first draft done. Don't think for a second if you say "Revisions are included" without specifying how many, that clients *won't* keep editing endlessly, soliciting the opinions of everyone from their vice-presidents down to the janitor along the way. They will. They have. And why wouldn't they?

By the way, don't itemize revision time with a specific number of hours on your estimate. What if you nail your first draft, with only minor tweaks the client can do himself? You risk him saying, "Well, since you didn't use those hours, we'll deduct them from the bill," essentially penalizing you for doing a good job.

Most FLCW's (including moi) provide two rounds of revisions. I've gone beyond that rarely—usually when the client changed direction, in which case, we added more hours. Occasionally, clients have wanted additional rounds beyond two. If it was minor stuff, I usually did it for free. But that was my choice, *not* "how it's done." Your call. Balance being an "easy-to-work-with" copywriter with getting paid what you're owed.

Speaking of revisions, know this: There's no such thing as "perfect" copy. So, while one could technically revise forever, each change only ensures the copy will be *different*, not necessarily *better*. It's a sickness. You end up obsessed, searching for the elusive perfect line. It probably doesn't exist. If it's good, leave it alone. As a rule, the more I edit something past the "good" stage, the worse it gets.

LOWER RATES FOR MEETING/RESEARCH TIME? The industry standard is to charge the same for research, background reading, or meeting time as for writing, and overwhelmingly, clients know that. The ones who push for a fee cut either aren't experienced or are hoping you're not. That said, there are few ironclad rules in this business, especially in the beginning. If they ask (rare), simply respond matter-of-factly that you do get full rate for those activities, and that little discussion should slink quietly away.

If it doesn't, say something along these lines: *When sitting in a first meeting, it's some of the most focused thinking I'll do on the project. Ideas are sprouting, concept directions are popping, a "voice" is forming, and all this is crucial to the final product.*

Same for research/background reading time, which usually means reading the material they've given you to get up to speed. While reading, I'm creatively percolating. That's worth your full rate. Of course, if my clients *could* see me in "concepting" mode, doodling in the dust on my desktop, making funny drum-like noises on my cheek, or humming "I Can See Clearly Now" in hopeful anticipation of wildly creative visions, they'd probably want a discount. Yet, those little M.O.'s are crucial to the process.

SHORT COPY, MORE TIME A marketing communications manager for a technology firm offered these estimating tips: "Writers need to be very clear with clients that writing short copy can actually be harder and take longer than writing long copy. They also need to explain that reading corporate literature and research is on the clock." Thank you.

Meaning, if someone's handing you a stack of stuff to read along with an hour-long interview with an article source, and expecting a one-page article, not only is research time billed at your full rate but writing one page might very well take longer than writing two or three. Make your life easier by asking enough questions of the client to get a solid sense of what they want to see in that one page.

Should you charge for travel to and from meetings? Generally speaking, yes. I hedge a bit, because regular clients usually get a break. For example, a 90-minute meeting and 30 minutes travel each way might end up being a total of two hours. Your call.

TIME FOR A RAISE? Consider this: If you bill 20 hours a week (about average once you're established), then your hourly rate times 1,000 is your annual income (20 hours x 50 weeks). $70/hr = $70K. $80/hr = $80K. When the time is right, don't let your own hesitance in charging a mere $10 more an hour take $10K out of your pocket. If your portfolio and reputation are growing, and you're getting no resistance to your rates, give yourself a $10–15 an hour raise, again, just for your internal calculations.

Ohio FLCW Jennifer Hodroge affirmed this in an email sent some time back: "A recent direct-mail postcard campaign (as you suggested in your book) resulted in a nice 100-hour contract. While putting the proposal together, and debating the hourly rate, I got your ezine and read about not being 'shy' to charge what you're worth. So, I quoted $15 more than I'd been charging and won the contract—and for $1,500 more!" Yowza.

Got Rate-Hike Anxiety?

I swallowed dryly, looked at my client, and declared, "I'm planning on raising my rates to $75 an hour (from $65). Would there be any problem with that?" Very commanding. "Actually," he replied, "we'd have a big problem with that." Okay, fine. I kept him at $65. That was years ago. Eventually I bumped his firm up to $85 (and $125 recently), but my initial stab at giving myself a raise was pretty lame.

An infinitely stronger (and easier!) way to do so, and the best I've heard, comes from marketing maven Marcia Yudkin, in her 6/07/06 "Marketing Minute" (subscribe at: **http://www.yudkin.com/markmin.htm**). Enjoy.

> *If I had snake-oil ambitions, I'd create a five-step process for successfully raising prices. First, work up elaborate reasons for the rise and sprinkle in heartfelt apologies. Express hope that clients will forgive you for this audacious step. Then, oh so gingerly, lay the foundation for your news, and so on. This report would sell.*

> *I know that because when I tell clients who are teetering from unprofitability how actually to raise their fees, they do not want to believe me.*

> *What's best: Make a simple, factual statement, like, "As of September 1, our fees will be $2,250 for Service A and $3,870 for Service B." No explanation, no apology. Then go on to the next item of business. That's it!*

> *Unless you're a public utility, you don't owe customers information about how you arrive at prices or why you run your business as you do. Apologies for prices position you as subservient to clients, rather than equal. Apologies also invite opinions and objections rather than the acceptance that follows the factual announcement ninety-nine times out of a hundred.*

What could be simpler? But it all starts with a belief that you're a professional, and deserving of professional compensation.

For those uncomfortable with the above direct approach, here are a few other suggestions: 1) *The Grace Period:* Send a note to clients announcing a rate hike some months in the future, letting them know you'll charge your current rates until then; or 2) *The Voucher:* Announce a rate hike in the immediate future, but allow clients to enjoy your current rates for their next job, whether that comes before or after the increase.

NEED WRITTEN CONTRACTS? Since starting in 1994, I've signed less than six formal contracts of any kind (and almost all came from the clients), and I've only had one—that's one, folks—situation where I got burned on a deal and arguably, a contract might not have even helped. Maybe it's my trusting nature, maybe a more casual attitude in the South —who knows? If things are more buttoned-up in your part of the country, then go with that prevailing climate.

Use a more formal contract when dealing with a new client or if the job is fairly large, complicated, and multi-faceted. But for your "regulars," formal contracts for each job aren't only unnecessary but will likely be insulting. If you have a good working relationship, and you've always been paid, what's the problem? And don't worry about the big Fortune 500. They've got the money. They didn't get big and successful by hosing their vendors. A more common problem with the big boys is slow payment. Smaller unknown firms are more worrisome. Get your "upfronts," and use this...

THE BID LETTER For most jobs, a "bid letter" is a perfectly adequate "contract," spelling out basic project parameters: fee, timing of payments, what the project entails, what's included for that price, and timetable. Instruct the client to sign it (so he can't come back and say you never told him X, Y or Z), make a copy, and fax or scan/email the original back to you. Here's a sample (note disclaimer at end):

WriteInc.
March 12, 2008
Mr. James Smith – Manager, Field Communications
ABC Wireless Products and Services
1234 Perimeter Canyon Parkway
Atlanta, Georgia 34567

Dear James,

It was a pleasure meeting you today and I appreciate the opportunity to bid on the ABC Wireless sales brochure project. As requested, this is a formal estimate for copywriting services. For the discussed tri-fold brochure (8½" x 11" with two vertical folds), I would like to offer a bid of $1,200–1,400.

This figure includes all concepting and copywriting, two rounds of revisions, and one additional meeting, if necessary. Additional revisions or meeting time would incur an extra charge.

One-half of the estimated fee range ($650) would be paid up-front prior to the beginning of work with the balance due and payable upon completion and delivery of final approved copy. Assuming I receive the up-front deposit by March 19, 2008, I will turn in a first draft by April 2, 2008. Once revisions have been returned, I will turn around the subsequent draft within three days or less.

Should you choose to terminate the project at any time and for any reason, as the writer, I will be entitled to full payment for all time invested to that point.

With experience both in writing marketing brochures and for the telecommunications industry, I feel confident in delivering a quality product that hits the mark. Given 15+ years of sales and marketing experience, I bring the crucial "write to sell" mindset to the table, always focused on powerfully and effectively communicating to your target audience.

Please sign below, make and keep a copy for yourself, and fax the signed original back to me at 404-987-6543. Thanks again and I look forward to working with you soon.

Sincerely,

Peter Bowerman

I have read, understood, and agree to the above bid:

_____

James Smith
Manager, Field Communications
ABC Wireless Products and Services

Date _____

THE PRECEDING IS NOT A LEGALLY APPROVED DOCUMENT. USE IT FOR GUIDELINE PURPOSES ONLY. I AM NOT AN ATTORNEY AND WILL NOT BE HELD RESPONSIBLE FOR ANY PROBLEMS, HASSLES, OR OTHER MESSES THAT YOU GET YOURSELF INTO OR THAT MAY ARISE FROM USING THIS DOCUMENT. CONSULT YOUR OWN ATTORNEY AND COVER YOUR OWN BUTT. I'M VERY SERIOUS. GOT IT? GOOD.

●   ●   ●

More in-depth contracts 🗄 may be a good idea for much larger jobs and in many cases, as mentioned, those contracts will come from the clients themselves. I've signed more client-generated contracts than ones I created myself.

Caveat: you'll notice that the bid letter calls for an upfront deposit before beginning work. While I've often walked out of an initial meeting with a deposit check (as a rule, clients will follow your lead; if you tell them an upfront deposit is required, they'll likely give you one), it won't always happen. If the client's established and comes with good references, maybe you bill them for the deposit, but start work before the check is in hand. The accounting systems of most firms—especially the big ones—are usually just not set up to cut a check on the spot or even have one in a week. So, be flexible.

Also note I don't mention any hourly rates in the letter. You're quoting a flat fee (with a range), based on internal calculations you've made based on your hourly rate. If they sign off on the flat fee, and it takes you less time than you calculated, you make more per hour. If it takes you longer, you make less. You'd bill the referenced "additional revisions or meeting time" at your hourly rate, but by wording it, "would incur an extra charge" as opposed to "at my hourly rate," you don't invite "What's-your-hourly-rate?" inquiries.

RUSH FEES Client calls you on Tuesday, needing a project done by Wednesday or Thursday. Or calls Friday, needing it Monday or Tuesday. Either scenario calls for an additional "rush fee" of 20 to 30 percent of the project cost (or more, if you can get it). That's how the world works.

Bidding & Billing When Working With GD's

A few FYI's about estimating and billing projects when teaming with graphic designers (GD's) or other MM's. There are no hard and fast rules; it can unfold in several ways.

Graphic Designer As Client

When the GD is my direct client—meaning, she, not the end user (EU), is paying me—my estimate typically amounts to little more than a fee range (e.g., $1500-1700, $2900-3300, etc.) she plugs into her master estimate to the EU. No contract or bid letter necessary. PLUS: Underscores how easy our job is. MINUS: To get paid, the GD typically has to bill the EU for partial payment, which adds time. And most GD's will play the "I-can't-pay-you-till-I-get-paid" game, which, while crummy, for one-person GD shops, is usually valid.

End User As Client

When the EU is the client for both you and the GD (i.e. they're paying you both), estimates are likely to be separate, with respective fees clearly delineated. Ideally, they should be combined into one document (or at least one email), to make it easy on the client. Even better, if the GD is using an attractive graphic frame for her estimate (often the case, and to be sent as a PDF), she can add your pages to her document, and make it all nice and pretty. Still distinct numbers, but representing a unified proposal, which reinforces the team aspect.

In this case, you'd both be billing the EU separately. Sure, the EU would probably prefer one bill, but in my experience, they're generally fine with two.

PLUS: When you're done, you can bill your piece, even if the design stuff drags on. MINUS: Your proposal needs to be a bit more involved, but a "bid letter" should still suffice (just lose the signoff line, and have just one signoff line for the whole proposal).

If a GD wants you to work directly through her (how I've worked with my main GD for 15-plus years), it's often because they plan on "marking you up" to the EU (charging the EU more for your services than you're charging them—standard procedure), and you may not have a choice in the matter. But if you *do* have a choice, opt for billing the EU directly. That way, you're only one layer away from your check, not two.

"Spec" Work—Yay or Nay? "Spec" work (speculative) typically means, 1) doing a project for which you'll be paid *only* if the client is satisfied, or 2) you're one of several writers "auditioning" for a job by providing a free sample of work. The client then decides who gets hired (and paid), and if you're chosen, you usually get paid for the sample work as well. Those not chosen receive nothing. Both extremely rare scenarios.

The first? Paid upon client satisfaction? Forget it. That's a sucker's game: it's far too easy (and common) for the client to *publicly* never be satisfied, and then privately use it later. With no paperwork, you have no recourse. *And* it sets a lousy precedent with client as dog and you as fire hydrant.

The second scenario? Why would any freelancers subject themselves to such indignity? After all, the creative industry is solidly against it, asserting that giving away anything devalues the profession and makes it harder for everyone to be taken seriously. True enough. *And* I have some philosophical objections to their stance. After all, times arise…

Obviously, if you're swamped, you don't need to do spec work. But say business is slow and you've got a shot at a big project (or a new arena of work) by investing a few hours of time. For many, bottom line considerations win out. And arguably, the mere existence of spec work could be evidence of a greater supply of writers than jobs. The libertarian in me says spec work isn't right or wrong. It just is. You do your thing and I'll do mine. Just don't decide for me. But, remember, *The Las Vegas Rule* applies: *Don't spend anything you're not willing to lose.*

Related to this is the idea of not giving away your creativity. Don't let clients milk you for more than they've contracted for (or *before* they've even contracted you, under the guise of "seeing where you're going with this thing"…). If they want the tour, they need to pay the toll. This is all part of developing a "well-fed writer" mentality. Your clients will only value your work to the extent that you do.

Kill Fees A note about the clause in the bid letter regarding payment in the event of project termination. "Kill fees" apply more to magazine writing: If a magazine kills a green-lighted and completed story for some reason (change of the issue's theme, new editor, Paris Hilton scoop, whatever), the writer typically gets a kill fee of roughly 15–40% of the original fee as sort of a consolation prize. In our business, if a project gets scrapped for any reason, you're entitled to be paid for the time you've put in thus far, and a full fee if you finished it.

I have colleagues who take it a step further: if a project is killed partway through, they bill for the *whole* job—and generally get it. Their rationale? *I set aside the time for this job, and possibly turned away other work to do so. The chance of filling this slot now is slim, so I'm entitled to the whole fee.* I agree. This attitude is just one more part of an overall mindset of valuing yourself as a writer and expecting clients to do the same.

Okay. Let's turn to billing, and tracking down your money…

Checks in the Mail…

A friend once shared a horror story about getting way behind on her billing because she was so busy (incredibly dumb reason; we're here to make money, so make collections a high priority). Anyway, by the time she finally got around to billing this one client for a bunch of work done months before, the company was tanking and her main contact had bailed. She went though hell getting paid, ultimately taking a bunch less than was coming to her. *Moral: Keep current on collections.*

When are you done with a job? When you ask the client if you can bill it and she says "Sure." Simple. But always ask. Don't assume. If you're on a PC, get a simple invoicing program like *My Invoices and Estimates Deluxe*, about $40. It makes billing easy (so you'll do it) and makes you look professional. On a Mac? Check out *Billings*. Both programs are quirky but solid once you break the code. If you have *Acrobat*® (or a free/low-cost PDF-making program like **www.PrimoPDF.com** or **www.cutepdf.com**), turn invoices into PDF's, email them, and shave two to three days off the payment cycle.

TIP: On any invoicing program, you input the terms: how many days the client has to pay. Put 15 days. If a company's system pays in 30 or 60, you'll get paid then. If it's flexible, you might get paid in 10. But you won't if you don't ask.

THE HARDWORKING INVOICE Georgia FLCW Terri Keller (**www.terrikeller.com**) offers up a great tip for turning invoices into selling tools. Clients will often cubbyhole you by the kinds of work you've done for them, not realizing you offer other services. Terri's strategy underscores the truism discussed earlier about it always being easier to land additional work from a current client than to find a new one.

She writes: "On every invoice, in an unobtrusive, nicely bordered, eye-catching square at the bottom, I put what I do. It's also on the back of my business card."

It reads:

> *Your business is much appreciated! If you should need help in the future, I provide the following services: advertising, annual reports, articles, booklets, brochures, business and personal communications, case studies, company and personal histories, creative concepting, executive profiles, newsletters, press/news releases, research, surveys, websites/content, and photography (to supplement written materials).*

> *Call today for a free consultation!*

> *We'll bring out the best in your business!*

MONEY ON THE TABLE Getting money upfront is standard in this business, though mostly with new clients and for larger jobs. Here are the basic rules:

1. **New Clients:** Regardless of the dollar amount of the job, get a third to a half up-front. If they balk, politely explain this is the industry standard and that, once you've worked together a bit, you'd be happy to bill them at project's end. Most won't have a problem with this. If it's a well-known company, maybe you skip it.

2. **Large Jobs ($2,500+):** A third to a half up-front. Good clients are unfazed by this request, though you may choose to let regular clients slide.

It's common to invoice bigger jobs in stages, because of longer time frames. Some (myself included) will bill in thirds, others in halves. With thirds, you get a third up-front, another third at first draft, and the final third upon completion. With halves, skip the first draft payment and get it on the front and back ends. Thirds are more comfortable for clients, who might be a tad nervous about paying for half a job before getting anything.

Invoice Before Starting? Get Paid Before Finishing?

Canadian FLCW Pete Savage (**www.petesavage.com**) shared his strategy for speeding up payment. On Option A, remember, as discussed, if it's a big household-name entity (i.e., you *will* get paid) whose accounting system likely can't cut a check that fast, having check in hand before starting work may not be possible *or* necessary. He writes:

"At the end of my agreements, just above the client sign-off line, I have two check boxes, with this copy:

For your convenience, two methods of invoicing are available. Please choose your preferred option:

Option A: Invoice us in two installments. 50% of the total project fee is invoiced now. The remaining balance will be invoiced upon project completion or 30 days from project start date (whichever comes first) and is payable net 15 days. Work for this project begins upon my receipt of this initial deposit check.

Option B: Invoice us once. 100% of the Total Project Fees amount is invoiced now, payable in 30 days.

"The result? It works like a charm and has sped up payments tremendously (15 to 30 days faster, depending on how you're currently invoicing). The client feels they have a choice, but both options are great for cash flow. To my surprise, some clients choose Option B. It's great to get permission to send an invoice for work you haven't even started *and* receive full payment for projects that aren't even complete!"

TRACKING THE DEADBEATS You mean, not everyone pays on time? No. Is it common? No, which is one of the best things about this business: high client caliber. By the way, I've always gotten paid—eventually—on every single job I've ever done. In this business, 30 days is the rule. Plenty will pay sooner, and a relatively small number will quite shamelessly cruise right past that guidepost. With ad agencies, sorry to say, 60–90 days is the rule. So, keep that in mind in light of the next discussion.

As a classic conflict avoider, I'm pretty laid-back about payment, and it's never come back to haunt me. Pick your comfort zone. If you're snail-mailing invoices, tack on an extra week in your mind for back-and-forth mail time. Bottom line, don't get all weird if the check doesn't show up exactly 30 days from the date printed on the invoice.

SECOND NOTICE Past 45 days, you've got a few choices. Send another bill, highlight the invoice date with a marker and attach a nice little note: "Thanks in advance for taking a minute to handle this." Or "Hope things are going well. When you get a minute, can you take care of this?" and end both notes with, "Look forward to working with you again soon." In most cases, that should get the job done.

Option two: call. With big companies, it's easier because you'll be dealing with the accounting department, not the person who can hire you again (which can make it awkward). Ask for accounts payable, and say, "Hi, Mary, this is Joe Blow, with Joe Blow Writes. Just checking on an invoice that's at about 45 days. It's invoice #13579, dated 4/17/08." Mary should be able to give you a good idea when it's coming.

SMALLER IS TRICKIER As discussed, one excuse for late payment you'll hear endlessly from smaller MM's: "We can't pay you till we get paid." Doesn't sound any more fair the hundredth time you hear it than it did the first. True, smaller design firms or ad agencies often don't have the resources to front all their vendors' money before they've received their money. That said, I've had plenty do just that.

The general consensus among my colleagues? It's B.S. If finished work was billed 30 days ago, you should get paid. Period. *And* plenty of companies will still pay you when they get paid. Sure, you can play hardball, demand your money and run the risk of alienating a client. Or you can roll with the punches, and ask that they keep you apprised.

One large design firm client of mine always plays that game. Sure, it sucks, but I've worked with them since 1994, and have always gotten paid eventually, so I leave it alone. Others might call me a pushover, doormat, or sucker. I'm okay with that. Pick your battles. There are worse things in life than well-paying, slow-paying clients. You decide what you'll put up with and what you won't.

OVER 60 DAYS? Once it goes over two months with a small company, the key is polite persistence. Be nice but pin them down as much as you can as to time frames. Where I lose patience fast is when someone avoids me, doesn't return my calls, etc. I can be exceptionally forgiving if someone's giving me regular updates.

. . .

Okay, now that we know what (and *how*) to charge, and how to get those nice checks coming in regularly, let's turn to networking: a bunch of strategies for meeting and staying plugged in to the people who can put money into your pocket...

Chapter 10

It started at a party over the onion dip. He was the fiancé of a friend of mine—and the owner of a small but growing commercial and residential security system provider. When he found out what I did, he chuckled and said, *Really. Hmmm. I've been working on a brochure for my company and not making much headway.*

We swapped cards, and $2,500 worth of brochure work later, I worked on a few other small projects for him. All from a social contact.

(NOTE: For an in-depth exploration of how this project unfolded (and it was an unusual one) along with many lessons learned and unusual marketing strategies employed, look in the *The Deluxe Well-Fed Tool Box* for "Multiple-Version Brochure Case Study" under "Real-World Case Studies.")

Fast-forward a few months. I get a call from a friend who works for a graphic design firm. Why I never contacted her before is beyond me. Her first question revealed how sorry a job I'd done of letting her—and no doubt others—know exactly what I did for a living: *Do you do anything besides technical writing?* she asked. Huh? How about anything *but* technical writing? Bottom line, I was hired to rework huge chunks of a big (household name) client's web site. Another $2,500.

HIDDEN CONNECTIONS Most everyone you know works for some company. Every one of them has a need—IF they want to stay competitive —to be constantly refining, improving, enhancing, growing and building on their body of written communications, as it appears in a variety of collateral materials (internal, external, print and web-based).

Have you tapped your social network? It's easy to compartmentalize our lives —put work here and friends there—and it can seem vaguely cheesy to hit up friends for business. Yet if those friends like and respect you, why wouldn't they want to help you out? Wouldn't you? More importantly, how many writers do they know? If you prefer warm calls to cold ones (who doesn't?), don't overlook the potential goldmine in your address book.

A few caveats on the "friend-ly" approach to prospecting. Be subtle. Remember, you should get the work *not* because you're someone's friend, but because you're competent and reliable. If you're new to the business and unproven in your friends' eyes, ask if they'd be comfortable steering you to the right person or department *and* to be honest with you if they're not.

By authentically giving them all the space in the world to say *No*, you increase the chance that they'll say *Yes* and, more importantly, preserve the friendship, regardless of their decision. If you have a web site, invite them to check it out to boost their confidence in you. Remember, their butt's on the line if you're hired and it doesn't go well. (Check out *The Deluxe Well-Fed Tool Box* ebook 📖 for a sample "Email/Letter to Friends and Business Contacts.")

BE COOL If you find yourself in a social/casual business setting—party, association meeting, networking function—softly seize the moment. Introduce yourself, swap cards, get the okay to give the person a call (and do just that within a few days at the most), then drop the subject. At a straight social function, say lightheartedly, *I promise, I'm not trying to turn this party into a business meeting*...and then continue as above with your story (see "Elevator speeches" ahead).

It starts with the right mindset: being open to opportunities, wherever they may be. Don't compartmentalize your life: *This is where I* work *or* socialize *or* work out, *but not where I might find business.* You never know. And don't just react—be proactive. Think of the communities and associations you belong to—full of people who already know and are comfortable with you—and contact them. One reader used her university alumni directory—a "background of relatedness"—to let fellow classmates know what their old pal was up to. A more receptive "warm-call" community. Why not?

DEEP NETWORKING Sometime back, I mentored a budding FLCW in California who, after three months of excellent progress, had yet to make his first cold call. He'd tapped fifteen years of contacts from software sales. He called the ones he knew, got five names from them, then five from them, etc. As long as he could drop somebody's name, even if he didn't know *that* person, it wasn't a cold call. One northeastern FLCW wrote me, saying, "I've not made any cold calls yet and have more work than I can handle."

Speaking of the above approach, if you get a referral from a client and make the call, here's what San Diego FLCW Jake Sibley suggests:

> *[If] you get the "barbed-wire" receptionist who asks, "And what is this regarding," simply say, "I was referred by Anthony Jones over at Advanced Wireless." Once you get to the prospect, if he or she asks how you know Anthony, just say "Oh, he and I were discussing the possibility of my doing some work for Advanced Wireless." The truth is you just cold called Advanced Wireless five minutes before and you don't really know Anthony from Adam, but so what?*

Anne Melfi, of Atlanta, talks about networking over cheese and crackers at a political get-together. Upon exchanging and viewing cards, the woman declared her need for marketing materials for a sideline catering company. Later that same month, Anne swapped contact info with a woman in a doctor's waiting room, landing a paying project from "a friend of a friend of a friend of a friend."

Mary Cvetan of Pittsburgh found that even volunteer work unrelated to her writing business pays—literally:

> *For the past 11 years, I've volunteered at a crisis/suicide hotline. One day, just two months into my freelance business, I was asked to evaluate some freshly trained new volunteers— a four-hour job. I grumbled but agreed and was paired with a woman named Gail, with whom I had a great time chatting.*

A few weeks later, I saw Gail again at the annual volunteer dinner and she invited me to sit with her and her husband, Tony, who asked me what I did for a living. I told him, and after a few moments of silence, he said, 'I have a name for you.'

Turns out Tony was the former big-wig of marketing at a huge local company. The following day, I called his former employee, who invited me in and gave me a very substantial project—one that I continue to show on sales calls today. Everyone knows the company, and the piece gives me major credibility.

Utah-based FLCW Chad Nielsen underscores the power of networking to lead to both paying jobs and valuable barter:

I've obtained two accounts from the guys I play pick-up basketball with. One's a real estate developer who needed PR support during a nine-month contract to run a large home-owners association. The other is a dentist involved with some cutting-edge technology who needs help getting the word out. I have a family of four so there will be no exchange of cash, but it's a great gig nonetheless. Make sure everybody knows who you are and what you do. Yes, even your friends!

Michele Ryan of Atlanta, during a conversation over margaritas with some of her neighbors, mentioned her new career. A year later, she explains, *I received a call from one of the lunch bunch with a local county Chamber. Several staff cutbacks, including their marketing communications person, left them with a daunting workload. My friend remembered our conversation and recommended me.* Her proposal for a steady five to seven hours a week at a healthy hourly rate was quickly and eagerly accepted.

LET 'EM KNOW WHAT YOU DO... Everyone knows a doctor, attorney, accountant, real estate agent or hair stylist. But a writer? Most people don't know many writers of any kind, much less a commercial writer. So, tell the world, and chances are excellent it'll be you that'll spring to mind if they cross paths with someone needing a writer. Even more reason to have **www.yourname.com** as your URL (*and* to hand out extra cards).

Thailand-based FLCW Dave Lowe seconds that motion, writing:

Though based in Bangkok, work takes me to Singapore and Vietnam frequently, as I used to live in both places. While in Singapore, I gave a business card to a friend who runs a *health club there. He didn't even need writers, but put it on his desk and went to lunch. A director for a new resort chain in Vietnam saw it and eventually I got $2,000 of work on three brochures and a web site. Hand out cards to everyone!*

Elevator Speeches & Verbal Taglines

The Networking Function (cue "Jaws" music...). For many, the idea of striding up to total strangers, introducing yourself, and discussing what you do is positively terrifying. Fine. You're not doomed to failure if you don't hit all these functions (I didn't), but getting more comfortable with the process will hasten the business-building process.

First step for in-person networking success: a good 15-second (or less) "elevator speech": a memorized—but naturally delivered—script, briefly describing what you do, and short enough to, theoretically, be delivered during the course of an elevator ride with a prospect. Come up with an even shorter version—a "verbal tagline"—for purely social functions. Here are a few good, real-world elevator speeches and verbal taglines:

I help companies become more profitable by helping them craft clear, concise, and effective sales and marketing messages in brochures, ads, newsletters, direct mail campaigns, web sites, or any other information-delivery vehicle.

Through creative, strategic copywriting services, I help my clients enhance their image in their industry and increase bottom-line profits.

I help my clients create and maintain a powerful brand presence in the marketplace through comprehensive and ongoing marketing campaigns.

I help businesses create training materials recognized as the most readable and user-friendly of any on the market.

I'm a really great writer with a little experience in everything from poetry, greeting cards, articles, a brochure here and there, an ad or two, and a bunch of other pretty cool stuff. Call me and we'll look in my bag of tricks and figure out how I can help you. I'm excited! Aren't you?

A little levity there. Though seriously, visit some writers' web sites and that's about how it sounds. Note that all the previous examples were specific *and* spoke to things important to most any audience. People really don't care about what you can do—just what you can do for *them*.

Features and benefits again. Instead of, *I write marketing brochures, ad copy and newsletters* (that's about YOU—features), try, *I help companies communicate more effectively in their marketing materials* (that's about THEM—benefits).

WHAT'S YOUR STRONG SUIT? At some point, figure out the specific talents and gifts you bring to the market. Maybe your specialty is converting complex language into simple, accessible copy. Perhaps you're a master of slogans or taglines. Or a maestro of compelling direct mail campaigns. Or THE "go-to" person for effective copy for the (blank) industry. Over time, you'll likely want to move in the direction of what you do well *and* enjoy the most. Make sure the world knows about it via an elevator speech.

For those of you groaning, rolling your eyes, and thinking about how you've become an obnoxious salesperson, complete with a pitch and everything, consider this: *you already have an elevator speech for your current or former role in life.* But this is different, isn't it? Let's probe a bit deeper here; it begins to get at a big fear of FLCW's starting out.

THIS TIME, IT'S PERSONAL Your present (or former) elevator speech likely allows you to merge your identity with that of your employer—stand behind the paternal pant legs, so to speak: *I'm a researcher at the CDC. I'm a reporter for the Sacramento Bee. I'm an English professor at Bowling Green. I'm an attorney with Dewey, Scroom & Howe.* Now, you're facing the world with nothing other than your own abilities to hide behind. Gee, maybe it's nothing more than a garden-variety identity crisis…

Before (or presently), you linked more of your identity than you'd probably care to admit to something *outside* of you. Now, it's just you. In the short run, it's like we're five, we've just taken off the training wheels, and we're wobbling a bit. An elevator speech is a good way to steady our nerves and start growing into this new identity of ours.

YOUR CHAMBER AWAITS Scope out your local Chamber of Commerce, which hosts a ton of networking functions—lunches, happy hours, monthly "grip 'n grins," etc. As Chambers differ vastly in makeup, fees and potential, visit as a guest before joining. In larger cities, count on paying at least $300 to join at the lowest level, which, realistically, is all a one-person shop needs. Sounds pricey, but one small job pays for it.

Like any networking opportunity, it's what you make it. Show up, get involved, look for opportunities to raise your visibility—whether it's speaking, contributing articles to a newsletter, volunteering, etc. As we've learned from the small-town folks, where joining Chambers is even more crucial, focus on building relationships and *serving*, as opposed to landing work. You'll come across as more genuine and, over time, the work *will* come.

AND OTHER GROUPS... Starting a business can be a difficult and often emotionally challenging process. It makes sense to find friends and allies on a similar path—people who want to share ideas and leads, and lend support as you all move forward. In Atlanta, I'm a member of *The Freelance Forum* (**www.freelanceforum.org**)—writers, graphic/web designers, photographers, illustrators, and others. For similar organizations in other major metros, see the list in Appendix A or just ask a few freelancers in your area.

SMART Networking...

All networking was not created equal. While I've heard plenty of Chamber/association networking success stories over the years (usually when people get actively involved in the organization, boosting their visibility), the "cattle call" networking event never did much for me—empirically or spiritually. Such events always feel so mercenary, full of mutual "objectifying": other attendees aren't humans, just potential sales.

WA graphic designer Mike Klassen guest-blogged (**www.wellfedwriter.com/blog**, 07/10/08) on this very subject, challenging FLCW's to rethink how they approach "networking," and offering up a few smart alternatives. Here's an excerpt...

The traditional Chamber networking event is typically promoted as a way to reach others with your products or services—in your case, writing. That'd be great if they promoted the event to everyone else as a way to hire you to write copy. But they don't, do they?

Nope. It's marketed as a way for everyone to sell what they have. For it to work, though, someone needs to be a buyer. But, *buying* something rarely enters anyone's mind.

Plus, many of these events are attended by small-business owners, most of whom can't afford our rates. To them, copywriting is an expense, not an investment. As long as they have spell-checking enabled on their PC, they'll tackle their writing tasks on their own.

Sure, there are success stories, but in my experience, and that of many colleagues, large scale successes (i.e., landing writing jobs) at "come one, come all" events are the exception, not the rule. Here's a better idea…

Look for networking events where those attending are likely to truly need you, already appreciate the value a writer brings, and *can* afford to pay you what you're worth. Let me give you two examples of what I call "off-the-beaten-path" networking:

A writer/marketer colleague attended a networking event for Americans and Canadians involved in cross-border trade, where attendees discussed trade regulations, security issues, marketing techniques, and more. While I'm sure sales were made, that wasn't the point of the event, and it wasn't marketed as such. Yet, arguably, everyone there placed a high value on writing skills in their efforts to promote and sell their products. My friend was the only one in the room providing that type of service. By the end of the evening, she had extremely high-quality leads to follow-up on.

A web site design colleague attended a seminar on online marketing. Attendees either had a product ready to market, or were looking to develop one. Since it was an "online" marketing event, how many attendees do you think might have had need for a web site designer? Like the other colleague I mentioned, this web designer left the event not only with lots of high-quality leads but also with a handful of immediate jobs.

So, yes, networking can occur anywhere. But if you're going to put your time into it, why not target networking events that increase your odds of success?

BUSINESS NETWORK INTERNATIONAL Speaking of "smart networking," BNI (Business Network International; **www.bni.com**) is an intriguing networking organization with 3,000 chapters worldwide. Each chapter (typically 20 to 30 members) meets weekly and *features only one member of any given profession*, so you won't be competing with fellow writers within your BNI chapter.

This is a serious organization, as evidenced by its membership fees (at press time, $350 for the first year, $275 for subsequent years). In addition to sharing ideas and contacts, members are *expected* to deliver referrals to other members, and anyone deemed to be a freeloader is punted.

Their motto: *Givers Gain.* Chapters differ in their potential, but the unique structure itself makes it worth a look.

VA FLCW (and BNI member) Randy Sly (**www.writeviewllc.com**) points out the hidden value of a BNI chapter: "When you're part of a group that's working hard to find you business, it's *not* about the people in the group and if *they* can hire you, but who they know who might be able to hire you."

Social Networking 101

LinkedIn. Facebook. Twitter. MySpace. Plaxo. Biznik. FastPitch. And more coming online daily (find all the above at **www.theirname.com**, except **www.fastpitchnetworking.com**).

True confession: as I write this, I'm not a member of any of the above. Gasp. I'm sure I'll break down at some point, but I haven't seen the light quite yet. Empirical results (i.e., paying clients/jobs) for social media sites are sketchy so far (though we'll explore one exceptional success story just ahead). But that mindset could be part of my problem…

Friend and Virginia FLCW Randy Sly, who maintains profiles on several social media sites, put it this way: "It's about relationships, not outcomes." Georgia FLCW James Palmer (**www.jamespalmer.com**) echoes that sentiment, observing, "It's a wait-and-see kind of thing. You can't have a desired outcome in mind like you could with a direct mail campaign. It's hard to track ROI. It's just another way of being visible."

PLANTING SEEDS A few days after posting a Facebook profile, Palmer got a promising writing inquiry from an Internet marketing firm after they visited his web site, and through his Biznik listing, he was contacted for a potential speaking gig. Nothing concrete, but connections forged. Same with Shel Horowitz, MA FLCW, business coach, and PR guru (**www.frugalmarketing.com**).

Shel notes: "Through my networking on Facebook and Plaxo, I've already been a guest on a business radio show; begun negotiations with a European meeting planner about speaking at his marketing conference in France; had an invitation to consider starting an East Coast office for a well-respected West Coast PR firm; and been networked to key people who are friends with people I've built relationships with. I haven't yet seen real dollars in my pocket, but I'm confident these or other opportunities will eventually gel."

STAYING IN TOUCH & IN SIGHT Dallas, TX FLCW Julie Ann Waid (www.waidwrites.com) sees LinkedIn as "a pretty great visibility tool. I've answered open questions posted within the network, and even got recruited into a group of expert writers and marketers after answering one. I've used it to contact decision makers; they've got a job section that lets you know when someone in your extended network works for a particular company, so you've got an instant 'warm' connection."

Says Colorado FLCW Casey Hibbard, "While I haven't gotten any jobs through LinkedIn, if your clients have a LI profile, it's a great way of keeping track of them as they move from job to job. Over time, that definitely *can* lead—even indirectly—to work.

Notes upstate NY FLCW Jill Gormley (www.jillgormley.com): "LinkedIn helps me get in touch with people I haven't heard from in years (e.g., college classmates), and has led to a couple of jobs. Also, I look at my connections' connections and contact directly those who seem to be likely prospects, using our mutual contact's name to 'warm up' the call or email. It eases the stress for a cold-call-phobe like me, has so far led to a couple of projects, and put me in the minds of folks likely to need me in the future."

ALL ABOUT VALUE NY FLCW Adam Farrah (www.technical-writer.net) offers up a useful mindset to adopt when dealing with networking sites: "The key operating concept to grasp with these sites is value. The juice in these sites is in *your ability to create value* for others in your network—present or future. That value can be as simple as pointing someone towards a web site that has some information they need, or as important as referring a potential client to a member of your network. And everything in between."

Adam offers up some good how-to resources for LinkedIn and Facebook users: **http://imonlinkedinnowwhat.com, http://facebookadvice.com**.

Like most things in life, put more in, get more out. As Adam puts it, "The way to be unsuccessful? Put up a profile and hunt around for people to ask for work. Or worse, do nothing and expect those who need your services to find you. The way to be successful (i.e., find clients) on these sites is to be valuable to your network. As you do, you display your knowledge and expertise and drive people to your profile."

QUANTIFIABLE SUCCESS In the case of LinkedIn and others, the true "put more in, get more out" strategy is to opt for their fee-based programs. Bay Area FLCW Kelly Parkinson (**www.copylicious.com**), who went the "upgrade" route, explains:

> *When I started my copywriting business, I didn't want to make cold calls. And direct mail, with its 2% response rate, seemed like a waste of money—and paper. One day I was clicking around LinkedIn's site and read that **InMails** (their proprietary emails) were 10 times more effective than cold calls. It seemed too good to be true, but for $50 a month and a guaranteed response, with the ability to cancel anytime, I was willing to give it a try. Turns out, **InMails** actually work. Over 6 months, I sent 32, got positive responses back from 13, and landed six new clients.*

Kelly notes that any changes in the LI system since she had her success could change results. And, she adds, "Obviously, results vary. LinkedIn isn't like applying a magical cream that instantly makes prospects fall in love with you. Specializing in an industry, having a website with relevant samples, and targeting the right people helps, too."

For all the details of Kelly's approach, visit **www.wellfedwriter.com/ sidedishes.shtml** and look for "How I used LinkedIn to get a 41% response rate & 6 new clients." While there, check out Kelly's great take on the mistakes people make on LinkedIn ("Are you making these mistakes on your LinkedIn profile?").

While social networking may as yet be short of definitive success stories, what's beyond debate is that people hire people, not just vendors, and prefer to hire those they know—either directly or through someone they know and trust. And if you can build your network, it *will* bear fruit eventually.

KICK-BUTT (AND FREE!) INDUSTRY REPORT My good friend, white paper guru and super-marketer Michael Stelzner (**www.whitepaper source.com**) released a killer free report on social media in late March of 2009: *Social Media Marketing Industry Report: How Marketers Are Using Social Media to Grow Their Businesses.* It contains the insights and input of 900 marketing folks about their use of social media in promoting their businesses. Check it out at **http://www.whitepapersource.com/ socialmediamarketing/report/**.

Your Own Writer's Group?

There are a lot of wonderful reasons—both personal and professional—for starting your own group. In a smaller market, where there may be fewer organized gatherings, it's a sound strategy for creating a community that can be nourishing on many levels.

On a Sunday morning in 1997, I welcomed six fellow scribes for brunch and the kickoff meeting of my newly-minted commercial writers group. During our collective portfolio "show-n-tell," we realized, to our delight, that we were all really good writers. A good omen. Well into our second decade now, there still six of us. I cannot recommend this idea highly enough. We were lucky—that we were all equally talented, and that we all really liked each other. It's comical watching the scheduling gymnastics we go through to find pot-luck dates that work for all of us; we all want all of us to be there.

THE STRUCTURE Those in larger metro areas can be choosier about who to invite than those in smaller markets. How to find these folks? I started with a few people I knew (and liked) through networking meetings, and trusted their judgment when they suggested others. Honesty is key. Ask around and pick only those you'd feel comfortable referring to your clients (which *will* probably happen). The last thing your reputation or bottom line needs is someone who could damage either—due to sloppy work or unethical behavior. Here's a list of criteria to keep in mind:

FRIENDS FIRST Gotta like each other. That means a minimum of egos, posturing, or the need to be the center of attention. Ideally, you want a group of quietly confident individuals with strong self-image.

EQUAL TALENTS Widely varying abilities can potentially be a spawning ground for insecurity, impatience, boredom, arrogance, and worse. Moreover, having an equally talented group allows you to focus outwardly on the possibilities and potential for the group, not inwardly on its limitations.

THE SAME DRUMMER Everyone should be an active, full-time commercial writer. A group with mixed disciplines and commitment levels might make for some interesting social interaction, but a more uniform profile will likely boost the professional paybacks of belonging. Consider including a range of expertise; our group has several generalists with varying industry experience plus a few more technically-oriented folks (*not* technical writers but high-tech marketing writers).

KEEP IT SMALL Six feels just about right (and not that it means anything, but there are three men and three women, three married and three single people). It could certainly work with a few more, but some of the benefits wouldn't be as easy to realize with a much larger group.

THE PAYOFFS At each of our Sunday pot-luck get-togethers, we eat well, talk shop, share ideas and leads, laugh and whine about clients, and have an all-round grand time. We've gotten a kick out of prospects who've called a number of us (we're visible in the same places) for possible jobs and said different things to each of us, not having a clue that we talk. But there are also serious professional payoffs that keep us together.

EVENING UP THE WORKLOAD Lead-sharing is a key benefit. Workloads vary over time. When swamped, it's great to be able to refer work to a trusted colleague. And clients appreciate it (and value you more) when you can offer a reliable referral when you're unavailable. And when you're a bit slack, it's nice to know you might get a job from one of your *compadres*, either because she's busy or because the project in question isn't a fit. I've referred plenty of leads to the group and have been sent plenty in return.

In fact, because I know folks just a phone call away with extensive experience in a particular industry, I may just steer those jobs to them, knowing they'll return the favor. Sure, sometimes I take the slightly "square peg" jobs if things are slower, but if I don't need it, now I've got options.

Needless to say, if we get referred to another's client, it remains their client. When I go on vacation, I leave contact info for two group members on my outgoing voice mail so clients have options. One member recovering from surgery referred a $5,000 direct mail campaign to me. Sweet. *And* was happy for me.

AN ONGOING SOUNDING BOARD Someone has a question about estimating a project (yes, even 20-year veterans don't have it all down pat). Or a dilemma about pricing a new category of work. Or wants to hear what the others know about XYZ Company. So we fire up the cyber-waves, share info, offer opinions, ease concerns, confirm suspicions, avoid troublesome clients and so much more. Truly invaluable—and the key is the small number. One message sent out to 25 people, with all the ensuing back-and-forth, would be irritating. With six, it's a few friends chatting.

THE POWER OF THE TEAM   While the following idea is strictly optional, a few years back, we took this group idea to a whole new level: a collaborative marketing campaign. We toyed with the idea three to four years earlier, but our hearts just weren't in it then. However, a tighter marketplace and increasing competition had us thinking about how we could package ourselves into a compelling offering for prospects and clients.

We'd often heard clients complain about the scarcity of good writers. Surely, we had a marketable product: a pool of six experienced, talented, and reliable writers who knew each other and each other's work. We could meet any client's need—individually or collectively. What a fabulous offer for the businessperson continually frustrated with incompetent, unprofessional, and unreliable scribes (and there are plenty). How much easier could life be, Mr. Prospect, with such a resource just a phone call away?

We created a name for our group—*Copyopolis*—and a series of six clever direct mail postcards (we each did one) leveraging the "six-great-writers-in-one-place" theme and put together a simple web site showcasing who we are and what we can provide (**www.copyopolis.com**).

The postcard mailings were spaced out according to a pre-determined schedule and sent to a list comprised of our own contacts and a list we bought. We've since done a bunch of advertising in targeted creative publications, which, when split six ways, is exceptionally budget-friendly. We approached one publication, offering to write occasional columns for the pub; we not only got a few hundred off our ad cost (a quarter-page four-color ad ran each of us $20–50 every two or three months), but added publicity as well.

Plus, we decided to kick in 3% of fees from any Copyopolis-generated project to a slush fund for any marketing/advertising expenses. You benefit, you share. Between expenses for printing, list, mailing, web site and ads, we've all invested around $2,000 each to date. We haven't gotten wildly rich, but we've all made back our investment at least two or three times over, if not more. And the 3% goes a long way to covering any ongoing costs, nicely limiting most out-of-pocket expenditures. Teaming truly is the way of the future.

Suggested Reading...

If you're already successfully working for yourself, *Free Agent Nation*, by Daniel H. Pink, offers up tons of great ideas to incorporate into your own business while reaffirming all the glorious benefits of self-employment. If you're still part of the salaried world but plotting your "jailbreak," the book will help you see yourself less as some intrepid pioneer, and more as a new player in a dynamic and rapidly expanding business sector—one with the power of a new consciousness on its side.

I love Pink's discussion of the vastly different paradigm of collaboration that exists in the salaried world vs. that in the free agent arena. In the former, you're thrown together with people you might very well not have chosen to work for or with. Coupled with the dog-eat-dog hierarchical structure of Corporate America, it's no wonder the average workplace brings out the worst in people (think "Dilbert" and "The Office"...).

By contrast, in the free agent arena, you build looser, more shifting alliances—totally by choice—based on mutual trust, benefit and complementary skills. You stay allied only as long as both sides win. Should someone betray that trust or prove unreliable, you simply sever the relationship. And that's how it is with graphic designers *and* my writer's group. We choose to stay partnered because the mutual rewards are clear and ongoing.

Okay, you're all hooked up now. So, let's switch gears. What if you're a cubicle dweller, or otherwise spoken for, job-wise, during some or all of the regular workweek? What are the chances of building the business part-time? Let's talk to some folks who have...

Chapter 11

The Question:

> *I've read your book and would love to carve out my own little island of freedom, flexibility, and financial security as a writer. But presently, I'm in a full-time job, working nine-to-five, five days a week. What's the answer?*

Having built the business full-time from Day One, I had to seek out those who'd built theirs part-time. Any way you cut it, it'll be tougher building your business this way than full-time—but if it's your only option, here are some ways to approach it.

- **Get Real.** Given the embryonic state of cloning technology, at present, you can only be in one place at a time. Being locked into a job during the same hours as your prospects and unavailable to take business calls makes things more difficult.

- **Get Honest.** Don't go out of your way to volunteer it, but if asked, be honest with people about your part-time status, and that you're best reached by email or after hours—even if it turns some clients off (and it will). And if you're earning a full-time salary in your 9-5 job, put in a full day's work, and if your budding writing biz takes time away from it, make it up after hours or on weekends.

- **Get a Web Site.** Crucial for *anyone* starting this business today, but mandatory for part-timers. A web site is like someone minding the store while you're out—which you'll be most of the working day. Make sure you have a decent number of good samples loaded up. It's hard enough building a business part-time without a weak portfolio working against you as well.

- **Get Smart.** If you can't make calls during the day, the obvious second choice is email prospecting. Build a list of target prospects through your city's *Book of Lists* (**www.amcity.com**), Chamber of Commerce listings, or other business directories that provide email addresses—obviously not possible with the Yellow Pages. If you want to target a particular industry, compile a list of companies, visit their sites, and contact key decision makers that way.

- **Get LinkedIn.** Or hooked up with other social networking sites like Plaxo, Facebook, etc. Virtual networking—free of time and space limitations—can be a great strategy for those with limited real-time availability. Given how exposed you are on sites like this, it's best when your full-time employer knows what you're up to. If you're not ready to come clean, then tread lightly, if at all.

- **Get Personal.** As discussed, the catchword with email prospecting is *personalize*. Spamming (i.e., unsolicited, impersonal bulk email) is just not worth it in terms of poor returns and bad PR. Send brief, personal notes to specific people, providing a link to your site (i.e., samples), and again, be honest about your time limitations. If you can find an email address, you might use the strategy discussed earlier: calling after hours, knowing you'll get voice mail, and then leaving a brief message stating who you are and that you'll be sending a follow-up email with a link to your site. And after hours, who knows who might answer the phone? It's often decision-makers—and overworked ones at that.

- **Get Flexible.** Unless you're planning on going full-time cold turkey at some point in the future, something's gotta give in your schedule. Try to work some flexibility into your schedule: an earlier/later arrival/departure to free up part of a day, a few days off a week, or telecommuting that allows you to do your FT job tasks after hours, freeing up prime-time hours for your growing writing gig.

- **Get Out There.** Try to attend after-hours networking functions—ideally, gatherings of folks in your industries of expertise—and where you might be the only writer. Hand out cards, and keep the radar up.

- **Get Outta Town.** As discussed, plenty of FLCW's pursue clients outside their main geographic area. If you're an east- or west-coaster, pursuing clients on the opposite coast can give you a three-hour working window before or after your normal workday to conduct business. So, keep that option open, especially if you've decided to pursue an industry with limited local prospects.

•   •   •

My First Test Case

Jim Meadows from Kansas City, Missouri (**www.jimfreelance.com**) contacted me several years back after reading *TWFW*. With 23 years of varied business experience under his belt, Jim was launching a FLCW business *while* employed full-time with AT&T. He was also an evangelist, a college instructor, a published author, *and* a husband and father. His goal? $2,000 to $3,000 monthly within four months—doable, given his experience.

He started cold calling in the fall, and six months later, he emailed me with this:

> *What you predicted is coming to pass. I'm exceeding my original goal. Just got a check today for $938 for some ad copy. Some current and future projects: press release for a medical center: $300. Mailer for a seminar presenter: $750. Marketing letter for a local trainer: $225. Quarterly newsletter for an association: $400. And coming up, a marketing booklet: $2,500. There are projects in the pipeline and lots on the horizon.* **And to think that I have accomplished all this with just a very part-time effort** (emphasis added).

Huh? Very *part-time*?! Somehow, I'd missed that *he'd continued to work full-time*. Wow. His schedule allowed him to come in to work late some days and leave earlier on others. He spent his freed-up morning hours cold calling, and did his writing at night.

Funny sidebar. I'd have Jim call in during live seminars, and have him tell his story over speakerphone (minus the FT job detail, but impressive even without it), then ask, *So Jim, what you do for living?* Puzzled faces all around, as Jim replied, *I work full-time at AT&T. I've been building this business strictly part-time.* I chuckled as jaws dropped all around. Suddenly, this opportunity went from doable to amazingly doable. How did this story unfold? These email snippets outline his plans, strategy, approach, and results.

September (one-month mark)

In the last three weeks I've made about 300 cold calls, yielding a database of 110 people interested enough to have me send materials, seven face-to-face meetings, and several clients with possible upcoming projects. I've had only one negative reaction to my $75 rate. My work experience has impressed prospective clients. I've got about 20 samples from my past lives and it seems to be enough.

December (three-and-a-half-month mark)

I've made about 1000 cold calls, resulting in a database of about 200 prospects, a few dozen personal meetings and a handful of small jobs. I've called every listing in the K.C. Yellow Pages for advertising, PR, marketing, events, and graphic designers, along with every company—public and private—in our local Book of Lists (and just on a Chamber of Commerce member list). Here's the 30-second pitch I use when I get voice mail during cold calling:

Hello, [Name]. My name is Jim Meadows. I am a freelance writer in the Kansas City area, checking in with your office to see if you need any project help. I have a 23-year career that has had me involved in all aspects of the writing and editing process, producing material for AT&T, Eastman Kodak, and other corporate and private clients. If I can help with a project, whether large or small, give me a call, XXX-XXX-XXXX. Feel free to visit my web site at **www.jimfreelance.com**. Thanks for your time, [Name], and you have a great day!

It seems to be effective, and I do get a lot of callbacks. I did a fresh mailing to every client and prospect in my database and I now have a web site.

December (one week later)

Today, I followed up by phone with 50 contacts on my hot-prospect database. Those gone for the holidays received a voice-mail reminder, and the ones I did reach were glad to hear from me; most said they anticipated projects in the New Year. I won't complain if it all hits at once, as you predict it might!

January (four-month mark)

You called it! Right after the first of the year, I started getting lots of activity: a direct mail project for an ad agency, a proofreading job and a marketing proposal for a seminar company. And the phone continues to ring. Of course, I'm not going to let up on the aggressive prospecting necessary to keep it going.

And then in March, Jim contacted me with the email you read previously. The following November, I got this update (note his comments about national marketing):

I've got about $10,000 in receivables, with more work coming from existing clients, and new ones in the wings. Still part-time. The vast majority of remote prospects aren't in the least put off that we're hundreds or thousands of miles apart.

I'm keeping the full-time job for now, but will likely cut the apron strings later. 1,000 cold calls have yielded 200 hot prospects, a steady stream of business and referrals that just seem to come out of the blue!

A few years later, Jim offered up these business-building gems:

• Do some *pro bono* work to build a portfolio.

• Stick to your guns on fees. There are plenty of people out there who will pay you well. I stuck to my $75 hourly rate, and while I've lost some potential clients over it, once they walked, it just opened my calendar for the more serious ones.

• In your research and marketing, try to identify companies with key contacts on-site around the clock. There may very well be some prospects that would appreciate a freelancer being available at odd hours.

• Make sure you're easy to reach. Provide your cell number on your outgoing office voice mail *(PB Note: OR just forward your office number to your cell, as I do).*

- Create a web site with samples to eliminate having to send physical packages. Targeted personalized email prospecting—advisable if building the business after-hours—is more fruitful with instantaneous "click-thru" access.

- Capitalize on whatever flexibility you have to shift hours or free up some weekday time, and then milk it for all it's worth.

- Consider having a family member or associate handle cold calling and meeting coordination during the day. It might even impress some prospects (*I'm his marketing assistant publicist* or *I'm her client coordinator.*)

- Believe the system works. Yes, I had more experience than many starting out, but closely following the blueprint laid out in *TWFW* is what brought me success.

- Marketing is crucial. Make the calls, no matter how unproductive it feels at times. Some of my best clients came from lists I initially looked at and thought, *I'm not going to pick up anyone here!* But I called anyway—and it paid off, big time.

- Leverage every resource, contact, and life experience you have. Identify the key qualities that will sell you to prospects, and capitalize on them in your marketing.

- Today's marketing plants the seeds of tomorrow's business. Keep it up. Every *No* gets you closer to a *Yes.* The law of averages is real: you must make X contacts to achieve Y number of clients. Even when you get busy with work, spend at least a few hours each week marketing—cold calling, mailings, etc.

- Continually research and network. I constantly scan the newspaper, business journals, radio and TV for leads (company start-ups, new marketing/creative directors, etc.). Attend professional business luncheons to grow your network.

- Everything you do and say must communicate professional reliability. Otherwise, why should someone hire you? If you're unsure of any aspect of that presentation, bounce it off a trusted business professional. Maintain the highest ethical and professional standards in every aspect of your business—it will serve you well.

•   •   •

From FT Job *and* PT FLCW to FT FLCW

When Ed Gandia (**www.edgandia.com**), a fellow Atlanta freelancer, shared his success story with me (below), I was blown away. Like Jim Meadows, he'd kept his FT job (software sales) while slowly building his FLCW business into a full-time income. In his first full year as a FLCW, he made over $163,000. Ponder that.

He's been incredibly successful, not because he's a slick salesman, but because he's a nice, down-to-earth guy who works smart *and* hard. I asked him to share his strategies for part-time business building. Tons of gems here for *anyone*. Subscribe to Ed's biweekly newsletter (**www.theprofitablefreelancer.com**) and as mentioned, score a free copy of his great report, "7 Steps to Landing More (and Better-Paying!) Freelance Projects."

Also, as mentioned in Chapter Two, check out Ed's ebook, *"Stop Wishing and Start Earning"*—his action plan for going from FT 9–5 job to FT FLCW (and $163K!). Check it out at **www.StopWishingandStartEarning.com**.

•   •   •

CAPITALIZING ON FLEXIBILITY   When I started my part-time FLCW business, I'd already been working from a home office for about four years, so that gave me some scheduling flexibility. And with my wife as a stay-at-home mom, I was the sole breadwinner. Not to say it was easy juggling the FT and PT gigs. I was a software sales rep—a job that demanded 10+ hours of work daily. Miss your targets and you're gone. Period.

So, while I could take FLCW calls during the day, I did the FLCW work from 7:30–10:00 p.m. on weekdays (exhausting, yes), and from 6:00 a.m. to 1:00 p.m. on Saturdays, with Sundays off (usually, but not always). Occasionally, I'd take a vacation day to complete a pressing project, and every few months, my wife would go to her mom's with my son, giving me more time to work. I planned my workload accordingly.

HOW DID I MARKET MYSELF?   While I set up a web email account for my FLCW email (and checked it three times daily), nearly all my marketing budget went to direct mail. Why? Because I could print, fold, stuff, and stamp letters at night. These very effective campaigns were my cold-calling "sales force" and helped me land a few clients quickly.

I contacted everyone in my network, shared what I was up to, and asked if they knew anyone who might need my services. While I wasn't expecting much there, a friend I met for lunch eventually led me to my two biggest clients (one still is). You never know. Find one person with the right contact who tells someone else, and you're in the door. And because you're a referral from a trusted source, you usually get your desired fee.

JUGGLING TIPS *Even if you work in a cubicle every day,* use technology to make a successful transition. A web-based email account, a simple web site and a BlackBerry can go a long way to making it happen. Be creative and disciplined. Some suggestions:

• Get a real domain and linked email address (ed@EdWritingServices.com, *not* EdWritingServices@yahoo.com). It costs little to look a lot more professional. Also, I used low-cost web hosting and templates to launch my first simple site. When I redesigned the site later, I traded services with a web designer.

• If it's not practical to access your FLCW web-based email a few times during the workday, get a BlackBerry and have your emails forwarded to it.

• Consider a bare-bones second line (with call forwarding) at home for your future FLCW biz, and forward calls to your cell/Blackberry during the day. Once you go solo, you'll be using the number clients and prospects are already familiar with.

• Don't tell prospects you're part-time. Most don't care—what they want is results, when promised. Plus, if you use technology wisely, and return calls and emails within four hours or so, it's not an issue. *Make* it an issue, and they'll go elsewhere. Client wants to meet you in person? Take some time off work and do it.

• Use direct mail! It allows you to do most of your prospecting in "off" hours. Use lunch, early a.m. or late afternoon to follow up with respondents. Best use of direct mail? A free report with valuable info for your target market. Make *that* the offer, *not* a "hard" offer in a letter (i.e., selling writing services directly).

• It's critical to keep track of available hours. I developed a spread-sheet-style calendar that let me see how projects were spread out daily and weekly, so I could tell when I'd have the time for a new project and when I could promise delivery. As your biz picks up, you'll have a thin margin of error, so you need to track time and commitments.

ETHICAL JUGGLING With few software industry contacts, I joined a local technology association and networked online via industry discussion forums. I attended a select few a.m. networking functions (taking off FT-job hours), but had to be extremely careful to avoid co-workers or job-related contacts. While I didn't tell my employer I was moonlighting, I'd never approach a company (to pitch writing) that competed with my employer.

Many say this can't be done. If you believe that, then it's true. But if you can visualize ways around these obstacles, you'll likely make it work. I did. And I did because I wanted it badly and refused to give up. Need some inspiration? Rent the movie "The Pursuit of Happyness" (based on a true story). Its core message: Others have had it harder...and did it.

Weekend Warrior

Maine 9–5 Cubicle Dweller Builds FLCW Biz Via Email

(PB: Those working FT for The Man, but wanting to build a writing business, need to be resourceful. Budding Auburn, Maine FLCW Brian Westbye (**www.greenbackmedia.com**) shared a strategy he's using to build his business on weekends. I'll let him explain...)

BW: Because I'm not around during business hours to cold call, every weekend I select a city and use Google to identify 100 graphic/web designers, a group you've spoken of having gotten a lot of work from. Makes sense: a good designer already has a built-in client base and new work coming in, *and*, they're not writers. So, I created a prospect email template, adapted from your basic cold-calling script:

Hello!

My name is Brian Westbye, and I'm a freelance copywriter in Auburn, ME. I wanted to take a moment to introduce myself and my company, Greenback Media, and to determine whether you have any ongoing or occasional needs for a good freelance writer to help create marketing collateral material: brochures, manuals, etc. I would love to discuss any opportunities you might have.

Since launching my business, I've worked on a wide range of projects, including membership renewal campaigns for the National Audubon Society, web site content for a multi-millionaire Australian web entrepreneur and product blurbs for an online emporium for baby gear. I'm confident I could help with any copywriting needs that you might have.

Please find below a link to my website. My résumé and pdf's of my work are available upon request. Thank you in advance, and I hope to talk soon.

(company name, his name, ph. #'s, EM, URL, LinkedIn URL)

• • •

I just plug in the address, the name of the contact if I can find it or, if not, just a general "Attn: Project Managers & Creative Directors." I schedule all 100 emails to go out at 8:00 p.m. EST Sunday night, so that my pitch will be one of the first things the client sees in their in-box on Monday morning.

While results vary, out of 100 emails sent, typically, 70–80 are no replies, while 10–15 are "we don't outsource" or "nothing now, but we'll keep you on file." Another 10–15 are "please send samples," and then nothing. Five to ten are "nothing now, but we may have some stuff coming up that might be a good fit."

So far I've landed one long-term client this way, for whom I'm writing all their product blurbs, and a web site for an orthodontist in L.A. (just puffing up about six paragraphs). Through the weekly emailings, I'm scheduling appointments with local prospects and phone calls with remote ones.

I'm getting a decent response, and some very promising leads, so I figure I'll keep on letting the numbers do the work for me. I'm getting there.

Reality Check: If you have a worthwhile dream, at some point, you will have to lead an unbalanced "overtime-rich" life—even if temporarily—to make it a reality. If you're unwilling to do so, it probably won't happen. Just know it's always easier to do it when building your own thing, as opposed to making someone else rich.

• • •

Okay, so what about those of you who live in smaller markets? Are you out of luck? Hardly—just read on. And if you're in a big city, DON'T skip the next chapter—there's lots of great advice for everyone.

Chapter 12

I live in the middle of Nowheresville, Montana (population 18). Can I build a writing business out here? No, probably not—if you're trying to draw only from local work (Billings, Montana, population 130,000, *maybe*, as we'll discover later). That said, there's a lot of middle ground between Nowheresville and New York or L.A. A lot of medium-sized cities and regions hold on to *beaucoup* freelance work.

Since I had no personal experience building a writing business in a small market or rural area, I found some impressive folks who have. Creative, ingenious, and resourceful. And yes, there are pluses and minuses to both big city and small market start-up.

THE DIFFERENCES Major metro areas have a lot more business *and* a lot more competition than a smaller burg, where you may be the only game in town. While big-city prospects typically know what a commercial freelancer does, you may need to educate small-town prospects about the value of hiring you. Bigger markets command higher fees, but costs of living will be dramatically lower in that small market. Big-market writers know it's all about marketing, direct mail and showing up consistently. Their small-town counterparts have learned the value of networking and relationships.

Through conversations with folks working in smaller markets, I've gleaned the following golden tips and strategies. But know this: *The following ideas are applicable to ANY marketing campaign in ANY size market* (and the same goes for larger-market strategies). They're just particularly crucial when building the business in a smaller market.

NETWORK Join the Chamber of Commerce and any other group that draws local businesspeople. Get involved, volunteer, be a presence, be generous. Seize opportunities to showcase your skills. People remember, and they talk.

BUILD RELATIONSHIPS While people everywhere are most likely to do business with those they know and like, this is especially true in a smaller market. View people as friends and neighbors first, possible sources of business second. Remember birthdays. Do small favors. Be that good neighbor. And yes, let people know what you do for a living.

EDUCATE Be sure the businesspeople around you know what's in it for them. Don't ask what they need—chances are, they might not perceive any needs. Instead, suggest projects. Show them before-and-after scenarios with other similar small businesses. Open their eyes. Let them picture it. Talk benefits (profits, enhanced reputation, life simplification), not features (writing services).

PERSIST Small-town folk often take a while to accept new ideas and people. Stay in the game. Even if you're not getting work or even a response from a particular business, keep in contact (unless they tell you to get lost). Over time, many will come around. Project a positive, low-key attitude. Foster the impression (and mean it) that it doesn't matter to you whether or not they ever do business with you, it's the relationship that matters.

STAY AWARE Keep your radar up for opportunities, but not in an overbearing way. Keep abreast of business openings, expansions or ownership changes—then send off a note of congratulations and/or suggest ways your services can support sustained business growth.

BARTER Small businesses with lower budgets may be happy to trade for your services. Ideally you want paid work, but if a restaurant, travel agency or health club you'd likely patronize is willing to barter—and the terms work—go for it. *Note: Barter is typically based on the retail price of both products/services, not a discounted rate.*

BRANCH OUT An obvious and highly recommended solution to the small-town dilemma is to prospect for work *anywhere* outside your area, even across the country. This can potentially offer the best of both worlds: you live wherever you want, including places with much lower costs of living than a major metro (and where prevailing rates for writers would likely be far lower) yet, given your big city clients, you'd very likely be able to command big city rates. Geography is quickly becoming a total non-issue for many clients.

Got this great note on this very subject from Nashville, TN FLCW Joyce Dierschke:

> *When I fell in love with Nashville and decided to move there, everyone thought I was nuts. I had just established my freelance business in Florida and had a stable of good-paying local clients. What was I thinking? Well, I was thinking that if I could build a business in Florida, I could do it in Nashville. The real surprise came when I told my clients I was leaving town. They all decided to come with me! Not literally, of course, but each said that they would rather work with me long distance than sign up with someone new. And, I'm still getting new South Florida clients through referrals. No one cares if I'm not there; we all meet up in cyberspace!*

When Austin, Texas-based Tom Myer launched his business, he made close to 350 calls in a few weeks, calling companies in over 30 states and landing close to $35K worth of work—the bulk of it beyond his home base (to see how far Tom's come since launching his business a few years back, check out **http://www.tripledogdaremedia.com/**).

Patricia Skinner (**www.wellwrittenwords.com**) lives in Amman, Jordan (yes, as in the Middle East), and she's built a thriving business as a SEO (search engine optimization) copywriter, with the bulk of her clients in the U.S.

Michelle Zavala (**www.studioz.ws**), a good friend and colleague in Texas, while living in Colorado Springs, had big clients in Virginia and Georgia. I remember her lamenting her lack of social life, given the 35 to 40 hours a week she was billing her Atlanta client (a mega computer firm), plus hours billed for the other two.

Incidentally, she picked up her Atlanta client through cold calling, and the Virginia client through a referral from another writer. Michelle notes, *Since she* (Casey Hibbard; more on her in Chapter 14) *focuses on case studies and I do creative/marketing copy, we frequently refer business to each other. Locally, I refer on tons of PR work and in turn, other referrals come to me.* Keep that in mind. Your fellow writers may be competitors, but they're colleagues as well (*and* I've gotten work referred to me by Casey as well!).

Besides smaller markets, remote prospecting will always be a likely scenario for another group: specialists in a niche industry who are running out of prospects in their local market. But that said, it could work for anyone, and the way you'd market yourself long-distance is the same as the way you'd market locally. Of course, a web site is imperative—given that it's THE single most expeditious way to neutralize the distance factor.

And often the work comes to you. I'm currently working for clients in Colorado (picked up through a graphic designer), California (through my web site), and Canada (through referral) and there are more in the works.

FROM THE TRENCHES What follows next are accounts from three impressively intrepid folks across the country (Ft. Myers, Florida; Sioux City, Iowa; and Fosston, Minnesota) who've built successful FLCW businesses in smaller markets. Again, I don't care what size your market area is, you will learn a lot from this crew.

Following that is another great small-market story—with a twist. If you've ever considered subcontracting—hiring other writers and making money on the spread between what you pay them and what you charge your clients—check it out.

●   ●   ●

Gulf Coast Gumption

LISA SPARKS – FT. MYERS, FLORIDA;
Integrity Writing (**www.integritywriting.com**)

How did you get started in the business?
When I first started as a FLCW, I was working in Philadelphia for one of the largest B2B newsletter publishers in the U.S. I learned I could competently handle a wide array of clients. After a move to Ft. Myers and a few unsuccessful attempts to land a job, I decided to do my own thing. Within three weeks, I had my first client.

Describe your geographic area and the challenges of working in southwest Florida.

Learning to market yourself, while crucial, is not that difficult. I attended free marketing seminars at a local college, trading ideas with other contractors or professors. I also get great advice from my clients…sometimes. When I first started out, they told me that the one big season is "snowbird" season—December to April—and after that, there's little work for ad agencies or contractors. But I still find work because I refuse to believe it.

Attitude separates you from the pack. Many competitors are more experienced or qualified, yet I keep plugging away. I have confidence when meeting with clients—and it shows. I typically come out with a signed letter of agreement and a deposit check.

Say "marketing" to a bunch of creatives and they panic. What's your definition?

Marketing means being outgoing, organized and prepared. Have a plan on how you're going to present yourself to the world. Have a clean and neat work space and take the time to set up processes and systems, whether it's a client info packet and how it's put together, how you approach a meeting, how you phone-prospect, what your 15- to 30-second elevator speech is (the sound bite that passionately explains what you do and what sets you apart from the competition, etc.) Get these things set and do them the same every time so they aren't so daunting anymore.

Network. That means thinking, *Even though these people might not bring me much business directly, by getting to know them, who knows who they might eventually refer me to?* Pound the pavement. And be patient—every action isn't necessarily going to lead to business, but it's all about momentum.

How do you overcome the challenges of working in a smaller market?

Be prepared to educate your clients about what copywriting is. Develop relationships with graphic designers so you can offer end-to-end solutions. Consider adding "project management" to your repertoire—nothing more than simply overseeing the project (a job that usually falls to the graphic designer).

Break everything down into bite-size pieces and think like the client. Pretend you know nothing about copywriting and ask yourself, *How would I explain this process to someone who's never dealt with a copywriter before, someone who doesn't think they need one?* Focus not on selling *your* services but on solving *their* problems (PB: again, *benefits* before *features*).

I always emphasize the time factor with clients. I find a lot of prospects that think they're great writers. I'll tell them, *Well, of course you don't necessarily need me from a writing standpoint* (often not true), *but given the demands of your core business, you just don't have enough time. As a smart businessperson, you need to focus on servicing your customers. I'll end up bringing in customers for you. How? Through my writing.* Just break it down into simple principles that every businessperson can understand.

Set up a small five-page web site that clearly explains what you do, what you've done in the past, and what you can offer. Also, collect email addresses through the site. A web site costs little to maintain and will convey professionalism to clients. I get back my investment many times over.

What are the challenges you face as an African-American FLCW?

It can present a challenge *and* an opportunity, because sometimes people want to give someone outside their own ethnic group a chance. People will often listen to me just because they want to hear what an African-American person will say! I think I'm the only AA-FLCW in Ft. Myers. That uniqueness often gets me in the door, but once there, the novelty quickly fades, and I have to almost *over*-deliver and be *more* professional than my white counterparts in order to close the deal.

I always dress in a suit, even though it's burning hot outside, at least for the initial meeting. I have to spend more time gaining trust, but once I get it, I can forge a pretty solid business relationship. People need to see I'm not a welfare mother; I'm not going to take their money and run. But there are those who'll believe those stereotypes, regardless, in which case it really doesn't matter how I present myself.

But most are practical businesspeople—the only color they see is green. Once you start talking about profitability and markets and how to get them there, it doesn't matter who you are. But to African-American writers, I'd say, be even more professional than you think is necessary to gain the client's trust and then keep those standards up, because old thinking can pop up anytime. It's not fair, but it's reality.

The monthly newsletter I started is an example of something that adds value and few others are doing. It's all part of always trying to bring benefits to my clients—this is how you can be a better businessperson, etc.

Have you ever run across some real prejudice in a client?

Yes, but in reverse. You go into a meeting to talk about business and all the prospect wants to talk about is civil rights and how they like black people and how they knew Martin Luther King and all that. They flip through your portfolio but they're not really looking and you want to say, *Are you interested in writing services?* Sometimes I've walked into an office for a meeting, after having only spoken to the client by phone, and the people are shocked when they see me. And I'm thinking, gosh, must be the nice dress I'm wearing!

I always try to turn the conversation back to business, and reinforce my professionalism at every opportunity. And I always follow up, though in many cases the client never calls back (which happens to ALL of us, so get used to it). There are times you'll hear a particular client has a huge copywriting budget, you meet with them and they try to get you to reduce your rates. I'd advise AA-FLCW's to not blame it on race, even if it feels that way. It's a daily fight to choose humanity and not to choose hate.

I've been tested a lot on my rates but I don't give in (often just the attitude you need to avoid problem clients). People will either respect that or they won't. But you can always walk away from a situation and feel good about it. That strategy is finally bearing fruit. Clients are coming from everywhere, mostly from my e-newsletter. Some have only met me at a few networking events, and all of a sudden they call out of the blue with a project for someone they know. And these people are more than willing to pay my rates.

What challenges do you face as a woman in the business?

I think it's easier to get a meeting out of a client if you're a woman. If it's a male client, they're sometimes just curious as to what you look like. It certainly doesn't mean you'll get work, but it can get you in the door. And a lot of my female clients will send work my way. They've actually come right out and said, *I'm glad you're doing this, and I want to give you business and I'm going to get my husband to do the same,* and so on.

How have you gone about landing most of your work?

In the beginning, it was phone prospecting. I'd call people and introduce myself and deliver a short script that fairly closely followed the script in *TWFW.* I lead with the fact that I do newsletters, then mention other types of work, like brochures, business letters and press releases. Sometimes, I'll simply ask for the marketing manager and not deliver a formal script at all.

But frankly, it's more fun and interesting to meet people face-to-face. So I go to Chamber meetings and hand out cards—and I can land four or five meetings out of a function. And regardless of whether I get work from them right away, I have a name and email address to add to my newsletter (with permission, of course). I wrote an article for the Chamber publication that went out to 1,500 businesses. It allowed me to promote my business *and* highlight all the benefits of dealing with a copywriter.

So, presently, I get most of my business and referrals from relationships I've formed at networking functions. They work wonders. They *do* produce business. AND I still do plenty of phone prospecting. My web site, coupled with my e-newsletter, is creating tons of business for me. It gives me a professional, polished look that prompts visitors to believe in my business. It's a great way to look "big" even when it's just me.

What do you wish you'd known when you started out?

It doesn't take slick sales ability to be successful, mainly because it's insincere. You only have to resort to that if you don't believe in what you're selling. I believe in myself and my abilities, so I don't need gimmicks.

What advice would you give to someone in your position starting out?

Look at things from a client's perspective. Ask yourself, *If I were a client, how would I like to be approached by a copywriter?* Know your audience. Don't focus on *I have to make money to pay my rent.* Believe me, they can sense it, and that will drive them away. Just be of service, and the rest will fall into place.

•   •   •

A Heartland Harvest

MARY GUINANE MCNAMARA – SIOUX CITY, IOWA;
The Write Answer (www.twacopywriting.com)

Because I live in a tri-state metro area with a population of only 100,000, I started out by networking and building relationships. Here, laying relationship groundwork is just as important as building a portfolio. A small market means that someone always knows someone.

GETTING STARTED Plan on slightly higher start-up costs because your initial impression, which needs to be strong, will have more ripple effects in a small community. Keep quality first rate in all your marketing materials, which may mean the added cost of professional printing and design. But, other professionals may be willing to barter for services, so added expense may only mean time spent instead of cash. If your marketing materials are done well, you'll attract clients who understand the value of quality. More than once, I had someone say, *I want a brochure like yours.* You can build your client list, network with other service providers, and get paid to build your portfolio by doing some of these simple projects for smaller businesses.

For my web site, I went to a well-known, award-winning designer with a reputation for quality. My web site still gets compliments. More importantly, he played mentor, fielding questions about bidding, local rates and his expectations for a good copywriter. I ended up working on projects with him and the graphic designer, who later went out on her own.

BUILDING MOMENTUM Though not billable, time spent at community events and networking functions weighs heavily in launching your business. In the beginning, view relationship building and networking as projects that need your time and attention.

I had a connection with the local Advertising Federation Club and helped them out with some freebie stuff. I was happily surprised when they paid for me to attend the District Conference, and I was asked to be the Program Chair on the Ad Fed Board. We only have about seven ad agencies in town, but they're all part of the club, and professional groups are a good way to make multiple connections at one meeting.

I also joined the Chamber, and helped with a *Buy Local* promotion along with other Ad Fed members. Lots of small businesses took notice, creating a follow-up gold mine!

Next, I joined the Junior League—very strong here. It helps balance my solitary work place and provides more networking opportunities. In this town—and most small towns—if you're in the good graces of the right groups, good things happen. In the Midwest, people are very loyal to the companies they patronize. In fact, the sales guys complain about how strong a factor that is when it's *not* in their favor.

VALUABLE VOLUNTEERING Don't underestimate the power of one job done free, but done well, for a committee; it can be as effective as time spent on cold calls or mailings. Volunteering feels good, but never give away anything less than your best work. Other committee members will appreciate your hard work, and who knows who they'll tell? They all have bosses and companies who just may need you, too.

Whatever you do, do it right. Your reputation will precede you by the time you're meeting with your third client in a small business community. Being professional at all times and producing solid work on deadline isn't just important, it's crucial.

Even if you don't plan to ever seek work from outside your market, build your knowledgebase by expanding your information network. Use the Internet to learn what happens in other markets, and find resources to help you think like your clients. Find message boards to network with copywriters in other markets. Use business and entrepreneur web sites and newsletters to find out what the decision makers you're meeting with are discussing. The more you know about their problems, the easier it is to offer them solutions.

I played the "new person" card as a copywriter, but made sure everyone I met knew that a high level of professionalism was my transferable skill. I may have changed industries, but simple things like thank-you letters and letting people know you followed up on the lead they gave you are always appreciated. It's okay to be new, but never let that translate into naïve or unprofessional behavior. Consider tapping community leaders for their expertise, but don't expect them to do your legwork for you. Figure out how you can reimburse them for their time with your skills. Focus on building a relationship with that person, not coming out of the meeting with a paying job.

BECOMING ESTABLISHED Don't evaluate the success of your first few years in business solely on income. Evaluate each project for its potential for repeat or referral business. One small job for a well-connected client may have a higher long-term return than a one-shot, big-ticket gig. Select new projects for the same reasons. It won't be long before the right people will be saying, *Oh, I've heard about your work.*

Think and act like a businessperson, not a freelancer, when you're with other businesspeople. The poor souls stuck in an office every day don't want to hear about you writing in your pajamas. They do enjoy an exchange on how your business is similar to theirs, so keep the conversation in their comfort zone. (You can always pity them later when you're doing the project you landed with them, in your PJs, of course.)

Be a source of solutions for clients, on committees and at networking functions. In a community where people cross paths often, you need to be part of the network. Find out the area of expertise of everyone you meet, then refer others to them. The more you know about what *other* people do well in your community, the more folks will think of *you* as a source of expertise and solutions.

BEYOND YOUR LOCAL MARKET With the Internet, living in a small market doesn't mean you're limited to a small pond to fish in for clients. Once you have some quality work samples, regardless of the clients they were done for, don't be shy about sharing them with prospects of all sizes. Use testimonials from satisfied clients to back up what you show them, and even the big guys will pay attention. Clients care about the quality of the work you've done much more than the size of your previous clients. By paying attention to the national market scene as you work with smaller clients, you'll be ready to jump to a larger market, should you decide to later. Having clients in big ponds and little ones can create a wonderful stream of varied projects and client interaction levels.

●   ●   ●

Minnesota Moxie

NATE FREDRICKSON – FOSSTON, MINNESOTA

(www.nmfredrickson.com)

I live in what is known as "Greater Minnesota"—meaning any rural community several hours north of Minneapolis (translation: not a Starbucks as far as the eye can see). As a sparsely populated region, there are fewer businesses of notable size from which to prospect. The upside is that there are few freelance writers with whom I have to compete.

One strategy I've used since returning to freelance work a little over a year ago has been to cultivate name recognition among local prospects by writing a weekly humor column for several regional newspapers. The financial compensation is insignificant, but most editors of small newspapers welcome the additional content without having to strain their very limited budgets. The positive exposure from the column has produced the desired results, and I have cultivated a number of long-term clients who use my services frequently, including a small regional vineyard and winery (in order to effectively write descriptions for their several wine varieties, the owners insist I try each of them. God bless market research).

Also, to take the burden of product development off the back of the client, I have partnered with a local graphic designer, and a web designer, along with radio and television producers, to become an unofficial ad agency of sorts. This has provided an excellent additional revenue source, as I charge an hourly fee for administering the client's project. Like St. Paul said, "Be all things to all people so that you might win some."

•   •   •

Subcontracting: A Small-Market Success Story

Over the years, I've gotten many emails (from marketing-loathing writers) asking if I'd ever considered subcontracting: hiring writers for projects and for less than I was charging the client. While it's certainly crossed my mind, I never made the leap. The following story—from someone who has, and in a BIG way—offers wonderful advice along with a great story.

A few years back, Dana Pulis wrote a piece for the ezine about her growing FLCW practice. More recently, I got a call from Dana that knocked my socks off. After topping out as a writer in a small market, this at-home mom with two toddlers had doubled her monthly income by subcontracting other writers. And that was just the beginning...

•   •   •

BABY STEPS Tired of urban sprawl and an unhealthy work/play balance, my husband and I quit our jobs and moved with our sons to the peace, quiet and real outdoors of Billings, Montana. It was a welcome change, but it wouldn't make the car payment or stave off the bank repo letters I received.

I graduated in journalism, was once a good writer, but hadn't penned a sentence in ten years. Desperate for a job, I went back to what I knew: newspapers. I made about $4,000 in 2001, doubled that in 2002 and 2003 with a bit of commercial work, and in 2004, finally went for it as a full-time FLCW. Before long, I was pulling in around $6,000 a month (yes, all from the Billings area!) and rarely working more than seven hours a day. Within two years, the workload quickly grew beyond what I could handle myself. I was charging $75 an hour and pushing $90K— about the limit of the Billings market. I faced a tough choice: find a way to keep growing or start turning clients away.

SUBCONTRACTING: RISKS & REWARDS Realizing I had some jobs I could farm out, I started looking for a writer. At first it was risky and uncomfortable trusting someone else. I focused on finding a writer who wasn't a threat—someone not as good but good enough. Mistake. I learned the hard way.

I went through several writers—two English students, an acquaintance, and a newspaper writer—people I could pay $20–25 an hour while charging the client $75 an hour. None were really great writers, and one even cost me a client. Still, within three months, by subcontracting, I went from roughly $200 to $2,000 a month. In March 2006, that figure doubled: I was making an extra $4,000 a month without ever picking up a pen!

More importantly, I started seeing a much bigger picture. My clients needed more than just writing; they needed marketing direction. So I read everything I could about marketing and started helping clients with marketing concepts and campaigns.

In May 2006 I was subcontracting two writers. I convinced my husband, who worked in corporate PR, to quit his job, and we started Write On Marketing. We partnered with a former client, contracting with their graphics group to expand our offering.

We also traded up—letting less expensive writers go and investing in more experienced ones. I got several good contacts through Peter—one he referred directly and two who contacted me after reading about me in his ezine. I paid each about $50 an hour—close to top dollar for Billings. I gave one of Peter's contacts—a solid writer and 30-year specialist in health care—nearly all I was making ($65 of $75 an hour).

That allowed me to focus on the client's marketing needs, *and* to develop a full-blown marketing contract with a new client who now pays me $90K a year (but would have been worth only $20K as a writer)

We spent the rest of 2006 transitioning our writing clients into marketing clients. As a writer, I had maxed out in this market at $85,000, but at the end of 2006, my income had nearly doubled—all by doing *less* writing!

In 2007, we hired a full-time writer, a graphic artist from the company we'd contracted with, and a marketing director. At the beginning of 2008, we were a seven-person firm, and continuing to grow. We're on track to net $400,000 this year, and $1 million in 2009—*pulling solely from the Billings market, population 130,000.*

Advice

Hire the best you can afford. If your subcontractors don't please your clients the way you please them, your clients will tell you, but it may be too late. If you're charging $75 an hour, find someone making similar and negotiate a $50 rate in return for handling the marketing end. You'll still make money, you'll get new clients, and just as importantly, you'll keep the ones you already have.

Don't be afraid to give it all away. At times, it's worth it to pay a writer nearly all you're making IF it frees you to focus on the client and land far more lucrative work.

Watch your ego. Hire the best, and then trust them to get the job done. You don't want to squelch them with a "Thanks-but-I'm-still-better" attitude.

Give subcontractors a trial run. Over several months, vet new subcontractors on a mix of the kinds of projects you'd be assigning them if you hired them full-time. Invite them to brainstorming meetings, ask them to do research, have them work on smaller projects. It's much easier (and less costly) to part ways at this stage than once you've assigned them a major client or hired them full-time.

Be prepared to hire and fire people. If you're uncomfortable with someone's work, don't hang in there with them. I did, and it cost me. Always err in favor of your business.

Make contacts with local magazine and newspaper editors. Writers in these professions are often in the early stages of getting published. Ask editors to recommend writers who are talented, versatile or specialized.

Tailor your contracts. Current trends are away from legalese. Search online for examples of subcontract agreements for writers. Since you're a writer, write up something in simple English that you and your subcontractors will be comfortable with. For a small fee, an attorney—or even a good paralegal—can ensure a contract is accurate and a fit for your needs.

Consult with business experts. If you continue hiring subcontractors and growing your business, your business structure may need to change. Most cities and some colleges have small business development offices with experts more than happy to offer free (or almost free) guidance. They might be able to help with creating contracts, too.

Hire a proofreader. Sometimes you get so invested in the work that you miss simple spelling and grammar mistakes. Make sure you tell the proofreader exactly what you do and don't want him to look for. A good source for proofreaders: **www.elance.com**.

Go Virtual. When it came time to form a company, we went "virtual." A computer network keeps us as connected as we need to be. When we *do* need a face-to-face, we meet in my home office. Not paying for an office lets me pay contractors and employees more, so I can keep hiring the best people. And frankly, not going to an office just makes us all happier.

PB Note: Interested in exploring subcontracting? Dana's available as a paid consultant to guide you through the ins and outs. Contact her through **www.kineticmg.com**.

•   •   •

Impressive bunch, eh? They've got to work extra hard to make it. Hopefully, you big-city folks appreciate all the advantages you have. Okay, so you've heard the hourly rate range in this business is $50–125+. If you're not at that upper level yet, have you wondered what it takes to hit it (*and* beyond)? Right this way…

Chapter 13

Got an email recently from a woman who'd come across my books, and was understandably excited about the opportunity to make a handsome wage doing something she loved and was good at. Referencing an oft-quoted fee range for the field of "$50–125 an hour," she asked, "What makes a $125-an-hour writer?" Good question. Who's got the best shot of hitting that $125 an hour level and beyond? Part of the answer is the groups we already discussed as having an easier go of this business, but there's more to say here.

Some readers of my earlier books may have gotten the wrong idea, so let's get the reality check out of the way. To earn $125+ an hour in this field requires more than simply the ability to put a decent sentence together. It takes either exceptional talent, a good grasp of marketing, specialized expertise or, ideally, some combination of the above. Let's take them one at a time.

TALENT: Some writers just have an innate gift, a sixth sense that allows them to effortlessly and unerringly craft just the right turn of phrase with the ideal words for the job, and with an engaging, genuine voice that draws readers in and keeps their attention. If you're one of those "naturals," that truly is half the battle. You can always learn the marketing. Speaking of which...

MARKETING SAVVY: On a par with talent is a good marketing sense. Together, they're a potent combination. The good news? Developing a marketing sense, as we discussed in Chapter Three, just isn't that difficult. You just need to be able to think *strategically* about a business. That simply means delving into a business with questions like:

What are you selling?

Who are prospects for your product/service?

What are the hot buttons for your audience?

Why do your customers do business with you?

What are your goals?

How have you tried to reach those goals in the past?

What's worked? What hasn't worked?

Who's your competition?

What do you do better than them?

What do they do better than you?

Plus anything else that can give you a better understanding of a company. You then use the answers to these and related questions in crafting your copy (per the "Discovery Questionnaire" we discussed in Chapter Seven). And no, not all projects require this, but if you're doing mostly marketing-oriented writing, assume this will be necessary.

Sure, some people have a native sense for marketing, and if you do, it'll be easier for you. If you're just *sure* you're not one of the anointed few, don't get all melodramatic and gloomy about it. Just ask the questions, listen to the answers, and apply what you've learned when you start writing. And read books to get better at it. Period.

SPECIALIZED KNOWLEDGE/EXPERTISE: True for careers in general. As discussed, if you're uncommonly well-versed in some specific body of knowledge by virtue of education, training and/or career experience, and can write about it with ease and clarity, you'll do well. Examples of such fields where knowledge + writing skills can = good money: healthcare, science, medicine, engineering, computer programming, software development, accounting, law, financial services, and many more.

"Spot Specializing," Anyone?

I've been a generalist forever, and like it that way. That said, I recently got a real taste of the financial rewards of specializing, or in this case, "Spot Specializing."

Over the previous four or five years, I've picked up more and more work doing taglines, company slogans, product/company naming, and book titling. Fun stuff. Like a little puzzle. "We want to incorporate this idea, and this one, and this, this, this and this. In four words or less." Love it. By the way, if you *don't*, sent that stuff my way. Seriously.

Anyway, about 18 months earlier, after realizing how many samples of this work I had, I created a separate portfolio—a hard-copy binder and a PDF for my online portfolio (**www.writeinc.biz**, *Portfolio, Naming/Taglines*, etc.). I wanted to see if I could land more of it.

About nine months later, I got a call from the creative director at a huge specialty marketing firm for an unusual gig: 150+ point-of-purchase displays for a supermarket, highlighting various tips, values, recipes, and product bundles. Each sign needed a snappy headline and a one-line snippet of body copy. Right up my alley.

She was interviewing three or four writers in all. I brought both portfolios—my standard one and the new one. She starts going through the new one, and I can tell it's working for her. A lot of focused nodding and "Oh, this is good," and "Nice work," and "Really good stuff." I got the job. AND at a most healthy hourly rate.

Clients DON'T want to hunt around endlessly for what they need. She was already overworked and overextended—hence the reason to hire someone in the first place—and she wanted the hiring process to go fast and successfully. I come along, show her exactly what she was looking for, and make it really easy for her to hire me.

As I write this, I've done two cycles, they loved my work, and I've been hired a bunch since by several different divisions of the company. Word got around. Total billings with them so far in less than 12 months? Nearly $20K. All because I took the time to pull out a specific chunk of my work and showcase it.

Any wheels turning? Got a specialty portfolio in the making? Or, as discussed in the chapter on web sites, how about a separate site for a particular specialty? The more clients believe you're THE expert in a certain industry or project type, the more likely they are to pick you from the crowd *and* pay you well. And you can *still* be a generalist.

P-C-O (*Professionalism/Competence/Ownership*): This one overlaps with the others. Those with talent, marketing savvy, and specialized knowledge are likely to exhibit P-C-O. By "ownership," I mean taking ownership of a project. If a client sees that you'll work well with little supervision, and won't be bugging them 10 times a day with questions you should have gotten answered in the first—and ideally, *only*—meeting, you've just made their lives easier—and that's the goal.

Some years back, my graphic designer and I landed a brochure project, despite being, according to my client, "the most expensive by far of anyone we interviewed," and with no relevant industry experience (one candidate had plenty). How did we do it? I'll tell you how...

We were prepared, professional, and we came in as a team. About one of the other candidates, the client said, "[She] had a lot of experience writing for our industry, but wasn't as organized or prepared as you, and wasn't part of a team." In addition, the clients liked our listening skills, saying, "When we told you what we wanted to accomplish, you listened to what we had said, took our ideas and then added to them."

All those things will absolutely allow you to charge more. In fact, check out the client's objection to one of the other teams they were considering: "Their bid was so much lower than yours, we had our doubts about whether they could get the job done for that price." The good clients *don't* buy on price. Play the price game and you turn your service into a commodity. And you'll lose, because there's always someone willing to do it cheaper.

Check out the 02/09/09 blog post at **www.wellfedwriter.com/blog**, "THIS Is What Clients Want. Are You Delivering It?" for a good example of "ownership" along with comments from others about how they deliver above-and-beyond service. As I discuss in the example in the post, after my client received copy from me that she didn't have to change a word of (rare, but nice), she told me, "That's why I love working with you. You 'get it' fast, work with virtually no supervision, and make my life really easy." Remember that.

(BONUS ATTRIBUTE #1) SPEED: This one won't earn you the big bucks by itself, but it can turbo-charge even modest levels of the ones above. Let me explain. I did several related projects recently for a product I'd written about previously. The estimates I offered were competitive for projects like these, but because I was "up to speed" already, I knocked them out in about half the time it might have taken someone new to the subject.

My effective hourly rate? Over $200 an hour. This is when the business gets really fun.

If you're a quick study *and* write fast, chances are good you can boost your hourly rate by whipping through projects—even in subjects new to you—faster than someone else might. Probably won't happen right out of the gate, but once established, it can be a most valuable secret weapon.

Michael Stelzner, the white paper guru, has worked the speed thing into a science. In the first Copywriting Success Summit (**www.copywriting summit.com**; check it out if you're new to the FLCW field, or you've been at it 2–3 years and are looking to take your business to the next level), he shared that he could knock out a white paper in 18–20 hours and his typical fee was $7,500 each (that's like $375+ an hour…). And he does four a month. 'Nuff said.

Oakland, CA FLCW Reese Minshew (**www.goeasywriter.com**) weighed in on this overall subject in a blog post some time back, writing, "In my experience, talent and speed are much less important than marketing savvy and specialized knowledge. I always relied on talent and speed, but didn't start making real inroads on that $125-per-hour mark until I could sport serious marketing chops, too. I highly recommend *The Personal MBA* (**www.personalmba.com**)—or at least the marketing books—to anyone serious about making money as a freelancer."

(**Bonus Attribute #2**) **Attitude:** So, I featured a cheeky Brit copywriter named Jon McCulloch (**www.jonmcculloch.com**) in my ezine sometime back. Jon charges—you ready for this?—$38K for a direct mail package that takes him about six weeks to do (amongst other projects). He's got clients backed up to work with him, because, I say, he's built a bit of mystique around his services. And yes, he's exceptionally good at what he does, so he can afford to have attitude.

When I asked him what clients get for $38K, he outlined the package components, adding, "plus all the advice they can eat (e.g., stop answering the bloody phone just because it rings!)." Hmmmm. Meaning what? You gotta love his reply. He wrote:

> *Peter: It's a positioning thing and a time-saving thing. Answering the phone is a huge time-waster, whether it's from existing clients, prospects, or my ex-wife. If everyone knows you'll pick up the phone and spend YOUR time talking every time they have a brain fart, they'll do it.*

Make it known that you don't answer the phone live except by appointment, and it marks you as a very busy, in-demand professional, and therefore desirable, no? It marks you out from all the hopefuls and wannabes who'll bend over both forwards and backwards to please a prospect. Set boundaries firmly and EARLY in the relationship.

If a prospect/client objected to not being able to call me every time he felt like it, I'd fire him on the spot. Because ultimately he'd end up thinking he owned my ass. You must NEVER allow a client to believe you need him more than he needs you (and even if you think that's actually true, it's a faulty perception on your part).

This is called "drawing your line in the sand." Jon understands human nature, and isn't the teeniest bit afraid to let people know he's a force to be reckoned with—both in what he can do for them and HOW he does business. Regardless of whether you're comfortable with the approach for yourself, there's a lot of wisdom here.

"Best-Bet Backgrounds" for the $125+ Level

As a long-time commercial freelancer, an author of books on the subject, and a coach for those starting and building a writing business, I've crossed paths with many hundreds of writers over the years. Along the way, I've noticed that there are several categories of folks who seem to have an easier path, not only in building the business in general, but in their earning power as well.

A short list of those groups is below. Now, if you don't find yourself in the following paragraphs, it doesn't mean you're doomed to failure. It'll just likely be more challenging for you. Just know it won't be a cakewalk for anyone, including the folks below.

IN-HOUSE MARKETING PEOPLE: Arguably the best background to hail from, these people are usually intimately familiar with the corporate culture and vernacular, the kinds of projects that need to get done, the requisite writing skill levels sought, and overall marketing strategy. Not to mention that they're usually ideally positioned to land writing work from former employers. Those who've done extensive writing in their jobs are even that much further ahead of the game, but even if they haven't, their familiarity with the game is a big asset.

CORPORATE STAFF WRITERS: These individuals have similar advantages to the above marketing folks, with the added edge of already being in a steady commercial writing groove—not always the case with marketers—which also spells the potential makings of a robust portfolio encompassing myriad project types. Where the marketing folks may have a plus over this group is in their general comfort level with marketing (i.e., the "marketing mindset").

AD AGENCY COPYWRITERS: Judging from all the "What-agency-did-you-come-out-of?" questions I got when I started out, ad agencies are common launching pads for our field. With similar advantages to staff writers, these folks also likely "get" the marketing piece as well. Minuses? The ad world is often egotistical, preening, and incestuous, leading to insular perspectives, condescending attitudes towards any writing other than ad copy, and an emphasis on creating clever (read: potentially award-winning) copy vs. *effective*, bottom-line-boosting copy.

JOURNALISTS: This group typically boasts excellent writing, editing and grammar skills, knows how to write engagingly, and is accustomed to deadlines—all pluses. They're also used to long hours, poor working conditions, and lousy pay—further motivation to switch careers, given the opposite reality in our field on all three. Minuses? Used to demonizing PR folks ("PR hacks"), they usually wrestle with the subjective and "sellout" nature of commercial freelancing (see sidebar below).

Attention: Ex-Journalists & Academics!

Sell Your Soul and Abandon Your Principles for a Few Bucks!

If you listen to some people (especially those hailing from journalism and higher education), the headline above is a pretty accurate assessment of what writing "commercially" truly entails. If it weren't for the fact that so many people actually buy this rubbish, it'd be comical.

Much of the basis for the "sellout" rap coming from journos and academics stems from their immersion in the principle that "objectivity is next to godliness" (course, everyone knows that no newspaper or university has any slant or bias whatsoever...). But, commercial writing—writing marketing materials for a company that's paying you—is most certainly not objective. Gasp.

In fact, that's correct. Marketing communications isn't journalism or an academic paper. It's not supposed to be objective. But that's a loooooong way from "selling your soul" or "abandoning your principles." I wish it were all so interesting, and one truly was always flirting with eternal damnation. Alas, no.

When I write, say, a brochure, ad, or case study for a company, I'm simply helping them put their best foot forward—showcasing the strengths and selling points of their product or service. I've never been asked to lie or even stretch the truth, and if I were, I'd walk.

In a typically prosaic scenario, I'd be highlighting the features and benefits of, say, a printing company's superior customer service and different offerings. Still my beating heart. I can hear Lucifer's chariots coming for me now.

Seriously, folks, let's pick our battles, and this isn't one of them. For a more in-depth discussion of this issue, check out "Sell Your Soul!" in Side Dishes at www.wellfedwriter.com/sidedishes.shtml.

PR Pros: This group typically has a lot of things in their corner: strong writing skills, deadline orientation, strong grasp of business and marketing principles (with a special appreciation of the "power of perception"), and familiarity with a variety of marketing materials, which are often produced in the marketing division of larger PR firms. As big PR firms scale back or their practitioners decide to run their own show, they're in a good position to thrive as a commercial freelancer.

Industry-Specific Experts: Do you have an extensive track record in some esoteric industry (especially a high-tech field) along with good writing skills and a willingness to use them to write about your field? That's a powerful mix. Plenty of people in specialized fields know their stuff. Precious few of those are also able to write well about their field. As such, Econ 101 dictates that those practitioners—assuming they're willing to let the world know they're out there—will generally thrive. And the marketing process for this group is generally easier, simply because both their audiences *and* their skills are so specific and well defined.

SALES PROFESSIONALS: I came out of this background. Those who do who understand the marketing fundamentals (audience, features/benefits, USP), can write well, *and* have no fear of marketing (i.e., cold calling, face-to-face networking, etc.) have some sizable advantages over those unaccustomed to those activities.

The biggest challenge for virtually all the above groups—given that they're likely coming from the salaried world (commission salespeople the exception)—will be making the transition to self-employment. That means the psychological/logistical/financial challenges of cutting the apron strings, handling all the nitty-gritty business start-up details, developing a healthy sense of one's own value in the marketplace, and successfully marketing one's skills to earn that value. All the areas, I humbly assert, where this book can help out...

The Great Debate: Generalist Or Specialist?

Should I specialize in a particular industry or project type? Or am I better off being a generalist and staying open to any project? Yes. As in, there's no right answer. It depends on your background, experience, education, and temperament.

As we discussed earlier, if you have specialized knowledge or skills, and can write clearly and coherently about it, you'll command higher rates than a generalist. Ditto for someone with a project specialty like speeches, white papers, case studies, direct response, industrial scriptwriting, etc. Remember Mike Stelzner? $375 an hour? Get known as "The ___ Guy/Gal," and you'll naturally make more.

I see the income hierarchy—from highest to lowest potential—as follows:

1) *Industry Focus:* Specializing in an industry or subset of one

2) *Project Focus:* Being a top writer of a particular project type

3) *General Focus:* Being open to all industries/project types

Generalist Pluses The big plus of being a generalist is the variety, which makes life interesting. Also, for 1 and 2 above, if an industry or project type takes a hit for some reason, things could dry up fast. Not so for generalists. But, the tradeoff is often lower income. Though, become the "go-to" writer for a big company with lots of projects to get done (remember, clients want to keep their lives simple), and you'll do just fine.

Do What Makes You Happy This is the key. If you just love telecommunications, or writing speeches makes your heart sing, then go for it. But don't specialize just because you'll make more money, if you don't enjoy the work. That's dumb. Then, you're little better than a cubicle slave—*and* your dislike of the work *will* affect your income.

By the same token, if you like the idea of variety (like I do) and being open to anything (ditto for me), then be a generalist (like I am), even if it might mean less money. After all, the main point of working for yourself is to enjoy what you do, no?

Would $60 an Hour Work? Remember: all the preceding is about what it takes to make $125+ an hour. What if you don't have any of those backgrounds? What if you're not a brilliant writer or one with sizzlin' marketing chops? Know that you *can* improve both of those, but let's be honest: some people will always be better than others. That's life. If that's the case, would you be happy with, say, $50–60 an hour?

That's the nice thing about this field. Two people from wildly different backgrounds—perhaps one boasting many of the advantages outlined above and the other less blessed—could both enter this field. One could earn $100–125+ an hour, the other a more modest $50–60, yet given their roots, both could be delighted at their respective outcomes. While this business isn't a cinch for anyone, even writers with modest skills can make an above-average wage. If that's you, maybe you'll never break the $100+ mark, but maybe that's okay.

A dear and talented fellow writer who does a lot of high-profile and high-paying magazine work, will poke gentle fun at our field, saying those who pursue it usually aren't good enough to write for top magazines. Don't agree completely, but there's some truth to it.

While the $125+ level typically demands strong or specialized writing skills, the $50–60 level is accessible to…lesser lights. And even that lower rate will usually earn you more per hour than a more talented feature writer. Just accept it—and cash the check.

•   •   •

Okay, so now we know what it'll take to make the big bucks. Let's turn to the actual projects we'd be writing. Not all-encompassing, but enough to give you a sense of the broad spectrum of possible work…

Chapter 14

YOU KNOW HOW TO WRITE, RIGHT? While there are dozens of possible project types in our field, if you're a good writer, it's much easier to learn the difference between them than to learn to write well in the first place. To a certain extent, writing is writing. If you're smart, you'll catch on as you go.

For a fun, educational look at the sheer scope of projects in the commercial writing world, check out the 8/7/08 blog post, "So, What Commercial Writing Projects Are You Working on These Days?" at **www.wellfedwriter.com/blog**.

Remember, there are three main categories of work: B2C (business-to-consumer), which is everything we, as consumers, see (i.e., ads, direct (okay, junk) mail, the occasional brochure, etc.). That's B2C. Which is dwarfed by B2B (business-to-business) marketing materials, which is all the projects created by businesses to market to other businesses. Finally, and huge as well, is *internal communications*—the enormous volume of projects created by companies to communicate with their own employees. Most of the project types we'll discuss ahead fall into one or all of the above categories.

If you decide to specialize in a particular project type (i.e., speeches, direct mail, white papers, etc.) experience will teach you more than I could ever tell you in a book. The thrust of this book continues to be the building and running of a commercial writing business. Pick up Bob Bly's *The Copywriter's Handbook* for the "how-to-write" details of many projects.

245

IT'S ALL SALES I work primarily in the marketing arena, and chances are good you'll be spending at least some of your time (if not most of it) there as well. That means writing pieces that help showcase the merits of a product/service/company and spur readers to take action (i.e., buy the product, visit the store, take a test drive, make the call, order the bigger brochure, return the reply card, whatever).

For all you ex-journalists or academics, that'll likely be an adjustment. *Not* some wholesale selling of one's soul, as some know-nothing cynics would have you believe, just an adjustment. Sheesh. Where *does* this stuff start?

ALWAYS THE FIRST QUESTION When I started out in this business, with meager portfolio and abundant enthusiasm, the one thing I leveraged to death was my 15 years of sales and marketing experience (more like 30+ years now, given that this business is also a sales and marketing venture).

I would tell clients that, because of my experience, I brought a sales and marketing mindset to the table: I write to sell, not just to communicate. And as discussed earlier, at the start of every project, the absolute first question is, "Who's the audience?" (the asking of which shows clients you have at least some clue what you're doing), followed by a bunch of related ones (see Chapter Seven). That information would then drive your tone and voice in the piece. Obviously, you'd write very differently to reach, say, breast cancer patients than you would builders, or sports fans, or teenage girls.

Got the Commercial Writing Chops?

At www.writeinc.biz, you'll find a portfolio representing a healthy chunk of my work over the years. After viewing these samples, you'll likely either be relieved or depressed—the former if you think you can write at least as well, or better, than me, and the latter if, well, you don't. In which case, just remember that while you do need to be a good writer for this field, you just don't have to be phenomenal to do well. Remember, in many industries, they're not looking for flashy, creative copy—just solid communication that conveys the important information.

When viewing the samples, note how copy is structured with notations such as *Cover Headline, Headline, Sub-head, Body Copy, Inside Left Panel Body Copy, Back Panel Copy, etc.* Study this format, as this is how you'd typically deliver copy to a client.

So, take a deep breath and go take a look. And while you're at it, go visit a bunch of FLCW sites I list in Chapter Four, and check out samples posted there. I'm sure you'll find writing ability that spans the gamut.

Okay, let's look at the different types of work we'll be doing. This is by no means a complete list, just some main project categories I've worked in over the years.

MARKETING BROCHURES Just about every company needs to create marketing brochures—and over time, more complex versions to reflect new directions, products, industry trends, and market demands. Often, the brochure a prospect sees is the first and only impression that person has of a company and its offering. So, it had better be good. A brochure provides info about, and lends legitimacy to, a company. A firm may operate out of a tiny office, but if they have a high-quality marketing brochure, they can appear larger and more established than they actually are.

Brochures can range from a simple tri-fold all the way up to large, multi-pagers with pockets, flaps, die-cuts, slip sheets, and every bell and whistle under the sun.

If a company has no marketing materials, a marketing brochure (or web site) is a logical place to start, and a logical first project to suggest. Do a good job on the first project and you'll position yourself well to pick up more work. Study the brochures in my online portfolio to get a better feel for things—*and* ones you get in the mail. Figure out which ones work on you and why, as well as which ones don't and why not.

CORPORATE IMAGE/IDENTITY PIECES As a company grows and carves out its niche, it'll often create a signature piece that captures its identity, its mission, its standing in the industry, and a brief overview of the product line (vs. a more-in-depth treatment in separate product brochures or sales sheets). They're still marketing brochures, just much more polished versions.

They tend to be slick, glossy, image-driven, light on copy, and are designed to leave the reader with any number of powerful and overriding impressions: professionalism, stability, creativity, reliability, international reputation, financial strength, etc. To write good image pieces, a writer needs to think "big picture," and be able to communicate in loftier, more top-line terms.

Often, a multi-page four-color brochure is the cornerstone of a corporate identity package, but perhaps the back cover will feature an inside flap/folder to hold smaller product-specific brochures, one-page spec sheets, and short case studies (more on these later)—all of which ideally share common design elements (this is where a talented graphic designer can start creating a company's "look"). The whole package works together cohesively to make a singular and powerful statement about the company.

Vanity Pieces? Cynics might assert that most corporate identity brochures are just fluff pieces—vehicles for ego gratification and to wow clients. While there's some truth to the charge, at the same time, for writers, this can be an exceptionally challenging and creative arena to operate in. Why? Because a company committed to getting at the heart of their mission must get at the heart of exactly what they do, don't do, and stand for.

You can play the role of facilitator, helping gel their thinking, and putting a voice to what's floating around in their collective psyches. There's no better feeling than coming up with a few lines that has the company president exclaim, "That's it! I couldn't put my finger on it, but you nailed it!" So, if you have a flair for the dramatic, hard-hitting, or heart-string-tugging nugget, this can be a fruitful avenue.

TRI-FOLD BROCHURES In the beginning, you'll likely be working with smaller firms who want/need their first marketing brochure: a tri-fold (i.e., an 8½" x 11" page turned length-wise, and folded twice—so why do they call it a tri-fold? Beats me—to make three panels). And yes, you can use an 11" x 14" and have a four-panel piece as well.

Here's a serviceable tri-fold "drill" in a nutshell. Keep front cover uncluttered: company name, tag line, URL, maybe a graphic. Period. Open the piece and the first panel you see is the flap folded in from the right. This flap serves two purposes: 1) an intro into, and set-up for, the main inside spread, and, 2) a summary of, and exit from, that spread.

Open that flap to the right and you're now looking at the three-panel "meat" of the piece. Try *not* to fill up every square inch of the space with copy. Break it up with white space and graphics. The first panel should be *benefits*-oriented; establish the challenge to be addressed. The second panel should get into the product service that addresses that need, and in the final panel, perhaps a few testimonials, and a "call-to-action" with contact info (URL and/or phone number). Keep the back flap uncluttered as well: full contact info for the company, and maybe a bio of principal(s), and nothing more. Not the *only* way to do this, but a tried-and-true formula. Check out "Three Real-World Projects" in *The Deluxe Well-Fed Tool Box* 🧰 for a step-by-step walk-through several actual tri-folds.

"10 Questions You Should Ask..."

An exceptionally effective device to use in marketing brochures promoting relatively simple businesses with lots of competition (e.g., house painting, home security systems, carpet cleaning, mortgages, etc.) is to create a list of the 10 (or 5, 7, or 12) "Questions You Should Ask of Any _____ Provider."

It sets your client's company up as the good guy, interested, first and foremost, in educating the consumer; highlights the benefits of working with your client's company vs. the competition (by asking/answering questions that showcase your client's strengths); and injects doubt about the competition.

I offer a more in-depth study 🧰 of this strategy in the *The Deluxe Well-Fed Tool Box* in two examples under "Real-World Case Studies.").

ADVERTISING COPY   Ad copy is some of the most fun and challenging work out there. As a rule, you have to be creative *and* persuasive—an often challenging combination. Study advertisements in magazines, news-papers, and billboards. Try viewing them from an academic perspective. Which ones get your attention? And why?

And remember, ads in national magazines are often written by the best in the business. Use this piece of information two ways. First, to explain why certain ads are so good (and to realize that you don't have to be nearly that good to write ad copy for smaller clients). Second, when you see a splashy, big budget ad or billboard that's lame, boring, or ineffec-tive—and there are plenty—know that you too can do this.

Of course, creativity doesn't necessarily translate to effective. Which explains why the advertising industry continues to lavish awards on campaigns deemed most clever and catchy, regardless of how ineffective they may have been in moving profit figures.

RESULTS MATTER (USUALLY)   If an ad designed to boost traffic and profits *doesn't*, who cares how many awards it wins? It's not effective. By the same token, if it's just solid, unflashy, meat 'n potatoes but brings them in the door or gets the phones ringing, then it's a good ad. Sure, a lot of advertising is done simply to boost brand awareness, and/or to keep up with the competition and, as such, it's not expected to boost sales/traffic.

Not comfortable writing catchy, funny stuff? Don't sweat it. Many companies just want straightforward ad copy that communicates the key sales messages and spurs the reader to action. If you come from a sales/marketing background like I do, you've got a head start. And remember: most of the companies you write for need to advertise sometime and somewhere, so once in the door, it's another project type to pursue.

As mentioned earlier, you likely won't be working on too many big national ad campaigns, unless you're so talented you can land freelance work with the big boys. More likely assignments for FLCW's will be smaller ads for small- to mid-size companies or peripheral "collateral" material for the big agencies.

As discussed, the smaller the company, the greater the chance your creativity will see the light of day. That's less likely with bigger firms, where legal and bureaucratic issues often rule the day, as they try to come up with something that hasn't been trademarked, will be totally unproblematic down the road, or hasn't been done before. Dream on.

Some years back, working through a design firm, I did a lot of headline concepting for the soft-drink behemoth. More often than not, I was coming up with a bunch of ideas for their POS (point-of-sale) store displays, most of which died on the vine. They have deep pockets and can afford to spend a healthy chunk of money to buy lots of ideas. If they get a few workable ones in the process, it's worth it.

GUIDELINES   With ad copy, again, first question is always, "Who's the audience?" Followed by "What's the purpose of the ad?" Image-building? Straight information? Retail sales ad? Special offer? Don't get complicated. Make *one* key point (ideally, a *benefit* to the reader), and build on that in the copy. Try to cover too much ground and you'll blunt the impact and lose reader interest. Try to rein in the "let's-cover-this-and-this-and-this" kind of client. Explain that that's what an ad *campaign* is for.

Always give clients a number of versions from which to choose. Chances are good that you'll agree on how many at the outset, but I always end up giving more. What's funny is that often, when I think I'm done, I'll come up with one last "throwaway" idea, and that's the one they love! So, be open to last-minute spontaneity.

RESOURCES *The Copywriter's Handbook* (Bob Bly); *Hey Whipple, Squeeze This* (Luke Sullivan); and *Creative Advertising: Ideas and Techniques From the World's Best Campaigns* (Mario Pricken). The last two, while geared just to ad copywriting, will help you hone your chops in *any* kind of persuasive copywriting.

NEWSLETTERS Where can you find this business? Everywhere. Every large corporation either is generating, or has the potential to generate, any number of newsletters, both internal (employee-directed) and external (customer-directed). And the best part about newsletters, by definition? They're recurring.

INTERNAL NEWSLETTERS These serve many purposes, and provide many things: information, inspiration, motivation, recognition, and employee input, and are vehicles for building *esprit de corps*. Today's ultra-competitive business climate requires companies to be nimble, cohesive, and responsive, and that means everyone "on the same page." A big company with many divisions could potentially have a publication for each division.

For a full year, I did a monthly internal newsletter for a division of a telecommunications giant that was touted as *the* communications vehicle for the group. It featured new product announcements and initiatives, profiles of new managers, and success stories to be modeled by the troops. I got paid $4,500 per issue for a project taking me roughly 35–40 hours of work a month. We like those.

As Intranets (a company's internal Internet) become standard fixtures in large firms (and even small ones), internal newsletters are likely to be web-based. The one I wrote appeared in print *and* online, with the latter providing more detail and expanded content. Print, however, is still valued for the "hard-copy-in-hand" factor. Intranet versions, while certainly convenient and low-cost, can get lost in the email crush.

EXTERNAL NEWSLETTERS These pieces, in addition to being informational, are typically designed to create a subtle yet powerful bond with customers, and make them feel they're part of a special group. The ultimate goal?

Customer retention: keeping those customers coming back and, hopefully, spreading the word. That was definitely the aim of a quarterly newsletter I did for the credit card division of a luxury auto manufacturer (gotta drive the car to get the card) for several years.

NEWSLETTER PROSPECTS EVERYWHERE Most mid- to large-sized companies are prospects for newsletter work—both internal and external. Oftentimes, an employee is writing a newsletter as an additional responsibility, but the company may be receptive to outsourcing the task. This is where it can get fun and profitable.

With the long-term gigs described above, the longer I did it, the more I learned about their businesses, and the more valuable I became to them. After learning what they stood for, how they operated, what was important to them, and what they could and couldn't say in print, my learning curve on new issues was virtually nil. Since I was doing good work, with minimal supervision, and dramatically simplifying their lives, it didn't make any sense for them to go somewhere else. True for any situation.

Eventually, in the case of the $4,500 gig, they pulled it in-house. Nothing is forever. But it sure was a great ride, and every FLCW's dream project: lucrative and recurring.

WHAT'S THE TONE? While many internal newsletters (especially if written in-house) tend to be dry—as if assuming employees *have* to read it—they should be just as engaging as their external counterparts. Employees need to be wooed like any other audience.

I always push for a more conversational, accessible tone. Be assertive on this. Fact: the more engaging it is, the more likely it'll be read (and objectives realized), the more positive employee feedback will be, and the more brilliant you'll look. Sometimes they go for it, sometimes they don't. With external pieces, it's even more critical. If you're trying to get your customers' attention, you'd better make it worth reading.

Read newsletters you get in the mail: airline frequent flyer pubs, inserts in your electric, gas, or telephone bill, and pieces from your insurance company, financial advisor, real estate agent, healthcare provider, etc. You'll get a good sense of both newsletter content and style, *and* see that writing quality varies widely. Where they're weak, why not call them up and find out who does their writing?

TEAM WITH A DESIGNER Chances are, big companies will already have the graphic side handled. Dealing with small- to medium-size firms, however, can offer golden opportunities to team up with a design compadre. Clients *love* end-to-end solutions.

Something to ponder: the external piece I did for the credit card company was produced by just a designer and me. The company had been using a big marketing firm for both the newsletter and direct mail campaigns, was paying dearly for it, *and* was unhappy with the result. I was brought into the deal by the designer, who was already there.

We ended up doing both projects, and delivered slick, sexy stuff— superior to what they were getting before—at a much lower cost. We got to be creative, were well paid, and collected some fab pieces for our books. These folks had the bucks to hire anyone, but chose us, and were delighted with the results. This is where it can go.

NUTS AND BOLTS Newsletters come in all sizes—two, four, six, eight (or some other multiple of two or four) pages. Many are a standard 8½" x 11" size, but "bill stuffers" are often smaller. With graphics factored in, figure approximately 500 words per page, give or take 50 (for 8½" x 11" versions). Like any job, price it in your head by the hour to come up with a flat rate (unless billing by the hour).

DIRECT MAIL Talk about accountability. Write a brochure, identity package, newsletter, or even an ad, and it's hard to gauge its effectiveness. Sure, with an ad, you can get a rough idea of its impact by increased sales, incoming calls, appointments, etc. Direct mail (DM)? Write a piece your client sends out to, say, 100,000 people, and within a few weeks, you know to the third or fourth decimal place how many people responded. Two main categories of direct mail are the long letter and the postcard. One at a time…

THE LONG LETTER One key DM category is *direct response*—with a long, multi-paged letter at its heart. Here, it's all about hard-hitting, attention-grabbing copy, both the catchy teaser on the envelope as well as the letter. Powerful, emotional hooks, heartstring-tugging copy, and a strong sales close. Nonprofits and purveyors of nutritional supplements and real estate investing programs are frequent users of direct response.

With nonprofits, it's all about their good works, noble cause, or the awful things their enemies (i.e., Republicans, evil real estate developers, the liberal media, etc.) are up to, all of which justify a healthy donation. Maybe an emotional pitch to support a foster child or to buy a money-making program ("You *do* want the best for your family, don't you?").

My experience with direct response is limited—unlike that of the following guest contributor. Bob Bly, the guy who's launched countless commercial freelancers' careers (including yours truly's) with his books, is recognized as the one of the world's foremost authorities on direct response copywriting. Here's a top-line primer from Bob…

Getting Started in Direct Response Copywriting

"Direct response," also known as "direct marketing," refers to any marketing that generates a direct inquiry for—or sale of—a product or service. In the old days, before the Internet, it was often called "mail order." You'd rent a mailing list, send out long-copy sales letters, and get back orders and checks in the mail.

This is in sharp contrast to "general" or "image" advertising, which seeks to build brand awareness but does not directly generate a sale or other action. For instance, when you hear a Coke commercial on the radio, there's no 800 number to call and order a case of Coke.

Direct response (DR) clients mainly care about one thing: can you write copy that beats their control? A "control" is their direct mail package they are using now to sell the product. It is the best-performing mail piece they have created to date, which is precisely why they're mailing *it* and not other mail pieces.

Direct mail is considered the "work horse" of direct marketing, but there are many other types of direct response promotions. Offline, we have TV and radio commercials, magazine and newspaper ads, inserts, and telemarketing. Online we use banner ads, e-newsletters, email marketing, and landing pages.

The mindset of much Madison Avenue advertising seems to be: how clever, funny, or creative can I make my commercial, and is it original enough to win an advertising award? The mindset of corporate marcom managers seems to be: how can I find a vendor who can turn things around quickly and provide the project management capabilities to make my life easier.

The mindset of direct marketers is: how can I write the strongest copy possible to sell this product and increase response rates while remaining legally compliant (e.g., no false claims, etc.). To be a direct response copywriter, you must focus on sales, not creativity. Forget branding, conversation, community, and other warm and fuzzy concepts.

You have to get inside the mind of the prospect, tap into powerful core emotions, and motivate them to pick up the phone and give you their credit card number. This is why direct response copywriters are in demand and command the highest fees.

While fees are all over the lot, a novice DR writer could charge as little as $1,000 for a one-page sales letter to generate leads. Experienced professionals charge anywhere from $5,000 to $10,000 and up to write a full-blown direct mail package (outer envelope, long sales letter, order form, sales brochure). Good freelance DR copywriters can earn $100,000 to $300,000 a year or more. A few earn seven figures.

The expression "copywriting is salesmanship in print" has been quoted more times than I can count. But it's not really true for many forms of copywriting. Much corporate communications and marcom really seems to be explaining or describing products, but not really selling them—not asking for the order. The salesperson does that.

With classic direct response, there IS no salesperson. Your sales letter must gain the reader's attention, engage his interest, create desire for the product, answer any objections, and get him to give you a check or his credit card number. This requires considerably more skill than writing, say, a press release announcing your quarterly results.

I have written extensively on how to get started as a freelance direct response copywriter. The quickest way to get more details is to download my ebook "Write & Grow Rich," available at: http://www.freelancewritingprofits.com/

NOTE: While direct response copywriting is what many people think of when they hear the term "copywriting" (thanks to companies like AWAI), Bly estimates that the DRC field accounts for roughly 3% of the overall "copywriting" universe—with most of the other 97% being the straight commercial freelancing covered in this book.

THE SELF-MAILER/POSTCARD   More and more companies are using self-mailers and postcards (usually oversize: 6" x 9") to deliver their messages. A self-mailer is a multi-panel brochure with one outside panel serving as the delivery/return address space. The piece can include all the components of a DM package—sales letter, brochure, perforated reply card—except in a much more compact form.

Writing postcard DM is like ad copywriting: catchy headline (front) and brief engaging body copy (back). That limited working space makes them ideal as awareness-building tools: reminding the world you're out there. Postcard DM is ideal for consumer-oriented businesses—print shops, insurance firms, health clubs, restaurants, automobile services, etc. Yet, given the ability to target corporate managers effectively through a good mailing list, they also work well in the B2B realm. In fact, know that there's a far larger universe of postcard direct mail (and hence, potential work) in the B2B arena.

A few years back, I did a postcard DM campaign for a software company whose flagship product was an accounting software program geared to small-to-medium manufacturing companies. Their key value proposition was that while accounting is viewed as a "necessary evil" by most companies, the smart ones (you, dear reader?) view accounting as a gateway to better decision-making ability, more control over operations, and greater profitability. So, we hit them with a provocative (okay, as provocative as accounting software can be…) bottom-line-oriented headline for the front:

Is Your Accounting System Leaving Money on the Table?

And a strong related follow-up headline for the reverse:

Unlock Hidden Profitability in Your Manufacturing Business

Talk in the language that gets their attention (sample at **www.writeinc.biz**, *Portfolio, Direct Mail, Peachtree Software*), and have them wonder…

THANKS TO THE INTERNET…   Postcards are even more popular now. After all, when most companies have web sites that tell their whole story, why spend a lot of time and money creating fat DM packages that probably won't get read anyway, when, instead, they can use a snappy postcard, rich in benefits-oriented copy, to steer people to their site? Where, chances are, the company can then capture their vital contact info.

I recently did a four-part combination postcard and self-mailer fundraising campaign for the Catholic charity, The St. Vincent de Paul Society in Atlanta (see sample at same link as above). We did three oversized postcards with the front featuring one-line teasers for stories of specific individuals helped by the Society's work. On the back, we fleshed out the stories, adding some boilerplate copy about the Society, and finishing up with a call-to-action that steered readers to the "Donate Now" link on their site.

The fourth piece in the series was the self-mailer: a tri-fold brochure with one final heartwarming tale, an expanded section on the Society's work, and finally, a physical reply envelope attached as a fourth panel to make it easy to send in a check.

WRITING STYLE With long-letter DM, it's all about powerful, hard-hitting, heartstring-tugging copy. For postcards, where space is at a premium, it's even more important that headlines be potent and copy be concise and direct. Again, study your junk mail. In any given week, you'll probably receive four or five examples in several categories.

PRESS RELEASES Or "news releases" as they're also known. Every business has to create a steady stream of releases—*the* primary vehicle for keeping media folks "in the know" of all noteworthy goings-on at a company. Big companies' media relations departments will typically write their releases, but even they occasionally get overloaded.

A 20-plus-year Atlanta PR veteran friend of mine, Beth Hawks (**www.corecommpr.com**), shared something interesting with me recently: "In public relations, we're always looking for a new angle or fresh approach that may catch an editor's eye. Freelancers are a great resource for those times when the workload is too heavy or things get stale internally. Even if the entire press release isn't used in its entirety, it's often worth the expense to have another point of view on a story." Straight from the horse's mouth.

Format and tone are everything in releases. Get the format wrong and media folks are likely to trash it. As for tone, the operative phrase is, "Just the facts, Ma'am…" Lose any whiff of "sales-y" or promotional tone and any subjective words (i.e., any adjectives gushing on about how great a company or their products are; the only exceptions are third-party testimonials in quotes), or it'll earn a quick trip to the circular file.

As discussed in our earlier sales/marketing chapter, ideally, try as much as possible to tie in a release with current trends, so it focuses on *benefits* to a larger audience. If you come from a PR background, you likely know how to write a decent release. If not, check out PR veteran Bill Stoller's great info-rich site, **www.publicityinsider.com**. And see *The Deluxe Well-Fed Tool Box* for *The Amazing Evolving Press Release*, four versions of a release promoting a self-published book (something I know a thing or two about), which range from gruesome on up to decent and serviceable.

Speaking of my friend Beth Hawks, I've included several of her releases in the *Tool Box* as well, including a few that represent a radical departure from the standard release format, but which, for her, have been a hit with journalists over the years.

WEB SITE COPY Given the oft-cited, ever-shrinking, gnat-sized human attention span, web copy needs to be short, punchy, easy-to-read "get-to-the-point-fast" copy. Short sentences, lots of bullets, lots of space. Big chunks of copy are deadly on the web. Write so that people can get in and out quickly.

More than most other arenas, web writing demands an ability to look at the site through typical "surfers'" eyes. Give them only what they want—and *need*—to know to move them along the sales cycle, not what you (and your client) want to tell them. Web work is everywhere. Used to be I'd pick up web work as I landed other work for a company, but these days, it's often the first call I get. Also check out web development companies as possible leads. Plenty of those around.

Bottom line, anytime you're in front of a client or prospect, ask about their web site. Of course, by that point, you should already know how well or poorly written their site is. If it's lousy, ask if they're open to reworking it, and if so, be ready to discuss how you might improve it. *And* casually ask who wrote it. If your contact wrote it and you start slamming it without knowing, you might just get off on the wrong foot.

Of course, if you don't have a lot of web experience, but do have some good clips of other work in the brief, crisp, snappy category, by all means share it, along with your persuasive assertion that, essentially, it's similar, which it is. A little secret: it's just not that hard to write effective web copy. The operative question is, "How can I convey the crucial information in the fewest words and most engaging manner possible?"

SEARCH & STUDY Visit lots of sites, especially the award-winning ones —designated by that little "Top 5% Site" logo. Google "Best Web Sites" (or similar). Usually, they're the best because (amongst other things) they're effectively written. Study them. Model them. And for a longer web writing primer, check out *The Deluxe Well-Fed Tool Box* 🗃.

CASE STUDIES As Casey Hibbard, Boulder, CO case study expert says, "Everyone loves to hear a great story about real people doing real things. The same goes in business." Case studies are becoming increasingly popular as companies look for engaging ways to tout their successes. And because case studies are basically articles, they're a great project type for current or ex-magazine writers looking to cut their teeth in the commercial world.

Casey (**www.compelling-cases.com**) is the author of the standout 2009 primer on case studies, *"Stories that Sell: Turn Satisfied Customers into Your Most Powerful Sales and Marketing Asset,"* designed for both companies looking to maximize the potential of case studies as well as copywriters wanting to add the project type to their mix. Visit **www.StoriesThatSellGuide.com**. I asked Casey to contribute a section. Read on…

Got a Knack for Storytelling? Give Case Studies a Try!

Customer case studies (a.k.a. "success stories") capture a customer's true experience using a product or service. From global corporations to one-person shops to nonprofits, many organizations create customer case studies to showcase their wares in action in a customer's setting—adding credibility, education, and validation to the rest of their marketing communications.

Organizations use case studies and case study content in various ways in their marketing, sales, and PR efforts. They can be run on the company's web site; emailed to prospects; left behind at sales appointments; handed out at trade shows; included in proposals; featured in company newsletters; reduced to bullets in PowerPoint presentations; sent to editors to pique their interest; turned into contributed articles; part of awards applications; and more.

WHAT THEY LOOK LIKE Going beyond the age-old testimonial, case studies can be anywhere from a few paragraphs to a dozen pages, with the typical one running two to three pages. The most successful case studies look like feature stories and follow a hero storyline, with the main characters being the featured customer company and individuals, and the products, services or service providers saving the day.

Include a mix of the following: who the customer is and what they do; their needs and challenges previously; why they chose the product or service; implementation/delivery of the solutions (if applicable); how the products or services work in the customer's environment; and the benefits and results that they have experienced.

Include engaging quotes from the customers, break it up with subheads, and include sidebar summaries. As with any communication, write for the audience. Craft your questions carefully to get all the relevant information in your interviews with customers.

While nearly any organization can benefit from case studies, the following are the best candidates: technology products/services, B2B solutions providers, consultants, marketing/advertising/design firms, and financial services entities.

WHAT YOU'LL EARN For the complete process (interviewing, writing, and then managing the review/edit/approval process with clients and featured end customers), the average two-page case study brings in anywhere from $700 to $1,500 each, depending on number of folks interviewed and complexity—not including design. Hourly rates average $75–100, with the higher end commanding upwards of $125/hr.

LEARN MORE Check out these sites for more information on case studies:

Articles and ebooks: www.compelling-cases.com/resources.html

A handbook for case study writers: www.forcopywritersonly.com/handbooks.html

Articles: http://www.thatwhitepaperguy.com/article_case_studies.html

Self-study course: www.casestudiesthatsell.com

To see sample stories, visit the sites of big companies and look for "case studies" or "success stories."

PB Note: Don't miss Casey's report 📒 in the *Tool Box* entitled, *"8 Tips for Case Studies that Compel and Sell,"* which takes this discussion to the next level.

WHITE PAPERS Entire books have been written about the art and science of this interesting, oft-misunderstood, and potentially quite lucrative writing niche. In truth, I've never done a white paper. Up till recently, white papers were mostly a high-tech thing, so they never appealed to me. They're becoming more mainstream now, so who knows? Might take a shot at it one day.

So, I'm no expert, but I know one: good friend Michael Stelzner, international authority on white papers, author of the excellent 2006 release, *Writing White Papers* (**www.writingwhitepapers.com**), and web master of the definitive web site on the subject, **www.whitepapersource.com** (plus editor of a newsletter and blog…).

I asked Michael to provide a top-line "who-what-when-where-why-and-how" Q&A overview of the field (below). If it all sounds intriguing, subscribe to his newsletter and blog, and consider investing in his book.

White Papers 101

Do you like to persuade? Want your writing to be referenced? Motivated by money?

If you answered yes, then give the white paper a try. Whether you are a seasoned journalist, a technical writer, a business communicator, a master of marketing messages, or a wanna–be writer, there's something for you in white papers.

What Is a White Paper? It's a cross between a magazine article and a corporate brochure. They blend the informative and authoritative content of an article with the persuasive elements of a company brochure. White papers are used to help educate and influence business prospects. They proliferate in the technology world, and are rapidly catching on in financial services, healthcare, insurance, and other B2B marketplaces.

Why the Fuss About White Papers? Simply put, white papers are hot, and corporations desperately need them. Consider this: in 2001, Google registered a mere one million hits on the term "white papers." By 2006, that number went beyond 300 million!

Why the growth? White papers help people make decisions, and are actively sought after. An astonishing 70% of information technology professionals rely on white papers to make purchasing decisions in the U.S. (*Source: ITtoolbox, 7/19/06*).

Add the need for quality lead generation: businesses are struggling to get their message in front of prospects. Research shows there's simply no better tool to attract leads than the white paper. In fact, a recent study concluded white papers were most valued by those at an early stage in the sales cycle—more than free trials, analyst reports and webinars (*Source: KnowledgeStorm/SiriusDecisions, 7/6/06*).

WHY WRITE WHITE PAPERS? Some key reasons writers are going for white papers:

- **Demand exceeds supply:** There are not enough writers who know how to write white papers. Businesses are aggressively looking to write more white papers. Master the art and count your dollars.

- **White papers bring prestige:** Many writers get bylines on white papers, bringing them significant recognition. If your paper is well received in the industry, or goes viral, your name will be associated with the ideas presented in the paper.

- **You can charge more for a white paper:** Since white papers help businesses generate leads and close sales, they're directly tied to revenue. For many businesses, just one or two sales from a white paper return the investment.

- **Businesses pay top dollar for white papers:** Word for word, nothing beats a white paper. A good white paper writer charges between $3,000 and $10,000 for a 10-pager—making it one of the most lucrative writing specialties out there.

- **White papers can be multi-purposed:** A well-written white paper can be converted into a contributed article or used as content on a web site. This adds more value to a white paper project.

- **Many businesses need multiple white papers:** If you prove yourself with an excellent white paper, there is a high likelihood the company will want others written. This can generate a consistent pipeline of work.

BUSINESS LETTERS Think about it: the goal of most business—or "sales"—letters we receive as consumers is to get us to pay attention and take some action. If it's a cover letter for a larger marketing package, its job might not only be to have the reader review the whole package, but also to frame *how* they do so (e.g., draw attention to certain package components, highlight info about the company, demonstrate a grasp of their customers' hot buttons, etc.). A well-written one can be the difference between a package getting tossed and one that's read and acted on. That's huge.

Vast Experience Unnecessary Don't have the extensive sales background you *think* it takes to write such letters? So what? If you have a decent grasp of the sales and marketing concepts discussed in Chapter Three (i.e., audience, features/benefits, USP), and feel confident you can harness those tools to get readers' attention and spur them to a desired action, you'll do fine.

Attention-Getting Openings for a Sales Letter

Here are a few proven ways to draw a reader into your letter and/or larger package…

1) **Stories:** How about a two-paragraph mini-case study about a client who had a business challenge and how this company's product/service solved it? Not only do stories engage readers, but if the issue discussed is a common one for this audience, it allows the reader to see themselves in the story, and "relating" is a key first step to an ultimate sale. After the story, you continue on with the rest of the letter. An example…

ABC Company had a big problem. Unauthorized Internet surfing and online joke swapping by their employees was squashing productivity. But it was hard to prove, and harder to catch someone in the act. Then, they heard about Cubuzz, the revolutionary automated system for discouraging time-draining web activities.

The company-wide installation, wired through a special "conductivity patch" installed on all employees' PC keyboards, was programmed to allow surfing on only approved sites. Surf to an unauthorized site and the employee receives a harmless (but quite painful) electric shock. Within a month, productivity had increased 25%.

2) **Questions/Bold Statements:** Questions, often combined with a strong declaration, make the reader think and form a response in their head. To be most effective, center the question/statement in larger bold type *above* the salutation. Some years back, I was asked to rework a letter crafted by a young, successful mortgage company seeking a capital partner. To get that potential partner's attention, the letter had to highlight the things that'd matter to that crowd.

The opening of the "Before" version looked like this:

Dear Mr._____,

Just over two years ago we founded and started Real Equity Financing Corp., Inc. and secured a license as a Mortgage Broker. During the past 28 months we have seen tremendous growth within the organization. Retail loan closings now exceed $10,000,000 per month with multiple sales locations in metro Atlanta and Charlotte, NC. If you have had any experience with mortgage retail, then you are probably aware of the significance of that pattern of growth and the ongoing potential with that level of volume.

Here's how I rewrote it:

A 2-year-old mortgage brokerage firm with monthly retail closings in excess of $10,000,000? And looking for a partner?

Dear Mr._____,

The past 28 months since we founded and launched Real Equity Financing Corp., Inc. have seen growth nothing short of phenomenal. Yes, $10,000,000+ in monthly retail loan closings from sales offices in metro Atlanta and Charlotte, NC. If you're familiar with mortgage retail, then you certainly recognize the significance of such numbers and the growth potential with this level of volume.

3) Statistics: An impressive, "I-didn't-know-that" stat that underscores a larger problem (which the company's product/service solves, of course) can make a reader take notice and think about something he hadn't considered before. For example, someone marketing writing workshops to corporations might start a letter with this:

Substandard employee writing skills cost U.S. businesses up to $2.7 billion in lost productivity annually. How much are you losing?

It's all about drawing readers in. Play with these ideas and see what you come up with…

EASIER LETTERS? Sometimes a client simply needs a well-written cover letter to a package of *requested* information. While such an audience is already inclined to read the info, the letter still needs to be persuasive. For starters, people often request literature just to get someone off the phone. But, even if they *were* genuinely interested, 1) you still have to re-energize their initial enthusiasm, which has no doubt cooled since the call, and 2) precisely *because* they're interested, you need to get 'em while they're hot.

But, don't agonize over making a letter perfect. Believe me, I've seen some business letters that are so frighteningly bad that simple coherence, proper grammar and spelling, and a reasonably logical flow would have made a 1000% improvement and thrilled the client to no end.

DOUBLE DUTY MAKES SENSE Letters aren't typically THE project you're hired to do, but rather an add-on to bigger projects. If you've just worked on a client's marketing brochure or corporate image piece, why not suggest that you also write the accompanying cover letter? It only makes sense to keep the tone and writing style consistent.

Besides, there are few things more tragic than a beautifully written brochure or identity package fronted by a clunky, bland, client-written cover letter. It's like an incompetent, inarticulate receptionist at a successful company. The old saying, "You don't get a second chance to make a first impression" was never truer than here.

Suggest it before you start the project and it'll demonstrate you have the crucial "big-picture" sales mentality. Plus, you'll make $200–400+ more, depending on your expertise and the client's budget.

As mentioned earlier, my standard opening paragraph to a variety of business correspondence (marketing, meeting/phone follow-up, etc.) is this:

> *As a freelance writer, my goal is to enhance your image, improve your profit picture, and make your life easier. If it carries your name, shouldn't it be the best reflection of you?*

Per the earlier discussion, notice the bold statement/question. I like its simplicity and how, right up front, it addresses those issues nearest and dearest to a client's heart: image/reputation, profit, and simplifying his/her life. I'm speaking to my audience.

MARKETING EMAILS/LANDING PAGES Email marketing has become increasingly popular with companies trying to reach targeted audiences. Emails need to be short, succinct, bulleted (ideally), benefits-rich copy. And wrapped up with a call-to-action to get prospects to click for more information and/or details on a special offer.

When they do click through, they're taken to a "landing page" that ushers them from email to web site, seamlessly continuing the conversation that began in the email. As opposed to the deadly mistake many companies make with email marketing: simply providing a link from the discussion/ offer to their web site, giving arriving prospects zero clue how to find out more about the thing that piqued their interest seconds earlier. At which point, they *will* leave. Tragically missed opportunities. See the 4/29/09 post at **www.wellfedwriter.com/blog** for an example.

Landing page copy should still be short, sweet, and bulleted—where feasible—but obviously, you can and should provide more detail so as to move the prospect further along the sales cycle, and closer to becoming an actual buyer.

I asked Atlanta FLCW Ed Gandia (**www.edgandia.com**), who specializes in this kind of writing, to comment on the above:

1) The reason for short, succinct emails is you're only trying to get readers interested enough to click through to the landing page. Period. Many clients (and writers!) want to say too much in the email, so they lose readers because it looks like too much work.

2) The ONLY goal of the landing page is to get the visitor to convert (i.e., buy the product, download the white paper, sign up for the webinar, etc.). To do this effectively, you must continue the conversation started in the email, reaffirm to the visitor that he's in the right place, offer additional details that wouldn't fit in the email, reiterate the benefits of taking the next step, and overcome last-minute objections/hesitation. Oh, and don't ask for 47 pieces of info. The less you ask, the higher the response rate.

3) While there's debate in this area, **MarketingSherpa** *(www.marketing sherpa.com) argues for keeping landing pages free of navigation and links to other pages, asserting that these items distract visitors and depress response. I agree. The page should be clean, inviting, and not full of sidebar copy and other clutter.* **MarketingSherpa** *and* **Marketing Experiments** *(www.market ingexperiments.com) have both done a lot of research on landing pages, and are good sources for info on what works/doesn't work.*

SPEECHES My sincere thanks to my good friend Erick Dittus, an Atlanta-based speechwriter for his extensive input on this section. I've done some speechwriting over the years, but Erick's written for 56 CEO's and almost 100 organizations, and for years, speechwriting accounted for roughly 95% of his business. Check out a few samples of Erick's speeches at **www.wellfedwriter.com/sidedishes.shtml**.

In my second year, as mentioned, I was hired by an event production company (EPC) to write the speech for a hotel chain's new EVP of marketing for a franchisee conference. An undefined scope (10-plus rewrites) meant I was paid by the hour. Final tally: $9,000. On the strength of that job, I landed an easier 20-minute speech for the GM of an international credit card company for their regional conference. Fee: $2,600.

These examples showcase two places to pick up speechwriting: middle and upper management of large corporations (along with the EPC's that work with the big boys). Additionally, small- to medium-size companies can be just as good prospects since they're less likely to have in-house writing staff, but they'll likely pay less, too.

According to Erick, at press time, a speech for a Fortune 500 or Top 10 not-for-profit (NFP) C-level exec (i.e., CEO, CFO, COO, CTO, etc.) should command $5,000 to $8,000, less for VP's on the fast track to the C-level. In-house speechwriters at a medium NFP can earn $60–70K, and up to $125K in a Fortune 500 firm. Some Fortune 100 speechwriters are pulling down over $200K a year (at that level, they own your butt…).

YOUR JOB Typically, when writing speeches, the client will supply you with large, meaty chunks of source material. If it's an internal speech (for their own people) promoting a new direction (or reinforcing an old one) or for a sales conference, that means getting facts, figures, and charts as a recap of the past year's (or quarter's) performance. And no, you're not expected to take all those graphics and format them into a *PowerPoint*; we're just writers. Sure, if you *do* learn *PowerPoint*, it's one more talent you can offer up.

Connecting the various sections with fluid bridge copy will generally be the easy part.

What's more challenging—and interesting—is creating a theme (if necessary) as well as a compelling opening and wrap-up that do more than just summarize. If you're entrusted with creating a theme, make sure the major players buy into that theme before you write the speech, and you'll avoid the anxiety of an 11th hour rewrite.

Make sure you ask scads of questions, many of them familiar:

1) WHO'S THE AUDIENCE(S)? What are their hot buttons and concerns? What don't they want to hear? With what feeling do you want them left? Are there important people (e.g., shareholders, employees, the media, government agencies) that also need to be considered? Sure, most of them won't be in the room, but they might get a copy or read snippets in somebody's blog.

In many instances, says Erick, C-level or senior executives receive a formal written request to speak at a high-profile event. Get that letter and read it closely. What do they want from the speaker? Desired speech length? Q&A after? If so, does the speaker want/need prep notes, bullets or full-blown text for that portion?

If the client (speaker) gives you vague answers about the event, ask to speak with the conference coordinator. There's often a big difference between the speech a client was planning to give and what the conference actually wanted.

Yet, regardless of the wishes of conference organizers, the client's the boss. As a rule, conference organizers are happy if the speaker just touches on some of their themes.

2) WHAT'S WORKED BEFORE IN GETTING THIS GROUP'S ATTENTION? (If there was a 'before.') What hasn't? It's no fun spending bunches of time conceptualizing a great theme only to hear, "Oh, we forgot to tell you (i.e., you never asked), we tried that last year and it tanked." Grrrr. Through the organizers or staff of past speakers at the event, try to get a copy of speeches that have succeeded in the past with this group.

3) CREATING A THEME? If so, factor concepting time into your bid. I used the theme of "Relationships" for one speech. I defined the word according to the dictionary and outlined the different company relationships: client/company, company/vendor, worker/co-worker, management/employee. Throughout, I kept tying things back to the theme, emphasizing the importance of relationships in a time when a firm's offerings were often a commodity, requiring a stronger competitive edge.

This might be a place to use a pithy quote from Bartlett's Quotations. Or one of those heartwarming, inspirational, clever email treasures you've saved over the years. I closed the piece with just such an e-gem—"The Goose Story" (Google it), a wonderfully illustrative example of teamwork from the animal kingdom.

4) WHAT STYLE AND TONE DO THEY WANT? Humorous, straightforward, modest, assertive, challenging? It's critically important that you capture the "voice" of the speaker, so he'll feel comfortable speaking the words you write. If he's familiar to his audience, it has to sound like words he'd say. If it sounds overscripted, it'll compromise credibility.

You'll get as much sense of the speaker's style from interacting with him and observing his mannerisms and bearing as you will from his actual answers to your questions. Talk with the people who know him well, as they may see things you won't hear from him.

All this assumes you'll be meeting with the speaker before you begin writing. If not, push for it (or at least a phone chat), explaining they'll get a stronger final product. If neither is possible, ask for videos of him answering questions—without a script—to get insights into how he really speaks (vocabulary, cadence, thought patterns) and his passions. Erick reports that, with C-level execs, in at least 25% of the cases, he doesn't get to meet with them until the first draft is written. Not ideal, but not uncommon.

5) ANY NEGATIVE AUDIENCE ATTITUDES OR SENSITIVE ISSUES THAT NEED TO BE ADDRESSED? (Could apply to any project, not just speeches.) I've been in several initial meetings where I've discovered a huge political issue (e.g., layoffs and the resultant anxiety, or a huge customer service issue that's caused a lot of ill will). If it's not addressed, the audience will simply tune out. Yet they sit there, ostrich-like, happy to deliver pabulum. Bring it up. Maybe they'll listen, maybe they won't. All you can do is go on record.

Being willing to bring up the uncomfortable issues—grounded in a commitment to a superior outcome—separates good copywriters from outstanding ones, and justifies higher fees. I say *not* taking the easy way out is part of our job.

Though sometimes, company lawyers have determined a certain subject is—for good reason—off-limits. That said, often what can't be included in a speech (which may be handed out to the media or posted online) can be artfully wedged into an answer during a Q&A. You can also get paid for writing these post-speech comments.

Most C-level clients, says Erick, expect speechwriters to be considerably more than just writers. Often, a client who realizes you've taken the time to understand the nuances of the business will ask your opinion about an issue separate from the speech content. The smart ones are always looking for fresh input. Give them authentic insight and you'll get asked back more often than your competitors.

One final rule. Always ask to write the speaker's introduction. At most events, the introducer, never having met the speaker, will simply read, word-for-word, the bio in the conference program. Yawn. Ask the introducer if you might write up "some ideas." Then create a 125- to 200-word (60–90 second) intro that'll make the audience want to listen to the words you've slaved over. The introducer will be happy you've got it covered, you'll make a few hundred extra dollars, and more importantly, because you added value to the event, you'll boost your reputation.

RESOURCES:

Speechwriter's Newsletter—According to Erick, "Regarding this profession, it's about the best thing going." **http://www.ragan newsletters.com**. Not cheap at $307 annually (2008), but a good investment, and they offer a no-obligation trial subscription.

The Speechwriter's Conference—Erick: "There are more speechwriters gathered there than at any other one place, except for maybe the Democratic and Republican Conventions. **http://www.ragan.com**, then *Events*, then *Conferences*.

Vital Speeches of the Day—Says Erick: "This is where you want your speeches published." **http://www04.mcmurry.com/product/VITAL**. Offering examples of the best speeches ever written, it features *The Speech of the Month* (audio). Subscriptions: $75 annually (12 issues).

GHOSTWRITING Speechwriting is actually a subset of the larger category of ghostwriting: writing something—speech, article, book—for someone who will put her name or voice to it as if she wrote it. Fact is, most people in corporate America aren't writers (beyond what they *have* to do), or more likely, they just don't have the time.

My first ghostwriting experience came three months into my career, when, as I shared earlier, I got the nod to ghostwrite a book for that local businessman who wanted to add "Author" to his credentials but wasn't a writer.

RIPE MARKETS For those inclined toward medicine or law, there are undoubtedly countless doctors and lawyers who want/need to get articles published regularly. They rarely have the time or inclination to do it, but they do have the money. Obviously, you need to be able to step in and, with a relatively small amount of background and supervision, crank something out.

Aside from contacting lawyers'/doctors' offices directly, hunt for this kind of work in companies for which you're doing other work. Again, if you can leverage past experience, even better. Ask your contacts in those firms if they know how that stuff gets done. Sure, in-house staff may handle it, but don't assume that's the norm.

UNUSUAL GIG Another interesting ghostwriting experience…The CEO of a local firm being considered for a prestigious CEO of the Year award in Atlanta needed to submit five 250- to 300-word essays. Not being a writer, he decided he'd hire one. While he ultimately didn't win (the competition was obviously stiff that year; translation: the copywriter had nothing to do with the outcome), he was delighted with what I came up with—as was I with the $1,750 fee for roughly half a week's work.

TRADE ARTICLES While most magazines offer pathetically low fees (i.e., $0.10–0.50 a word) in relation to the effort expended, writing articles for trade publications can nicely boost those fees. As a rule, don't settle for any less than $1 a word (those who've been at a particular niche for a while can routinely earn $2+ a word). Here's where someone coming from a particular industry like retail, high-tech, financial services, or healthcare can do well.

A SWEET DEAL Often, a trade publication is a wholly owned (but unpublicized) subsidiary of a company who uses the pub as a venue for promoting their own products and services. Smart little arrangement. They might do a piece that highlights the growing trend towards an innovative technology—a trend which, when acknowledged and acted on by readers, will create a demand for the very products and services they sell.

Since the publication is viewed as an advertising medium of sorts, one that should yield real bottom-line profits, they can afford to pay well. A few years into my career, I was earning over $1 a word for the trade pieces I landed. I have a colleague who writes regularly for a trade pub serving the livestock industry. Regardless of the length, she always gets $2,000 for each one. Her motto: "I don't pick up a pen for less than $500." Hey, more power to her. So it's out there.

DVD/VIDEO/CD SCRIPTING   As web sites pervaded, video production took a big hit. But recently, video's experienced a resurgence, due, paradoxically, *to* the Internet. Putting video on the web used to be a problem, since video can hog the Internet pipeline. Faster, inexpensive connectivity has solved the bandwidth problem and faster computers process the video more quickly on the user's end. So, video rises again, and that spells writing opportunities with companies large and small.

Instead of trying to explain a product or service to a prospect in, say, India, a U.S. company can demonstrate benefits and features instantly with a click of a mouse. The following video, audio or multimedia formats are being used extensively, and all require copy or scripting by *someone*.

DVD's   Big companies create a healthy number of DVD's for both internal and external use—either done in-house or outsourced. Typically, a company would create a DVD to showcase products, services, a message from the president, education, training, company histories, pictures with captions, videos, etc.

The Advantages of DVD (Marketing)   Because DVD's are menu-driven, allowing the viewer to "click 'n choose" what they want to watch, they're used increasingly in the sales arena. A salesperson can show different prospects—with different needs and "hot buttons"—different things. DVD's portability allows for viewing anywhere, and its uniformity means everyone watches the same thing.

The Advantages of DVD (Training)   Here, DVD's can be designed so students can't move to the next module until they pass the present module's test or review. That said, because DVD's are non-linear, viewers can choose where they want to go vs. the fixed path of video. Since the viewer has choices, the material has to be compelling and user-friendly. Ergo, the need for writing creativity here is high.

VIDEO RISING   You can do a lot of cool things with a video clip. Longer chunks (five-plus minutes) can go on DVD's, while shorter ones can be posted streaming on a web site, included in an email signature (below), or downloaded onto public venues such as YouTube (used by smaller creative firms as a surrogate web site because the hosting is free, and it provides a medium to market services to, potentially, millions).

Straight video will undoubtedly continue to hold a strong position when a linear story needs to be told, if a company doesn't have the budget to go interactive, or if a piece needs to evoke strong emotions or tell a compelling story slowly and progressively.

VIDEO EMAIL SIGNATURES The piece of real estate at the bottom of an email is prime property. In much the same way an email signature may include a web link, links to short video clips are showing up more and more in many companies' email signatures. Brevity is key. The video email signature may link to a 30- to 60-second commercial, a brief two-minute new product teaser, or a marketing brochure turned into a mini-pitch. To keep things fresh, companies will periodically change the video clip, and that translates into repeat writing opportunities.

To land any of the above, contact a company's marketing or marketing communications department. And once you're in the door of a company and have a feel for their goals and directions, don't be afraid to suggest some of the above. Other possible prospects? Video and/or multimedia production companies, web developers and sound studios.

AUDIO CD'S As dowdy and old-fashioned as audio CD's now seem compared to their flashy multimedia DVD brethren, there's still a strong demand for the medium. Just think about all the poor souls sitting in traffic every day. Motivational speakers and other how-to gurus are good prospects. Many understand the value of doing a professionally produced program, complete with high-quality production and writing. National (**www.nsaspeaker.org**), regional, and state speakers associations and speakers bureaus (**www.nsb.com**) are great places to track down speakers and gurus.

HOW DO YOU WRITE FOR VIDEO? Short sentences, simple structure, and few $50 words. A well-written video script is written for the junior high school level. Why? When someone watches video, his attention is split between sights *and* sounds. Hence, you need to make it easy for your viewer to hang with it and get the message. Make your sentences too long or too complex, and your audience will tune out.

VIDEO FORMAT #1 The standard video script format is side-by-side, like so:

VIDEO	AUDIO
Med CU (close-up) of Graphic Designer sitting at monitor kneading a pile of Play-Doh and placing the pieces in his nose.	The story begins in the same place where all large-format poster production starts: at your designer's PC or Mac. The image is manipulated in the same manner.
Designer puts a fresh pile of Play-Doh in the little grinder and, using the star-shaped attachment, cranks out long, starry ropes.	After the image is enhanced through the dynamic Diffusion Software, it is then processed through RasterServe, the state-of-the-art digital imaging software.
Designer presses ball of Play-Doh into a piece of newspaper, peels it off, leaving the reverse image of the front page.	Once through these steps, the image moves on to your Xerox Versatec or Calcomp electrostatic printer.

This format allows for easy juxtaposition of the video and audio components, as well as any text (i.e., bullet points, pithy quotes, dramatic questions, etc.) that will appear on the screen along with the video images and audio soundtrack.

PROBLEM/SOLUTION Now, in *Word*, you'd use a table to create this format, which creates two independent columns (VIDEO/AUDIO), where one isn't affected by the other. The only problem with this approach is that when the page you're working on 'breaks' to the next as you get to the bottom, the program occasionally ends up vanishing your text. It's there, and you'll probably get it back, but until you do, it can most assuredly mess with your inner peace. If you know you'll be doing a lot of scriptwriting, check out this link: **http://filmmakerstore.com/swvideo.htm** (featuring a two-column scriptwriting template).

VIDEO FORMAT #2 If you have a simple script to write, with only video and audio (no text/bullets appearing on the screen), you can likely get away with a much simpler format I picked up from an experienced video producer years back. You just type your audio portion and preface it with the video directions in caps:

CUT TO VAN PULLING UP TO FACILITY. SHOT OF DRIVER LOOKING AROUND AS HE PULLS FLASK OUT AND TAKES LONG DRAW. UNSTEADY BUT SMILING, HE GETS OUT AND HELPS PATIENT TO RECEPTION AREA.

Once you arrive, your professional driver will happily escort you to the reception area. When your surgery is finished, he'll be waiting for you! Just a few cups of coffee and he'll be as good as new!

STAFF IN MOUSE EARS ENGAGED IN SPITBALL FIGHT STOPS SUDDENLY AND SMILINGLY GREETS PATIENT. PICKING UP PHONE AND SPEAKING (BKGRND. TALK SAYING "MS. JONES IS HERE FOR HER PROCEDURE.")

Our courteous and professional staff is expecting you, and after signing in, they'll notify the surgical coordinator that you've arrived for your appointment.

Much easier, no? You can also use it as the format for a preliminary script, converting it to side-by-side when you have all the video direction and on-screen text set.

NEED A VIDEOGRAPHER? If you land a project that needs an experienced videographer (especially if you're in the Atlanta area, but he travels anywhere), you couldn't do much better than my long-time friend and experienced pro, Bob Hamilton (who offered up beaucoup industry insights for this section). See **www.infocuscommunications.com**.

RADIO SPOTS Writing radio spots is similar to writing for video, since both are written for the ear. While video has the visual competing with the audio, radio competes with whatever the listener is doing—working, driving, puttering around the house, etc. As such, radio spots need to be simply written and easy to follow by a distracted listener. Best way to determine which companies may need help? Tune in. It'll be mostly consumer products: retail, automobiles, leisure travel, financial services, banks, etc.

Writing radio spots can be big fun, especially when clients let you get creative, and most are open to that. Humor works, because an entertained listener is an attentive listener. But remember, funny is good only if the spot achieves the desired result: boosting sales, calls, interest, etc. If you're unsure of your abilities in this arena, just listen to the lame, awful stuff that often circulates on the airwaves and you'll get your confidence back in a hurry.

As a rule, you'll be writing 30- or 60-second spots (actually 27–28 and 57–58 seconds, respectively. Always build a spot around the core information: the who, what, where, when, why, how, and how much of a product or service. Think of creative ways to position those key facts within a compelling (which can mean funny) storyline. Keep the copy simple. No big words or long phrases. Check out my portfolio for samples.

"ON-HOLD" MESSAGES An interesting variation on radio copy is "on-hold" messages—what people hear when they call a company and are put on hold. Sure, many companies still use Muzak or a radio station, but more and more are taking advantage of the captive audience to deliver low-key sales messages, new product announcements, product or customer service enhancements, etc.

Small- to medium-size companies with a limited and easily definable product line are often the companies best suited for this kind of writing. Your best bet is to pick up this work as an add-on to other work you're doing for a company. Ask if they're currently doing it, and if not, suggest it. You'll not only pick up extra work, but you'll also be viewed much more as a consultant than a writer. Again, samples at **www.writeinc.biz**.

EVENT SCRIPTING For six years, I scripted the annual awards ceremony of a prominent Atlanta business organization, an event sponsored by the state branch of Junior Achievement. I did another such project for the annual two-day regional conference of a fast food company in Atlanta. I was initially involved with the creative brainstorming of the show's theme and structure—a two-page treatment. Once the client bought off on the concept, my next task was to actually script every moment of the two-day event.

Much more than just a parade of speakers, it featured an involved talk-show format, with 12 distinct segments. The script included all the 'blocking'—i.e., "Host walks onstage, a small elevated platform with host desk and three comfortable chairs. Host banters with audience about morning session before introducing first guest"—and the bridge copy: intros and exits to and from each guest's presentation or interview.

Each of the speakers/guests provided their own copy points and answers to questions. Since most weren't writers, it was my job to clean up their masterpieces, work them into the overall flow of the program, and make it all sound conversational, while preserving a uniform tone throughout.

It was a chance to get creative with the directions and details of the event, and happily, few of my suggestions were nixed.

The big event production companies (EPC's) we discussed earlier are a primary source of this kind of work, along with many other types of projects: brochures, speeches, convention literature, etc. Additionally, think of any firm that puts on a well-orchestrated multi-media event each year. Remember: the Junior Achievement event involved three totally distinct writing tasks plus a few others I didn't do.

HI-LEVEL PROPOSALS   If a major event production company is pitching a Fortune 500 company on securing all its trade show business for the next four years (an actual proposal I worked on), it won't be a two-page flyer. Try a binder with ten+ sections covering every aspect of the process: introduction, rationale, creative ideas, drawings, photos of other work, production details, financial details/breakdown, summary, etc.

Often, you're looking at a gargantuan coordinating effort to bring all the disparate pieces together in one "voice"—a uniform tone and flow to the whole document. Sounds complex, but it's still just writing. There might be a different tone for the creative brief section than for production details, but it's writing nonetheless.

WELL-PAID FRUSTRATION   A few years into my career, I had an intense week-long proposal writing experience. Twelve departments contributed sections to a 1000+ page document. I was writing sales-oriented copy for several segments while managing the project's assembly. In the end, however, the client didn't tap my strengths—my writing ability and sales perspective—but rather, I was handling technical issues of formatting and importing documents, areas where I wasn't nearly as comfortable.

I shared my frustration at mid-week with the project leader, who'd brought me in on two days notice and *knew* of my technical limitations. He said, "It's well-paid frustration, no?" True. Sixty-five hours in six days at about $70/hr. Somehow I found the strength to go on.

Goes with the territory. A super-fun and rewarding project might not pay well (although sometimes does), while a taxing, "can't-wait-for-this-to-be-over" scenario will put a bundle in your pocket. It all works out.

"TREATMENTS" Not all proposals are like the Manhattan Yellow Pages. Another type—just a few pages long—is the "treatment," which a creative firm might be asked to write (and in turn, might outsource) to outline their vision for a particular project. For example, an event production company might suggest a theme, and how they'd execute, in top-line terms, a particular event, conference, product roll-out, etc. If the client likes the direction, they might then ask for a full-blown proposal.

BLOG WRITING Talk about a ubiquitous medium. While the overwhelming bulk of activity in the blogosphere is dreck—pointless blatherings of people whose opinions few care about—serious, well-written blogs have come to play a critical role in much of today's media mix.

Thanks to RSS (Really Simple Syndication), which can broadcast a message across the 'Net, many companies are realizing the potential of blogs to increase web traffic. But, like so many other writing projects that companies don't have the time or resources to do in-house, blogs are a great candidate for outsourcing. And given that many blogs are updated two to three times a week (not that I think that's necessary), it could be steady work. And work best not left to an in-house staffer, for whom blog writing is likely just one of many responsibilities.

WHY DO A BLOG? A colleague of mine landed a steady gig writing blog copy (at $100 an hour) for a service business, which used blogging to underscore their bottom-line benefits. They took their overall "value proposition" and sliced it up into separate blog posts. Remember, an average blog entry is short—150 to 300 words. Blogs can be a great way for a company to get a leg up on the competition. By underscoring issues of importance to their target audience, a company can elevate themselves above the din.

If you're already doing work for a company you suspect would benefit from a blog, why not suggest it? Or, if you have a personal interest in, say, politics, the environment, animal rights, etc., or a formidable knowledgebase in a specific or esoteric industry or industry segment, why not approach players in that arena with the blog idea? There isn't a company out there that wouldn't like to strengthen the relationship with their audience and drive more traffic to their site, and blogs can potentially do that. I say potentially, because blog content has to be good, and worth taking the time to read.

RESOURCES For an excellent primer on the art and science of blogging as it relates to corporations, check out online marketing guru Debbie Weil's book, *The Corporate Blogging Book* (**www.thecorporateblogging book.com**). While geared to corporate types wanting to know what starting a blog entails, obviously, it'll give you the tools and simple technical know-how to be able to make persuasive how-to and why-to pitches to those prospects. Convince someone of the bottom-line benefits, along with your ability to pull it off, technically and content-wise, and you might just land a juicy ongoing gig.

Also check out my friend Stephane Grenier's great book (which I titled/subtitled): *Blog Blazers* (**www.blogblazers.com**) for input from the world's top bloggers. Educate yourself further on blogs at three of the more serious blogging sites: **www.typepad.com**, **www.wordpress.com**, and **www.blogger.com** (the first two are considered more serious choices by many when setting up a blog).

TAGLINES/NAMING A copywriting specialty few FLCW's like *and* are good at. I'm one of them. Probably wouldn't build a dedicated business around it, but it's a fun and potentially lucrative part of my mix (as discussed last chapter in "Spot Specializing").

Crafting a company tagline entails capturing and "nuggetizing" several different key messages into one, succinct, catchy, benefits-oriented blurb (but don't sacrifice clarity or benefits for "catchy." Bad tradeoff…). The right tagline can literally put a company on the map (Think, "GE. We bring good things to life.®" "Avis. We try harder.®" "Burger King. Have it your way.®" "Virginia is for lovers.®")

Naming is just as, if not more challenging than taglines, and much more is at stake—a company's very identity. To get a feel for the process and see tons of real-world examples, check out **www.namestormers.com**, a big player in the naming/tagline arena. Couldn't find prices, but **www.creatingnewnames.com** gets $7,500 for a name. Also see my work in naming/taglines/book titling at **www.writeinc.biz**.

TECHNICAL WRITING Another enormous arena of writing—sort of the quieter, more studious cousin of commercial freelancing—is technical writing. Not where my interests lie, but there's work aplenty: technical manuals, software documentation, product spec sheets, user guides, online help modules (what you get to when you click the "Help" button on a software program), web-based reference material, and more. You need a solid grasp of technical issues, whether the arena is telecommunications, software, manufacturing, or others.

You need to really like this stuff, because in contrast to the one- or two-week time frames in commercial writing, technical writing projects are typically months long in scope. The pay scale for technical writers (TW's) tends to be lower than creative marketing rates—$35–60/hr depending on the project and the writer's experience.

LONGER GIGS Most TW's use third-party agents/brokers (or "job shops") who specialize in matching writers with projects. TW's tend to be reluctant marketers, both because of the typically introverted "techy" personality and because long projects preclude the need to always be marketing. And according to some insiders, roughly 90% of TW's work onsite with companies, due to quirks in the tax laws (which I won't get into here).

Only about 10% are truly freelance, meaning they, 1) do work for more than one client; 2) don't work onsite in a client's office; and 3) don't go through the job shops for their jobs, but rather approach the companies directly. Those freelancers generally make more than contract TW's (roughly $50–75 vs. the $35–60 discussed earlier). Why? Because the job shops are significantly marking up their TW talent to their end clients, and a freelancer can charge more than what a contract TW would get, and still be well below what that company would pay to the job shop.

YOUR OWN ASSOCIATION If you want to find out more about technical writing than I could possibly share, then check out the Society for Technical Communication (**www.stc.org**).

You'll find publications, articles, networking, conferences, and links to local chapters, typically with sites of their own.

NOTE: There's a big difference between technical writing and *high-tech marketing writing*. The former is much less persuasive or "sales-y" than the latter, though the writer still has to clarify, warn, and subtly motivate. Pick up a manual for a software program and you'll know what I mean.

By contrast, high-tech marketing writing is like any other creative/ marketing writing, but for high-tech products. If you like the high-tech arena, have a good grasp of the technological issues and can write from a "features/benefits" sales perspective, you'll enjoy higher rates than technical writing. And given that it's harder for high-tech companies to find people who both know technology *and* can write persuasively about it, those who can do both can make more than the average commercial freelancer.

CAVEAT ESCRITOR Technical writing is a highly *tools-based* profession, meaning an employer is likely to be more interested in your mastery of multiple software applications than your ability to truly write well. One FLCW (and ex-TW) I know takes on gigs in both arenas, but shakes his head at the TW field, saying, "It's a strange animal; I'm just not sure they care very much how effective the writing is."

If you're a writer at heart, you'll probably tire quickly of the tools-orientation of TW. And, in fact, many former TW's indeed left the field precisely because they were—first and foremost—writers, and they wanted to get back to wordsmithing. Can't blame them.

•   •   •

While I've covered a broad spectrum of the kinds of projects you'll come across as a FLCW, you'll certainly discover new arenas and new kinds of work on your own, and as business changes and evolves. Well, we're almost done here…

Chapter 15

"The 5% Rule: Why Success is Easy"

Marcia Yudkin's 9/12/07 issue of *The Marketing Minute* (well worth subscribing to; visit **http://www.yudkin.com/ marketing.htm**) had the above title. She wrote (in part):

When L.A. filmmaker Jeff Bollow moved to Sydney, Australia a couple of years ago, he planned to launch an independent feature film studio but couldn't find enough commercially suitable screenplays. To beef up the supply, he began teaching screenwriting workshops in his new homeland.

Four years later, he had trained 641 workshop participants, but he still did not have a dependable stable of screenwriters. Although nearly everyone in the workshops loved the training, less than 5% of participants did anything with what they learned.

[T]his outcome has nothing to do with Australia or with screenwriting. It's human nature. And where Bollow lamented his 95% wasted energy, I see vast opportunity for the 5%. When you not only take action, but do it well, you'll find yourself way, way ahead of colleagues.

Reminds me of emails I've gotten over the years: "Given that the success of *The Well-Fed Writer* has no doubt unleashed zillions of copywriters out into the world, is this still a good opportunity or is the market saturated?" Saturated? That's funny.

Okay, here's the short answer: No, Mr. Worrywart, the market is not saturated. Yes, this is still a good opportunity. As Ms. Yudkin points out above, well south of five percent of folks who read *any* how-to guide—particularly one requiring some serious "getting-off-your-butt"—will ever do anything with their newfound knowledge.

Now, the bad news is that most of you reading these words will never pursue this business. But, the really good news is that if you're one of the few who do get in gear, you've got far less competition than you might ever imagine. Coupled with the reality of just how much work is out there, the good news positively swamps the bad.

Of course, let's not forget the 95/5 reality: any writing direction that pays $50 to $125 an hour or more, is flexible, home-based, and can potentially earn you six figures annually in the space of a few short years, by definition is not going to be a cakewalk. As I'm fond of saying, if it were, everyone would be doing it, and we'd all be making ten bucks an hour. It takes a lot of hard work. No way around it.

Plus the cold, cruel reality is that it'll be harder for some, easier for others, and that's life. If you have no writing experience, are deathly afraid of marketing yourself, live in the middle of nowhere, or have never worked for yourself, then you'll have a tougher go of it than someone for whom the opposite is true. At this moment, in terms of your particular background, education, experience, portfolio, and circumstances, it is what it is. Everyone has things that work *for* them and *against* them. Again, c'est la vie. What matters is what you're going to do about it.

ONE OF THREE GROUPS If you've read the book cover-to-cover (thank you), you're likely in one of three groups. The first group enjoyed the book, found it interesting *and* knows it's not for them. Thanks for taking the time. Live long and prosper.

Group #2 finds the whole idea intriguing but there are a lot of obstacles (current job, family obligations, financial reality, etc.) you've got to handle before you can more forward. Group #3? You're pretty excited right now. And not real light and breezy.

As you've read the book, you've likely found yourself saying, "I can do this. I can *do* this!" Your head's aswirl with, "What if…maybe…it might just work…" You're in a place of head-bursting possibility, alternately giddy and terrified, envisioning mind-blowing success and catastrophic failure. Is it really as great as it sounds, you wonder. It is. I and countless others are reminded daily of how great our lives are.

When we stop and think about the world we've left behind—one of alarm clocks, rush hour, cubicles, performance reviews, office politics, two weeks vacation, fast food lunches at our desks, little personal time, and all the other trappings of a "challenging and rewarding corporate career," we often have to pinch ourselves.

Not trying to be glib here. Many of you have realities that require scenarios like the above, and I'd never belittle the commitments you've made to those who depend on you. I simply want to share a pretty wonderful possibility—one that can often yield the same or greater income while providing lifestyle benefits most would kill for.

BAD DAYS AT THE BEACH   No, this career path isn't some nonstop funfest (what is?), but it's like that old bumper sticker: "A Bad Day at the Beach is Better than a Good Day at the Office." Plenty of days, I'm not excited about what I'm doing or for whom I'm doing it, but they're just bad days at the beach. Kind of like being with someone you love who occasionally irritates you vs. someone you can't stand who constantly irritates you.

Reminds me of a line from a program by Marianne Williamson—the new-age author of *Return to Love*. If you feel unmotivated, lazy, and discontented in what you're doing, she says, chances are good that you're not fundamentally an unmotivated, lazy, and discontented person. Rather, "you just don't want to *be* there."

Nevertheless, we keep jamming our round-peg selves into square-hole careers, pump ourselves up with the latest pop platitudes, and then wonder why the good positive feelings last about as long as the happy gas after you leave the dentist's office. Try doing something you really enjoy and watch those positive feelings and general upbeat attitude about life put down roots.

If you're a good writer, a decent, honest, humble, reliable human being, willing to work hard and learn new skills, this life is yours for the taking. The only way you'll fail is if you never try or quit early. But here's the good news: all you *can* control is the actions you take and that, in fact, is more than enough to be successful.

JUST START The toughest part of any process is the beginning. I've heard from plenty of folks who've said, *Gee, I put off starting forever, making it out to be this big scary thing. Once I finally took the plunge, it wasn't nearly as difficult as I built it up to be.* Well, it almost never is. Real life can rarely compete with our over-active imaginations.

What about the subtitle of my book (unchanged from the first version)? "Financial Self-Sufficiency as a Freelance Writer in Six Months or Less." Is that still doable? Good question. I threw that very question out to my readers in a blog post. Check out what they said (45 comments worth!) on the 6/12/08 post at **http://www.wellfedwriter.com/blog**.

While, arguably, the business is harder than when I started 15 years ago, many folks felt I should keep the same title, since I did it in less than four months, and my book, as a blueprint for how I made it happen, ends up being inspirational. Depending on your background and experience, six months is still possible, but know that it could take longer. As always, my fellow "in-the-trenchers" know best, so check out their input.

NEED SOME GUIDANCE?–Just an FYI (okay, a self-serving FYI…). If you think you'd find some value in a coach looking over your shoulder as you get out of the gate (or even down the road), I have offered one-on-one mentoring since 2002. Judging by the feedback, I seem to be pretty good at it. Check out the details, what I can help you with, and yes, all that feedback at the Mentoring link at **www.wellfedwriter.com**. And speaking of help…

UNEXPECTED ALLIES If you've decided you're going for it, this book is a pretty solid roadmap to take you there. That said, it's you and you alone who will pull it off. Just know that when you decide to do it, you unleash powerful and wonderful allies who, unpredictably and unexpectedly, will help you along. I'm reminded of a poem written by W.N. Murray of the Scottish Himalayan Mountain Expedition:

Until one is committed
there is hesitancy,
the chance to draw back, always ineffectiveness

Concerning all acts of initiative and creation
there is one elementary truth,
the ignorance of which kills countless ideas
and splendid plans:
that the moment one commits oneself,
then Providence moves too.

All sorts of things occur to help one
that would otherwise have never occurred.
A whole stream of events issues from the decision,
of unforeseen incidents and meetings,
and material assistance
which no man could have dreamt would have come his way

I also have a deep respect for one of Goethe's couplets:

"Whatever you can do, or dream you can—begin it.
Boldness has genius, power and magic in it."

It's true. It really works that way. Commit yourself, and things start happening. Make it happen, and let me know about it.

Appendix A

The following is the farthest thing from an exhaustive compilation of resources for writers, and not every one of them is exclusively geared toward commercial writers. That said, they were all recommended by successful FLCW's as being of value. I'm virtually 100% certain that anyone reading this will exclaim, "I can't believe he didn't include _____!" C'est la vie. Find a more comprehensive list of writing resources at www.wellfedwriter.com ("Links").

Books

The Copywriter's Handbook by Bob Bly
A classic on the how-to of business writing.

Selling Your Services by Bob Bly
Great insights on giving quotes—especially high ones—and justifying prices, along with the psychology of winning clients.

Start and Run a Copywriting Business by Steve Slaunwhite
Great primer from seasoned B2B copywriting veteran.

Writing White Papers: How to Capture Readers and Keep Them Engaged by Michael Stelzner
THE white paper guru writes THE book on the subject.

Hey Whipple, Squeeze This: A Guide to Creating Great Ads by Luke Sullivan
Wonderful book with gems on every page to help you improve not just ads, but anything you write.

The Nitty-gritty of Writing for the Search Engines by Jill Whelan
From "The 'first lady' of search marketing." (**www.highrankings.com**)

How to Start a Home-Based Writing Business by Lucy V. Parker
Great book with success worksheets and a lot of good nuts 'n bolts info.

Book Yourself Solid: The Fastest, Easiest, and Most Reliable System for Getting More Clients Than You Can Handle Even if You Hate Marketing and Selling by Michael Port and Tim Sanders.
"…simple, yet effective techniques for creating relentless demand…"

Booked Beyond Solid: Your Business, Your Life, Your Way—It's All Inside by Michael Port as well.
"…Discover your ability to innovate in your business…" Visit Michael's site (**www.michaelport.com**) for a refreshingly different view on sales and marketing.

Marketing Strategies for Writers by Michael Sedge
Mostly geared to magazine writers but with enough fabulously entertaining lessons on being outrageously bold that ANY writer looking to profit from their writing can benefit.

Get Clients Now! by C.J. Hayden.
Bestseller by business coach C.J. Hayden for consultants, coaches, salespeople, and anyone who markets a service business.

Cold Calling for Women: Opening Doors & Closing Sales by Wendy Weiss

How to be Your Own Publicist by Jessica Hatchigan
Do-it-yourself playbook shares insider secrets for scoring positive publicity.

The 22 Immutable Laws of Marketing: Violate Them At Your Own Risk by Al Reis & Jack Trout (authors of *Positioning*)

Wizard of Ads: Turning Words Into Magic and Dreamers in Millionaires by Roy Williams
Challenging insights for anyone who communicates for a living.

Ogilvy on Advertising by David Ogilvy
THE classic work on advertising.

Direct Marketing by Howard Nash
Considered by many to be "the bible of direct marketing."

The Anti 9-to-5 Guide by Michelle Goodman
Geared toward women, but with enough good stuff for guys, too.
(blog: **www.anti9to5guide.com**)

Atlas Shrugged by Ayn Rand
The classic novel about business and economics as it relates to the way the world works.

7 Habits Of Highly Successful People by Stephen Covey

Purple Cow by Seth Godin
Drives home the importance of differentiating your offering from competitors.

Cold Calling Techniques That Really Work! by Stephan Schiffman
Proven techniques for reaching decision makers and making appointments (*and* pitches).

Zing: Five Steps and 101 Tips for Creativity on Command by Sam Harrison
Great guide to jumpstart your creative juices.

Don't Make Me Think by Steve Krug
Says one reader: "If you read just one book on web usability, make it this one."
www.sensible.com/index.html

Web Word Wizardry by Rachel McAlpine
A must-have how-to for web content writing.

Ready, Aim Specialize: Create Your Own Writing Specialty and Make More Money by Kelly James-Enger
For magazine freelancers (many still do a bit of that…)

Reference Books

The Synonym Finder by J.I. Rodale
PB: This nearly 1400-page beauty is, hands-down, the most often used reference book on my shelf. Arranged like a dictionary for easy use.

Woe Is I: The Grammarphobe's Guide to Better English in Plain English by Patricia T. O'Conner.
Very practical and delightfully written.

Simpson's Contemporary Quotations: The Most Notable Quotes Since 1950
By James B. Simpson

Words That Sell: The Thesaurus to Help You Promote Your Products, Services, and Ideas by Richard Bayan

The Associated Press Stylebook and Libel Manual, from Addison Wesley

Newton's Telecom Dictionary
An informative and entertaining reference for anyone who writes for the telecomm industry.

Web Sites

www.wellfedwriter.com – Goes without saying...

www.bly.com – Bob Bly's site—the guy who launched it all—the original commercial writer and author (or co-author) of 55+ books on writing and business. Great articles, tips, resources.

www.forcopywritersonly.com – Top copywriter and copywriter trainer Steve Slaunwhite's great site. Ezine, free "success kit," reports, courses, books, etc.

www.whitepapersource.com – The top site for everything about writing white papers, from Michael Stelzner, recognized international authority on the niche.

www.yudkin.com – Published! and Creative Marketing Solutions, both by 20-plus-year veteran freelancer Marcia Yudkin, offer dozens of useful articles on making a living as a freelance writer. Subscribe to her *Marketing Minute* at **www.yudkin.com/markmin.htm.**

www.writingformoney.com – The Internet newsletter that shows you how to make money and live a great life as a freelance writer.

www.writedirections.com – Classes, how-to articles, writing resources, coaching/consulting and free newsletters loaded with tips, tool, and leads!

www.writingcareer.com – Expert career advice for writers and freelance writers.

www.absolutewrite.com (both free and premium versions)

www.marketingprofs.com – Marketing know-how from professionals and professors.

www.marketingsherpa.com – critically acclaimed site "specializing in tracking what works in all aspects of marketing (and what does not)."

www.personalmba.com – Tagline: "DIY Business Education & Training —What You Need to Know to Succeed."

www.aboutfreelancewriting.com – Anne Wayman's great site, full of resources for freelancers, including job leads three times weekly (some of interest to FLCW's).

www.freelancewritinggigs.com – Deb Ng's great site. Started to help writers (mostly at-home moms) find decent paying jobs; has become a top online writing community.

www.writersweekly.com – The FREE marketing e-mag for writers, published by freelance writing maven Angela Adair-Hoy.

www.writing-world.com (formerly Inkspot.com) – The Writer's Resource —One of THE premier and most respected sites for writers: articles, links, resources, and networking.

www.worldwidefreelance.com – Award-winning site for freelancers.

www.writersmanual.com – The bragging zone for writers worldwide."

www.writingfordollars.com – Find current markets that pay; how to market what you write and earn more; tips for entering high paying markets; and interviews with successful writing professionals.

www.writersdigest.com – Writer's Digest, the world's leading magazine for writers.

www.writers-editors.com – Where editors, businesses, and creative directors can locate writers, copy editors, proofreaders, ad copywriters, ghostwriters and PR help.

dobkin.com – The website for "Marketing Master" Jeffrey Dobkin, author of *How to Market a Product for Under $500* and *Uncommon Marketing Techniques*. Site houses a bunch of excellent (and free) articles on various aspects of the marketing process.

www.abraham.com – Actionable strategies from marketing guru Jay Abraham to "grow your business beyond anything you ever expected or even hoped."

www.cargillsells.com – Gill Cargill, a top sales training professional, and according to one reader, "a fabulous resource for anyone who needs to market his or her business."

http://filmmakerstore.com/swvideo.htm – Features an application with 12 script templates for $129, including a two-column format for video.

http://bartleby.com/141/ – The Elements of Style (now it's online!)

http://dictionary.reference.com – Dictionary.com

www.apostropheabuse.com – For those who cringe at incorrect apostrophe use.

www.westegg.com/cliché – The Cliché Finder. Need a little inspiration to write a headline or improve your copy? Clichés might just be what you need.

www.squidoo.com/businesscliches – Encyclopedia of Business Clichés: Seth Godin sets the record straight on the most useful and useless business clichés.

www.espindle.org/roots.html – Root-word reference complements naming exercises.

www.freedict.com/onldict/lat.html – An English-to-Latin dictionary offers copywriters easy access to word definitions.

www.quotation-marks.blogspot.com – A blog about unnecessary quotation marks.

www.visualthesaurus.com – A great resource to help with brainstorming names, taglines, or when you just need to find the right word.

Web/Online Copywriting Resources

www.useit.com/papers/webwriting/ – Jakob Nielsen is a guru in the field of web usability. This page on his site has links to numerous articles, books, and guides.

www.gerrymcgovern.com – Gerry McGovern, web content guru, provides info and resources on creating a more customer-centric web site.

http://www.highrankings.com/seo-resources – Search Engine Optimization expert Jill Whelan's resources link: SEO classes, workshops, forum, FAQ's, and glossary.

Social/Business Networking Sites

LINKEDIN: www.linkedin.com – THE business person's social networking site.

FACEBOOK: www.facebook.com – Not as serious as LinkedIn, but wildly popular.

TWITTER: www.twitter.com – Says one user: "Twitter is the telegraph system of Web 2.0."

PLAXO: www.plaxo.com – "Connect to your family, friends, and business network."

Others worth a look, though many have a focus that's more social than business: **www.MySpace.com, www.Ryze.com, www.Tribe.net, www.Friendster.com, www.Classmates.com, www.Xanga.com, www.Orkut.com.**

Writing/Marketing E-Newsletters

THE WELL-FED E-PUB (MONTHLY)
Editor: Peter Bowerman
Website: http://www.wellfedwriter.com
Focus: Copywriting

BOB BLY'S DIRECT RESPONSE LETTER (MONTHLY)
Editor: Bob Bly
Website: http://www.bly.com
Focus: Copywriting

THE WHITEPAPERSOURCE NEWSLETTER (MONTHLY)
Editor: Michael Stelzner
Website: http://www.whitepapersource.com/newsletter.html
Focus: White paper writing and related news, articles, and marketing

THE MARKETING MINUTE (WEEKLY)
Editor: Marcia Yudkin
Website: http://www.yudkin.com/markmin.htm
Focus: General Marketing with an emphasis on writing

MARKETING SHERPA [EMAIL SHERPA] (WEEKLY)
Managing Editor: Anne Holland
Website: http://www.marketingsherpa.com
Focus: Email Marketing

THE PROFITABLE FREELANCER (BIWEEKLY)
Editor: Ed Gandia
Website: http://theprofitablefreelancer.com
Focus: Copywriting

EXCESS VOICE NEWSLETTER (BIWEEKLY)
Editor: Nick Usborne
Website: http://www.nickusborne.com/excess_voice.htm
Focus: Copywriting

eNEWSLETTER JOURNAL (MONTHLY)
Editor: Meryl K. Evans
Website: http://www.internetviz.com
Focus: Email Newsletters (Ezines)

WORDBIZ REPORT (WEEKLY)
Editor: Debbie Weil
Website: http://www.wordbiz.com
Focus: Business Writing

BENCIVENGA BULLETS (PERIODICALLY) (HIGHLY RECOMMENDED)
Editor: Gary Bencivenga – World-Renowned Copywriter
Website: http://bencivengabullets.com
Focus: Copywriting

MARKETINGPROFS TODAY (WEEKLY)
Editor: Ann Handley
Website: http://www.marketingprofs.com
Focus: General Marketing Tips from Industry Experts

THE PUBLICITY HOUND'S TIPS OF THE WEEK (WEEKLY)
Editor: Joan Stewart
Website: http://www.publicityhound.com
Focus: Effective Public Relations

Editor: Harmony Major
Website: http://www.harmonymajor.com
Focus: Internet Marketing

Writing Blogs

The Well-Fed Writer Blog: **www.wellfedwriter.com/blog**

Bob Bly's Blog: **http://bly.com/blog/**

Michael Stelzner's Blog: **www.writingwhitepapers.com/blog/**

Casey Hibbard's Case Study Blog:
http://successstorymarketing.typepad.com/ssm

Inkthinker Blog (by buddy Kristin King): **www.inkthinkerblog.com**

THE 2008 TOP 10 BLOGS FOR WRITERS: Compiled by Michael Stelzner
(Not all are commercial in scope, but all are worth a visit)
Link: **www.writingwhitepapers.com/blog/2008/09/??/top-10 blogo
for-writers-winners**

1) *CopyBlogger:* **www.copyblogger.com**

2) *Men with Pens:* **http://menwithpens.ca**

3) *Freelance Writing Jobs:* **www.freelancewritinggigs.com**

4) *Write to Done:* **http://writetodone.com**

5) *Confident Writing:* **http://confidentwriting.com/blog**

6) *The Renegade Writer:* **http://therenegadewriter.com**

7) *Remarkable Communication:* **www.remarkable-communication.com**

8) *The Writing Journey:* **http://writing-journey.com**

9) *Freelance Parent:* **www.sparkplugging.com/freelance-parent**

10) *Urban Muse:* **www.urbanmusewriter.com**

Writers Groups

A short list of regional and national writing/business organizations. Some may be more commercial in nature than others. PLEASE remember: Every group has a different profile and "vibe." Respect their right to NOT accept everyone if, in their estimation and for whatever reason, it's just not a fit. Remember, you can always start your own group.

Chicago

IWOC (Independent Writers of Chicago): **www.iwoc.org**
CADM (Chicago Association of Direct Marketing): **www.cadm.org**

Ohio

Downtown Writers (Columbus-based): **www.downtownwriters.com**

Washington, DC

American Independent Writers: **www.americanindependentwriters.org**
(Now national, but still physically located in the Washington, DC area.)

Tampa Bay, FL

Bay Area Professional Writers Guild: **www.bapwg.org**

New Jersey

New Jersey Creatives: **www.njcreatives.org**
Professional Writers Alliance (PWA) of Mercer County: **www.pwawriters.org**.
Communications, Advertising and Marketing Association: **www.njcama.org**
NOWA – Network of Writers and Artists: **www.nowa.org**

Atlanta

The Freelance Forum: **www.freelanceforum.org**
Creativity Atlanta: **www.atlantaadclub.org**

Seattle

Freelance-Seattle.net: **www.freelance-seattle.net** – Two-branch listserv: discussions/project postings.

Seattle Writergrrls: **www.seattlewritergrrls.org** – Not purely commercial, but good for keeping the creative side of our jobs fresh.

NATIONWIDE (FIND LOCAL CHAPTERS)

American Independent Writers – formerly Washington (DC) Independent Writers: **www.americanindependentwriters.org**

IABC – International Association of Business Communicators: **www.iabc.com**

PRSA – Public Relations Society of America: **www.prsa.org**

BMA – Business Marketing Association: **www.marketing.org**

BNI – Business Network International: **www.bni.com**

EFA – Editorial Freelancers Association: **http://the-efa.org**

STC – Society for Technical Communication: **www.stc.org**

Law Marketing Discussion List: **www.lawmarketing.com**

(For those wanting to write for law firms or entities providing services to law firms.)

Conferences/Seminars

COPYWRITING SUCCESS SUMMIT: **www.copywritingsummit.com**

This projected annual event, produced by white paper guru Michael Stelzner, kicked off in October 2008 with a main faculty roster that included Bob Bly, Steve Slaunwhite, Michael and me. It was a "virtual" event (phone and web-based), and the first of its kind for *our kinds—commercial copywriters*. The 2008 program earned a staggering 99% "I'd-come-back-again" rate. Michael does the *White Paper Summit* each year as well—check it out at **www.whitepaper summit.com**.

At-Home-Working-Mom Links

www.WAHM.com: The Online Magazine for Work-At-Home Moms!

www.bizymoms.com: You Can Have It All! Be a Work-At-Home Mom!

www.momwriters.com: For Those Writing With Children Underfoot.

www.hbwm.com: Committed to Bringing Working Moms Closer to Their Children.

www.momsnetwork.com: One of the Original Sites for Work-At-Home Moms.

www.homeworkingmom.com: A Mom's First Step to Working at Home.

Appendix B

I dearly love to hear about writers succeeding. Does my heart good. That's what this appendix is all about: writers across the country (and beyond), with vastly different circumstances and backgrounds, all making it happen—and on their terms.

In the pages that follow, you'll hear from both general and niche practitioners (including a few nonprofit niche-rs), as well as At-Home Moms & Dads. And for all you journalists out there, your erstwhile brethren are well-represented in these stories. And virtually all of them started their journey with a copy of *The Well-Fed Writer*. Love that.

What you see here are abstracts—the bare essentials of their story. Visit the *Side Dishes* link (**www.wellfedwriter.com/sidedishes.shtml**) for the full text of their stories. Enjoy.

• • •

NANCY ADAMS
Higgins Lake, Michigan
www.writemind.net

THINK YOU CAN'T BE A SUCCESSFUL FLCW IN THE MIDDLE OF A FOREST? THINK AGAIN.

Following 25 years of full-time employment, I "retired" at age 53 to begin a career as a freelance copywriter. With no commercial writing experience, no portfolio, no clients, and no academic degree, I set out to pursue my long-held dream of making a living by doing what I love. My business capital was the inspiration I'd gleaned from TWFW, confidence in my skill as an effective writer, determination...and little else.

At first, marketing was a problem. I live in a sparsely populated, seasonal resort area, and I was wary of making face-to-face sales calls, so I planned to conduct virtually all of my business via the Internet. Initially I found work on bidding sites like Elance and Guru. I accepted lower rates for the opportunity to gain experience and build a portfolio, a compromise that paid off when several of those early projects led to ongoing client relationships.

Today I have a growing client list and plenty of work. I'm more selective in the projects I pursue, and my fees are based on market rates. I've never looked back, not for a moment, and I'm living my dream each day.

• • •

KENT AUSTIN
Lewes, East Sussex, England
www.copy-doctor.co.uk

A PORTABLE WELL-FED FEAST FOR FLCW IN THE UK

These days I have as much work as I can handle at roughly $80+ (US) an hour. My assignments span the copywriting gamut: hard-nosed sales letters, web sites, brochures, and any number of joint ventures with creative agencies. Most recently, I've completed ghostwriting a book on political corruption for a Nigerian politician.

Am I some kind of super-achiever? Far from it. Has it always been this good? No. Did I ever feel like giving up along the way? More than once. Would I trade this lifestyle for any other? Read on.

I bought *TWFW*. Starting from scratch and with virtually no money, I followed Peter's advice. I was self-sufficient as a freelance commercial writer within six months. It's a fact. You don't have to take Peter's word for it. This deal works—on both sides of the Atlantic. All it takes is a will to succeed and a little imagination.

• • •

MARIAN CALABRO
Hasbrouck Heights, New Jersey (NYC area):
www.CorporateHistory.net

DISCOVERING YOUR NICHE: AN "AHA!" MOMENT

CorporateHistory.net produces histories that help organizations profit from their past—visual, reader-friendly, marketing-savvy books, and other history-oriented materials. Our clients include Fortune 500s, nonprofits, and family businesses.

I started in this niche as a subcontracted author. The field was a natural because I had publishing and corporate communications experience; I was also a proven writer of highly readable history books. My business partner is a former ad agency creative director. This work calls for very strong skills in research and interviewing, as well as the ability to extract and shape a compelling narrative from masses of raw material—and to put it all together with sophisticated design.

Most of our business comes from referrals and web site inquiries. The pitching process often requires detailed proposals, careful estimating, teleconferences, or meetings. And clients rarely make decisions overnight! The advantage is that the projects are fascinating, long-lasting, and lucrative. Looking just at the writing side, a history book specialist can earn a nice five-figure annual income. Experienced, busy writers can make more. To get started, try to interest current clients in history-themed marketing.

• • •

MARY CVETAN
Pittsburgh, Pennsylvania
www.cvetan.com

ONE-ON-ONE BUSINESS TRAINING AND NETWORKING HELP BUILD WRITER'S BUSINESS

I worked for 11 years as a marketing communications and public relations writer for a large hospital system. Some friends started freelance graphic design businesses and did very well, so I decided to follow suit. I prepared for a year (researching, taking classes, saving money) prior to launching my FLCW business.

Today, I write marketing and sales collateral, from web site content to sales letters to brochures to white papers; I edit technical documents (300–1,000 pages), such as government reports and proposals; and I write press releases and pitch story ideas to the news media to obtain publicity for clients. The workflow can be very unpredictable, but the potential is $3,000 to $10,000 a month. Sales and marketing and administrative activities (and rest!) can eat up a lot of time.

I built the business with networking, including joining a small business networking group and a chamber in my first year, and later becoming a leader in the local International Association of Business Communicators (IABC) chapter. I have never made a cold call and have done just two mailings in six years. Two things that helped me immensely were taking sales training and finding good mentors—and, of course, reading Peter's books!

•   •   •

MARCI DIEHL
Canandaigua, New York
www.marcidiehl.com

VETERAN FREELANCER MAKES TRANSITION FROM MAGAZINES TO COMMERCIAL WRITING

I started writing professionally as a very young woman, 10 years into marriage to my college sweetheart, a professional golfer on the PGA Tour. Media and businesses surround the Tour, and I learned how diverse corporations use media and sports to connect and market. I began my writing career in magazines and spent 15 years writing freelance for local, regional, and national publications. But divorce "detoured" me into working for a staffing company that asked me for help with their advertising because I was "the creative one." When hard times meant the elimination of my position, I took my portfolio on the road, networked, and set up shop in a corner of my dining room as a FLCW.

Eleven years later, I still have a home office and head up projects as a FLCW and creative director, collaborating with other professionals in broadcast, print, trade, digital, and on the web. My experience in magazines is now being put to use by a new magazine launch. They've asked me to write (freelance, of course), edit, and help to shape the direction. Last year I finally grossed six figures, but other years have been lean ($25,000 to $35,000). Very low overhead helps, but there are always years when I wonder if I can keep working as a FLCW. Then I remember how much I love working from home and having the freedom, variety, and client relationships I experience. Priceless.

•   •   •

CHERYL DUNKERTON
Toronto, Canada
www.advocatecopy.com

NONPROFIT NICHE BRINGS SUCCESS AND PERSONAL SATISFACTION TO CANADIAN FLCW

A seminar given by Peter Bowerman first opened up my eyes to the possibilities that awaited in FLCW. However, I spent the next two years pursuing other goals by working in international development in Outer Mongolia. Upon my return to Canada, I pitched articles about my time in Mongolia to various magazines and a newspaper, and all articles were accepted and published within months. I began to see that I could create a job for myself that combined my belief in working for social change and my passion for writing. Before setting up AdvocateCopy, which serves not-for-profit organizations, I spent several months studying copywriting and doing my own extensive market research while continuing to teach full time.

My first copywriting assignment was working on a planned giving campaign for a major Canadian museum. The project went very well, and since then 80 percent of my work has been working on similar campaigns in the Canadian health sector. Although I'm still teaching part-time at the local university, my income potential is around $500 to $1,500 per project.

I am very proud of the fact that my writing contributes towards raising thousands of dollars for organizations whose reason for being is to improve the lives of others.

•   •   •

JEFFREY DUROSKO
Pittsburgh, Pennsylvania
www.duroskoPR.com

FROM JOURNALIST TO VP TO BETTER (FLCW) LIFE

After many years of planning and hoping, I made the leap into the commercial writing business by walking into my boss's office (the CEO of a billion-dollar public company) and telling him I was resigning to pursue my dream. In one hand I had a letter of resignation and in the other a proposal to continue working with the organization. I had lined up one other client prior to that event, and my CEO bought the proposal on the spot.

Today I'm so busy that I subcontract work to three other professionals in my area and am billing at $150 per hour. I'm earning much more than I was when gainfully employed and have carved out a lifestyle that includes taking my oldest daughter to school every day, and generally more family time and happiness all around. I have spent very little time marketing myself as the word of mouth has spread.

My initial thrust to contact all the folks with whom I had a relationship at my last position yielded clients across the US. Most of my clients are retainer clients, and my assignments range from writing projects to strategic communications consulting.

•   •   •

MERYL K. EVANS
Plano, Texas
www.meryl.net

DIVERSIFYING RATHER THAN SPECIALIZING SUITS TEXAS FLCW JUST FINE

I never wanted to go into business, knowing it involved administration like accounting. Furthermore, as a profoundly deaf person, how was I going to build up sales if I must rely on relay services to make phone calls? After my second child arrived, I convinced my inflexible company to let me switch to part-time.

While on maternity leave, I began work on a certificate in Internet Technologies from NYU to support my goal to become a web designer. After doing several web design projects, I decided it was more frustrating than enjoyable. Accidentally, I discovered that I liked writing about web design. Slowly, I earned more paid writing assignments. The corporate part-time job let me build the writing business. I continued part-time until the company forced me to return full-time. By then, I had plenty of business writing experience and a healthy portfolio. Only I couldn't quit my job because my husband didn't have health benefits. We had three kids, so it was an important issue. When my husband landed a job with decent benefits, I retired from corporate America for the freelance life full-time. The business has thrived since, and I made as much in my first full year as a freelancer as I did in the corporate world full-time.

●   ●   ●

CASEY HIBBARD
Boulder, Colorado
www.compelling-cases.com

CASE STUDIES "LOVE AT FIRST WRITE" FOR FORMER JOURNALIST

With a background in marcom writing and journalism, I jumped into FLCW. At first, I wrote anything and everything for anyone for not very much money. But I soon leveraged my experience in writing about technology for brochures, web site copy, press releases, and case studies for tech companies while increasing my rates. I discovered I LOVE case studies! Soon I chose to focus exclusively on them with the idea that my specialization would separate me from the crowd and help those needing case studies remember to call me.

It worked nicely. Renamed and branded, I have built very steady work creating success stories and case studies for companies around the world, all from my home. I even wrote a book on the topic of customer stories, "Stories That Sell: Turn Satisfied Customers into Your Most Powerful Sales & Marketing Asset." My clients hire me to interview their satisfied customers, write a compelling story, and manage the process until the featured customer approves it. New business comes in via referrals, targeted cold calling, my web site, or articles I write. My income potential ranges from $85 to $105 an hour depending on the industry and complexity. I'm now moving for the second time and taking my business easily with me!

•   •   •

ANDREW HINDES
Los Angeles, California
www.theinhousewriter.com

EX-JOURNALIST BUILDS THRIVING FLCW BUSINESS WITH HOLLYWOOD ROOTS
Before starting The In-House Writer, I spent eight years as a Los Angeles-based full-time entertainment journalist, including a stint at Hollywood trade paper *Variety*. While I enjoyed the work, the pay wasn't enough to support my family, and the long hours meant I didn't spend much time with my kids. As my last full-time job wound down, I read *The Well-Fed Writer* and decided to give freelance copywriting a shot. I called all the contacts I had made as a journalist and slowly started landing a few assignments. Four years later, business is booming. I've provided PR and corporate communications copy for all of the major Hollywood film studios as well as numerous networks, production companies, talent agencies, and PR firms. More recently, I've expanded beyond entertainment into other business sectors, including technology, travel, financial services, and nonprofits. I've never had the guts to make cold calls, so I focus on making sure my existing clients are so happy with the quality of writing and service I provide they keep coming back and referring their friends and associates. It works: I make a living writing and get to work at home and spend time with my family.

•   •   •

Doug Jenner
Hitchin, Herts, England
www.bestwords.co.uk

Former English Teacher in UK Turns Writing Dreams into Reality

"So Doug, let's get this right: You're NOT actually a high school English teacher anymore? Now you're a…what is it? A *copywriter*?" (Cue next question.)

I was holidaying in Australia visiting family and friends, having lived in the UK for over 10 years. They'd all known me as a teacher, and with over 20 years in the job, that was a big part of how they identified me.

So now they were full of questions, like how had I made such a fundamental career shift in just one year. Answering their questions helped me answer my own. How HAD I made it?

Writing for a living was something I'd dreamt of for a long time. I suspected I had the ability. But I didn't fully believe it. Something that helped me develop that belief was the process of self-marketing. Standing up at networking meetings, calling hundreds of prospective clients, and saying "I am a good writer who can meet your needs" got me a long way up that mountain of self-belief.

Now, a couple of years into a very successful career, it still helps me to get through those moments of self-doubt.

•   •   •

Donna Kaluzniak
Jacksonville Beach, Florida
www.CopywritingSolutionsServices.com

Building a Part-Time FLCW Business with Retirement in Mind

I love my job as a utility director for a small city—I really do!

But after 28 years of being on call 24/7, attending night meetings, and working mega-hours, it was time for a change. So, I started Copywriting Solutions as a part-time business.

At age 53, my plan is to build my writing business to the point where I can take the early retirement program in a few years and have the time and location flexibility that goes with a writing career.

Cold calling on nights and weekends was a challenge for me. I got most of my business through Chamber of Commerce functions and joining Business Network International. I worked on a wide variety of assignments my first year—from online technical courses and training manuals to web copy, press releases, and brochures. I wanted a boost, so I worked with a business coach to develop a marketing plan that keeps me on track.

If you're not ready to give up your day job, it's easy to start a part-time writing business that can supplement your income or transition to a full-time copywriting career. All it takes is determination, organization, and some time management. I expect to make about $10,000 to $12,000 this year, but it could be more if I boost my marketing efforts.

•   •   •

JANICE KING
Seattle, Washington
www.writespark.com and **www.writinghightech.com**

NARROWING IN ON A SPECIALTY CAN PRODUCE GLOBAL RESULTS

I became a freelance writer when I was laid off from a corporate job. Since then, I have also become an author; my most recent book is *Copywriting That Sells High Tech*. All of my clients are large technology companies. I work on a broad range of sales and PR materials: brochures and data sheets, press releases, magazine articles, web content, and especially case studies and white papers.

One advantage of working with large companies is internal referrals. I've had relationships with some companies for five, ten, or even more years simply by working in different divisions.

My industry focus has always made it necessary—and rewarding—for me to pursue clients in other states, even other countries. I believe that clients of all types are now more willing to work with remote writers, especially for projects that require special expertise.

Writing for technology companies continues to bring me the satisfaction of intellectual challenge, terrific clients, and ongoing company relationships that have brought me freelance success for nearly 20 years.

•   •   •

HEIDI LaFLECHE
Watertown, Massachusetts
www.worryfreewriting.com

FEEL-GOOD FLCW SUCCESS FOR FORMER MASSACHUSETTS JOURNALIST

When I was diagnosed with breast cancer, my dream of becoming a full-time freelance writer could no longer be put on hold. I'd worked as a staff writer/editor for magazines, newspapers, a nonprofit, and dot-coms. I'd enjoyed a stint as a Boston correspondent for *People* magazine. I had the skills, the experience, and the contacts to make a go of it.

After reading TWFW, I knew the earning potential was not in journalism but in commercial writing. I viewed my journalism experience as an asset. I could tell a good story. I liked interviewing people. My writing was readable and factual. I did not expect to hit roadblocks *because of* my journalism background.

I had marketing professionals tell me I was too inexperienced to compete in an urban market, including an agency person who flat-out spat out, "*We don't hire journalists.*" Despite the naysayers, I knew I could be successful; I just needed to figure out how to differentiate myself in a crowded market.

In a one-on-one coaching session, Peter Bowerman helped me realize the thing of value I could offer to business was the thing I did best: human-interest writing. I repackaged my services with a new brochure and web site, and now the work for employee profiles, success stories, etc., is plentiful and well paying. And I've been able to fill my schedule by networking with just my existing contacts.

•   •   •

KRISTEN KING
Ruther Glen, Virginia
www.inkthinkercommunications.com

FREELANCING FRESH FROM COLLEGE, FLCW (NOW 27) DRIVES, THRIVES AND DIVERSIFIES

I started freelancing just out of college with great skills but limited professional experience. I ended up getting a full-time medical editing job to expand my résumé, still freelancing on the side. I started out at $50/hour. Before long, I was turning down so much work for lack of time that I realized I could freelance full time if I didn't have my day job. I quit my job and raised my freelance rates to $100/hour, and I haven't regretted it for a second.

I live in a rural area 30+ miles from the nearest city, but through my online presence, I've built an international client base with customers across the US and Canada, Europe, and as far away as New Zealand. My first website, **www.kristenkingfreelancing.com**, was my 24/7 marketing department during the 20 months I was moonlighting, snagging me clients even though I was unavailable during regular business hours, and it was named a finalist in the 2006 Writer's Digest Best Writer's Website Contest.

Since then, my work has grown to include not just writing and editing, but also consulting and speaking. I still maintain my award-winning blog for writers, **www.inkthinkerblog.com**, and now I market my business through **www.inkthinkercommunications.com**.

•   •   •

DARCY MAULSBY
Lake City, Iowa
www.darcymaulsby.com

FLCW SUCCESS IN THE LAND OF DRIVE-BY TRACTORS

When I was laid off from my job as a content editor at a dot-com, I was inspired by *The Well-Fed Writer* to hang out my own shingle rather than go through the demoralizing process of hunting for a job. From my home in the country near the small town of Granger, Iowa, I began building my commercial writing business. I've never regretted my decision.

I was able to build my client base in under a year to include marketing companies and advertising agencies from Des Moines, Iowa, to Sioux Falls, SD. Along the way I also landed some national clients, including the National Pork Board. (I write their web features, magazine articles, and newsletters.) Through the years, I've written for real estate firms, cooperatives, retirement communities, and insurance companies. For someone who loves to learn and enjoys plenty of variety, this arrangement suits me well and keeps the creative juices flowing, which benefits my clients.

When my husband and I decided to move back to my hometown of Lake City, Iowa (population 1,800), it was such a relief to have a lucrative job that was also portable. Today my client base extends from South Dakota to North Carolina, and I continue to grow the business, even from an area that's so rural that tractors regularly drive by my home office window!

· · ·

JACQUE RILEY
Columbia, South Carolina
www.rileycommunications.com

GIVING UP THE DIRECTOR-LEVEL JOB FOR NEW CAREER AS A FLCW

I can vouch for the fact that corporate communications directors regularly hire freelancers because I used to be one. Groomed for the marketing management track since college, I nonchalantly distributed $15,000 brochure budgets and scrambled to find content for pamphlets, magazines, and annual reports.

Despite my interactions with the freelance community, I never considered freelance commercial writing as a career option until I became increasingly frustrated with my job. Would I always have to hire people to do the fun, creative things while I went to budget meetings?

With $1,000 and a three-month timeline, I decided to venture out on my own. In addition to writing, I capitalized on my design training to offer a complete suite of marketing services to the small business community. As I approach my one-year anniversary in business, I have more work than I can handle and have decided to raise my rates to $125 an hour. By viewing my start-up as a career rather than a hobby, I've been able to pursue what I love and help other South Carolina business owners thrive.

• • •

DAVE TANDET
Santa Monica, California
www.davidtandet.com

WHY YOU SHOULD ALWAYS LISTEN TO YOUR PARENTS

After my dad gave Peter Bowerman's seminar two thumbs up, I decided I'd have to see "The Well-Fed Writer" myself. Four years later, I'm a full-time freelance commercial writer.

My work as a paralegal at a Los Angeles litigation firm gave me plenty of practice writing on schedule. Not that I needed it my first umpteen months as a professional copywriter. But the vision of making a living writing for my own clients? Too cool to let slip away. So I cold called, met with fellow "Well-Fed" readers, and read my monthly "Well-Fed E-Pub."

When I saw the item in "The Well-Fed E-Pub" about Bobby Hickman exhibiting at a Staples, it inspired me to do likewise. I dropped Peter a note about it. A mention in a later E-Pub led an L.A. reader to call and meet me for coffee.

A year later? That acquaintance was the editor of well-respected L.A. publication. Her recommendation got me a gig doing freelance PR for a large medical institution. It's opened the way to other healthcare writing and marketing communications in all areas. One of my clients is a Los Angeles City Council member. The point of all this, I suppose, is not that you'll get a break because you read the Well-Fed E-Pub. It's that you might. Because that "lucky" break can come from anywhere. Even when you're not looking.

• • •

LISA MANYON
Lewiston, Idaho
www.writeoncreative.com

WRITING CAREER NO LONGER JUST A DREAM FOR THIS IDAHOAN

When my career peaked in the local advertising agency arena (population less than 100,000), I revisited my dream of writing for a living, and *The Well-Fed Writer* gelled that direction. I left my job, created a strong Internet presence, and started doing freelance gigs for clients across the nation.

It takes money to make money. So, I joined the National Association of Women Writers (**www.NAWW.org**) and invested in mentorship with industry experts like Lorrie Morgan-Ferrero, for whom I crafted a press release for her mentorship program, and with whom I conducted a teleconference about my POWER Planning Process. I also acted as team leader for her Red Hot Copywriting Bootcamp.

My national connections increased credibility locally. I created and implemented a training series, which is included in my ebook for the Idaho Small Business Development Center.

Plus, I don't forget those who have helped along the way and send thank-you cards for any occasion (Peter doesn't call me the "Thank-You-Card Queen" for no reason!).

With these tactics and more, I've doubled my hourly rate, bid copywriting on a per project basis, and regularly land new writing gigs locally and nationally.

•   •   •

ANNE DEETER GALLAHER
Mechanicsburg, Pennsylvania
www.deetergallahergroup.com

NO LIMITS FOR THIS PENNSYLVANIA FREELANCER-TURNED-ENTERPRISE

I began as a freelance writer doing a quarterly newsletter for a nonprofit youth ministry. They were great, but funds were always limited and $25 an hour seemed like a lot of money to charge. Now with two of my three sons in college, I am focused on producing excellent marketing materials for superior clients for above-average fees. I tell my clients that I am the Jaguar of marketing—I'm not for everyone, but for those who appreciate sophisticated and highly valued communications, I'm the firm for you. I have won some great awards for my pieces and am proud of all my work.

I am very active with businesswomen, especially On-Rampers (women returning to the workforce), and serve on several regional boards. I have been honored as one of the Best 50 Women in Business in Pennsylvania by the Department of Community and Economic Development and the state's five business journal publications. Not bad for someone who started by reading TWFW and who only had one business course in college. I was surprised to learn that central Pennsylvania readers of Harrisburg

Magazine recently voted me Reader's Choice Role Model. I was humbled and privileged to be thought of so highly. I tell young people: Only in America! There are no limits that you can't overcome.

• • •

At-Home Moms & Dads

MICHAELE CHARLES
Denver, Colorado
www.voicecommunications.org

NEW MOM PARLAYS BUSINESS EXPERIENCE INTO FLCW SUCCESS

I started freelancing two years ago while working full-time as a recruiter. I'd been writing fiction and decided that with my business experience (five years in accounting, two years in recruiting), commercial writing might be for me. I approached my company about doing some internal writing, and I tapped friends and former co-workers for pro bono projects (marketing materials, newsletters, web site copy, etc.).

Aside from my full-time job, the biggest challenge I faced was my newest job: PARENTHOOD. I started this "side" freelancing when my daughter was four months old. I was working full-time with one day at home, and when my day at home was a slow recruiting day, I'd call people about doing some writing for them.

I built up a pretty good little portfolio in those several months and decided to quit my job and pull my baby from daycare. I relied on the grandparents for babysitting, and I worked at night, when my daughter napped, and early mornings until my husband went to work.

I now have several regular (paying) clients, and I've hired a nanny for 25 to 30 hours a week. Initially, I quoted $55 an hour but now quote $65 with no issue. Being persistent and believing that it WILL happen is a formula for success. I do believe that.

• • •

Amy M. Dawson
Alpharetta, Georgia
www.amymacpr.com

At-Home FLCW Mom Commands $50K Working Just 15 Hours a Week

Every morning, I walk my kids to the bus stop, come home for another cup of coffee, clock three hours of freelance copywriting at $75 to $125 an hour (depending on the scope of the project), and still have time to go for a run before I pick up the kids from school.

My trick for having a career and being a stay-at-home mom? Know what your writing is worth and demand it. Many at-home moms think transitioning back into the work world is an impossible mountain to climb. Not so. A mere six weeks after starting my business, I filled my calendar with 15 hours of steady, weekly work.

I'd been out of the work force for almost seven years when I started freelancing, which meant I really needed to jazz up my portfolio with up-to-date clips. I scooped up any *pro bono* projects I could: I wrote news releases for my brother's political campaign and volunteered as the vice president of communications for the local Junior League, then filed all the writing samples in my portfolio. I did work at a much-reduced rate for other family members and nonprofits, and I pitched my previous experience to executives I knew in the area.

Many talented at-home moms believe no company will work with a mom who has been out of the 8-to-5 world for several years. Don't sell yourself short! Exude professionalism and deliver on-target results, and even the most buttoned-up corporate suits won't care where you are doing the work—just that the job gets done right.

•   •   •

Jonelle Foutz
Yakima, Washington
www.writemindonline.com

Well-Fed Mom in Small Market Gives Thanks

As a stay-at-home mom in semi-rural Yakima, Washington, I've turned my education and experience into a successful copywriting business by tapping into a basic human need—the need to be appreciated. Simple thank-you notes are at the core of my success story.

With solid writing skills, a positive attitude, and a copy of *The Well-Fed Writer* as my guide, I wrote letters, made phone calls, and scheduled meetings all over town. I built a web site. I sent a thank-you note to anyone who talked with me.

I got a few small jobs in the beginning, but nothing steady. I wrote more letters, made more phone calls, and scheduled more meetings. And I sent more thank-you notes to the people I'd done work for. Soon, those people started calling me back. My best marketing strategy turned out to be simple and sincere—taking the time to say "thank you."

I now have several steady clients (at $50 per hour). Working part time from home, I have the flexibility I need to accommodate my family's active schedule, and if I get any busier, I'm going to have to give up one of my other jobs…housework. And yes, I'm thankful!

•   •   •

LINDA B. LLOYD
Tooele, Utah
www.seagullmarketinggraphics.com

AT-HOME MOM PERSEVERES TO MAKE DREAM LIFESTYLE A REALITY

I am the mother of two young boys, 11 and 13, and within a period of six months, I was widowed and lost my father, who we were caring for. This left me in the position of either going to work at a 9-to-5 (I had always been an at-home mom for my boys) or finding something I could do and still be at home with my boys. Due to the tragedy that had filled our lives at that time, I really felt the need to be home with the boys, for us to be together.

I seriously took a look at copywriting, and after taking a course and coaching program, I am now making good money. I have five contracts—two in negotiation and three firm. I also have a number of prospects asking me to contact them. All of these are ranging well over the $125 an hour mark. I am grateful that I was able to find this field and actually able to make a living. From where I stand, there is more than enough work out there for everyone. Even web sites or letters written today will need to be revised tomorrow.

•   •   •

MELANIE R. NEGRIN
Randolph, New Jersey
www.merocune.com

AT-HOME MOM FOCUSES ON FAMILY-FRIENDLY NONPROFIT NICHE

I began Merocuné Marketing and Public Relations after the birth of my daughter Kaila. I developed my creative portfolio and business-building skills in the year and a half after my daughter was born by identifying nonprofit organizations with missions I was passionate about and who needed marketing, writing, or design expertise.

When our family savings fell to uncomfortable levels and I learned I was pregnant with our son Nathaniel, I found a full-time public relations position in real estate. After Nathaniel's arrival, the position was eliminated, and this employer became my first paying freelance client.

Since then, I have established a reputable and consistently growing company with more than 20 paying clients—all repeat customers—located across the United States and in some international countries. My company specializes in developing marketing and development communications that build community awareness, brand equity, and financial sustainability for nonprofit organizations and entrepreneurial businesses. I love what I do every day, and I am inspired by helping others make their charitable missions come true. Being able to make a difference from home while I enjoy the company of my children, now ages 5 and 3, is a gift.

•   •   •

EDMUND R. SCHUBERT
Greensboro, North Carolina
www.writewellcc.com

AT-HOME DAD BUILDS FLCW CAREER FROM CREATIVE ROOTS

I was a stay-at-home dad looking for a way to generate part-time income from home. I needed to be there for my kids, but after twelve years of running my own business (before the kids were born), I also felt the need to do more. I had always enjoyed writing and had published several short stories, but wasn't making any money doing that. Then I met Peter

Bowerman at the North Carolina Writer's Network Fall Conference, and he showed me how I could apply my writing skills to commercial writing. Here was the best of both worlds: making money doing something I enjoyed and being able to do it from home, on my own schedule.

To make a long story short, within six months of meeting Peter I started editing a regional business magazine on a freelance basis, and the contacts I made as a result of that work landed me additional projects working with graphic designers, ad agencies, and other businesses in the area. I write and edit web sites, flyers, handouts for trade shows, executive summaries, newsletter material, etc., charging between $65 and $75 per hour depending on the size of the project and the client's turnaround time.

•   •   •

MARY SHAW
Norwalk, Connecticut
www.shawcopy.com

AT-HOME MOM COMMANDS FT SALARY WORKING PT HOURS

I was an agency web producer working 70 hours a week when my three-year-old daughter got really sick with viral pneumonia. Then my day-care provider quit. Bottom line, I had to find a solution fast and thought starting my own copywriting business would work.

Copywriting appealed to me because I had done a lot of writing over the course of my career, and I thought it would be a flexible work-from-home opportunity. I read Peter's books and Steve Slaunwhite's *Start and Run a Copywriting Business* and got busy building my portfolio. Leveraging industry contacts, I had three paying clients two weeks before I quit my job. My rates are $65 to $85 an hour. I'm on track to make at least $50,000 this year and haven't worked more than 20 hours a week since quitting my job nearly two years ago.

My goal was to work part-time from home, and I currently have more work than I can handle. The best part is my incredibly flexible lifestyle: my daughter snuggles up to me and my laptop whenever she wants; it's easy to schedule my work around her activities; my husband loves that I'm home; and I'm much happier in general.

•   •   •

CLAIRE SMITH
New Zealand
www.evolutioncopywriting.co.nz

AT-HOME MOM IN NEW ZEALAND TURNS HOBBY INTO THRIVING BUSINESS

Before leaving my full-time sales job within the veterinary industry, my writing experience consisted of a Diploma in Freelance Journalism (done on a part-time basis through a local correspondence school), a few published magazine articles, and an encouraging report from my primary school English teacher. I'd always enjoyed writing but assumed that a career in writing was reserved for those who'd endured many years of university and had done the hard yards in agencies building up impressive portfolios.

After having three children, I made the inevitable decision that I simply couldn't manage full-time work anymore. I started researching copywriting as a career after a friend asked me to write her husband's real estate newsletters. The more I learnt about it, the more I knew that it was exactly what I wanted to do. I made plans to ditch my sales job and set myself up in business. In the first few months, I struggled to find work and thought I'd made a huge mistake, but before long the work began streaming in. Two years down the track, I'm making considerably more money than I've ever made before, and I'm turning work away on a regular basis. I can't imagine a better way to make a living!

•   •   •

JOSEPH RATLIFF
Lacey, WA
http://josephratliff.com

FLCW AND INTERNET MARKETING CONSULTANT IS HOME FOR HIS KIDS

Being a full-time FLCW allows me to control my schedule fully, which includes being a "stay at home" Dad for my two boys. Totally awesome.

In late 2000, I started coaching businesses on their marketing processes part-time. After a little while in this part-time venture, many of my clients requested that I provide copywriting services for them as a value added service. Doing both types of business operations part-time was time draining though.

I also found out that I developed a passion for writing marketing materials. So I made the decision to focus on writing, and adding consulting as a value added proposition, and make a go of it full-time.

In the beginning I made a crucial error in allowing my database to empty of useable leads to prospect. I had to resort to cold calling, which I was not a big fan of at the time.

Until I read *TWFW*. Long story short, I made the transition from part-time to full-time much easier than I had initially thought. Cold calling is not as difficult as I had made it. I landed 4 clients in my first week, and have never looked back since.

Now, using more of the techniques from TWFW, freelance commercial writing makes up an average of $5300.00 or more a month in my business (I still consult for internet marketers as well). My business is quite successful, full-time, and in part due to the information and engaging writings in both original *Well-Fed* books.

Thank you, Peter, for giving me the "boot" I needed to put my business into high gear. I refer to both *The Well Fed Writer* and *Back For Seconds* quite often still.

Appendix C

Readers of my original *WFW* titles will recall *The Well-Fed Tool Box*, the killer companion ebook bursting with all the tools you need—forms, letters, contracts, questionnaires, hot linked-resources, and much more—to ease your passage to "Well-Fed World." With this new edition of *TWFW* comes *The Deluxe Well-Fed Tool Box*, 120+ pages, also updated and expanded, and also printable and cut 'n pastable.

In addition to all the components of the original *Tool Box* (including a bunch of stuff from the book that you'll say, "Gee, it'd be great to have *that* in an electronic form"), you'll find new tools and reports covering a wide spectrum of issues and challenges near and dear to the FLCW life: business structures, insurance, improving your writing skills, why you shouldn't worry about the economy, the power of testimonials, writing for the web, and a lot more.

I'll wager you'll find yourself referring to this beauty as much as the book itself.

Check it out (and purchase it as an instant download) at **www.wellfedwriter.com/toolbox.shtml**.

Oh, and for about the price of a cheap pizza night out: $29.95. I'm an idiot.

Heck, I should've packaged *The Well-Fed Writer* and *The Deluxe Well-Fed Tool Box* together as a "Success System"—complete with one of those long-letter web sites that builds the case during an endless scroll, culminating in one of those calls-to-action that ask, "*What would all this be worth? For all the time, money, and hassle, it'll surely save you, at least $1,000, right? Well, forget $1,000, or even $500, or even $250. How about $139?*" I'd probably have made a fortune.

But, I didn't. Instead, for less than half that, you get both (AND the *Time Line* coming up...). I make a few bucks and you get a killer package for jump-starting a whole new lucrative career as a writer. Woo-hoo. Win-win.

So, what's in it? Check out the list below. The exact Tool Box contents and order may change for the final version, but rest assured, it will contain all you see here and perhaps more (and yes, several of the reports are adapted from sections that appeared in the two original books but didn't make it into this one due to space constraints). For final contents, visit the link mentioned earlier.

The Deluxe Well-Fed Tool Box

TABLE OF CONTENTS

- Expanded Cold-Calling Guide (from Chapter Six):
- Writer's Résumé Guidelines & Format
- Customized Follow-up Snail-Mail Letters (after meetings/prospecting)
- Email Follow-up Notes to Phone Prospecting
- Email to Friends Announcing New Business
- The "Bid Letter" (text of the simple "contract" adequate for 95% of writing jobs)
- Sample Contract (for the other 5% requiring a bit more)
- "Discovery Questionnaire" (to simplify life and make you look brilliant to clients)
- Phone Interview Advance Questionnaire
- Video Scripting Formats
- Writers' Self-Check List (25 tips to fresher, more engaging, error-free writing)

- *Word* Keyboard Shortcuts: The Basics

- Writing/Marketing Resources (Appendix A from book, but all links are hot!)

- Your Colleagues' Web Sites (from Chapter Four, again, with all links hot)

- Project Description Form (to fill out at start of project to capture key info)

- The Amazing Evolving Press Release (four samples: from gruesome to good)

- The Super-Duper Press-Release Producer! (a cool, easy-to-use tool!)

- Alternative Press Release Format (a new and powerful variation on the original)

"Three Real-World Projects":

Follow the creative execution of three actual commercial writing projects

- Tri-Fold Brochure for a Residential Painting Company

- Tri-Fold Brochure for a Family Therapist

- Marketing Brochure for a Residential/Commercial Security Firm: Discover how they got four brochures for a bit more than the price of one…

8 Kick-Butt Reports:

REPORT #1: WELL-FED BUSINESS STARTUP
The Fine Print about Business Structures, Taxes, Retirement and Insurance

REPORT #2: WELL-FED DO'S AND DON'TS
15+ Tips to Having a High-Profit, High-Satisfaction, Low-Stress FLCW Career

REPORT #3: "IT'S NOT THE ECONOMY, STUPID!"
Why the Economy Doesn't Have Much Impact on Your Writing Business (Really!)

REPORT #4: WRITE BETTER, EARN MORE
10 Tips To Improving Your Writing (and Making More Money As A FLCW)

REPORT #5: LET YOUR CUSTOMER SELL YOU:
Using Testimonials to Land More Business

REPORT #6: WRITING FOR THE WEB:

A Top-Line Primer For Writing More Effective And Engaging Web Copy
By Andrea Harris (Guest Contributor)

REPORT #7: 8 TIPS FOR CASE STUDIES THAT COMPEL AND SELL

By Casey Hibbard (Guest Contributor)

REPORT #8: MAXIMIZE YOUR "NETWORKING ROI"!

12 Steps to Uncommon Networking Success
By Mike Klassen (Guest Contributor)

Again, check it out at **http://www.wellfedwriter.com/toolbox.shtml**.

But, not so fast. Got one other goody I think you're going to want…

**"THE WELL-FED WRITER TIME LINE"
(A.K.A. THE ANTIDOTE TO "OVERWHELM")**

Starting a commercial freelancing business can be an overwhelming process—sort of a "where-do-I-start?" proposition. Way I figured it, a quick reference guide laying out the key chronological highlights of the business-building process in an easy-to-follow format would be useful in ratcheting down the anxiety level, no?

Got the idea for this from the *Time Line* appendix in *The Well-Fed Self-Publisher,* which has earned gushing kudos from users for its wonderful ability to simplify and demystify a complex, scary process into a far more manageable one.

I thought, why not come up with one for commercial freelancers that lays out all the milestones from way before you launch your business to after you've got it up, running and profitable? You'll see a brief description of the step along with parenthetical page numbers referring back to the place in the book that discusses it in greater detail.

Check it out at **www.wellfedwriter.com/timeline.shtml**. Cost? Just $14.95. Pretty cheap peace of mind, if you ask me. Buy both the *Tool Box* and *Time Line* and you'll save even more. For more details on all of it, visit either product link above…

And with that, I leave you with this:

Good luck and may all your writing be well-fed…

Index

X–Z